# THIS IS YOUR
# EVEREST

# THIS IS YOUR
# EVEREST

## THE LIONS, THE SPRINGBOKS AND
## THE EPIC TOUR OF 1997

TOM ENGLISH

PETER BURNS

**POLARIS**
PUBLISHING

POLARIS PUBLISHING LTD

c/o Aberdein Considine

2nd Floor, Elder House

Multrees Walk

Edinburgh

EH1 3DX

Distributed by Birlinn Limited

www.polarispublishing.com

Text copyright © Tom English and Peter Burns, 2021

ISBN: 9781913538125

eBook ISBN: 9781913538132

British Library Cataloguing-in-Publication Data
A catalogue record for this book is available on request from the British Library.

Designed and typeset by Polaris Publishing, Edinburgh

Printed and bound in Great Britain

by Clays Ltd, Elcograf S.p.A.

# CONTENTS

PROLOGUE                                                                      1

ONE: THE DEATH OF DANIEL BONGANE                                              4

TWO: IT'S THE KAFFIRS, MAN                                                   19

THREE: EIGHT BOKS OF THE APOCALYPSE                                          28

FOUR: TELFER                                                                 50

FIVE: IT HAD TO BE JOHNNO                                                    59

SIX: WE DOUBLED DOWN, REMORTGAGED THE HOUSE                                  81

SEVEN: KOBUS WIESE IS ANGRY                                                  92

EIGHT: HE KEPT HIS DEAFNESS SECRET                                          108

NINE: ONE–ALL, WANKER!                                                      120

TEN: WE NEEDED TO SUFFER                                                    131

ELEVEN: SOMETHING WASN'T RIGHT                                              154

TWELVE: VICTORY IS A FORMALITY, SAYS OS DU RANDT                            164

THIRTEEN: TOM SMITH, BOSTON STRANGLER                                       172

FOURTEEN:  LAWRENCE DALLAGLIO AND HIS JUTTY-OUT JAW                         189

FIFTEEN: DO A JOB ON JOOST                                                  206

SIXTEEN: EVEREST                                                            218

SEVENTEEN: I TROD IN A DOG SHIT                                             253

EIGHTEEN: GARY TEICHMANN'S PAIN                                             265

NINETEEN: THE ASSASSIN JERRY GUSCOTT                                        274

TWENTY: COME ON JIM, WE'RE LEAVING                                          313

TWENTY-ONE: TRAGEDY OF THE FALLEN BOKS                                      331

TWENTY-TWO: WONDERWALL                                                      348

EPILOGUE: THE '97 LIONS WILL BE REMEMBERED FOREVER                          361

ACKNOWLEDGEMENTS                                                            368

BIBLIOGRAPHY                                                                371

*To my lovely mum, Anne, for everything.*
TE


*To Julie, Isla and Hector.*
PB

*A Lion in South Africa is special.*
*The Lions are special; the legends go with it.*

**IAN McGEECHAN**

# PROLOGUE

IN A CONFERENCE room deep in the bowels of the Lions' team hotel in Cape Town, Jim Telfer was positioning chairs, setting them out in rows, then in a single line, muttering to himself the whole time, oblivious to the camera trained upon him. 'We've got to be sharp as a fucking knife . . . There's no way we go back . . . We take every step forward . . .'

Preparing his final address before the Lions ran out to play South Africa in Newlands in the first Test of the momentous summer of 1997, Telfer was in a world of his own. For more than a month he had pushed his players harder than he'd ever pushed players before – and that was saying something. Just behind him there was a flip chart. On it he had written some put-downs taken directly from the South African press. Meat and drink to the great man.

Hadn't he feasted on this stuff when coaching Scotland to a Grand Slam in 1984, hadn't he made hay with talk of England's supremacy when assisting Ian McGeechan in another Scottish Slam in 1990? Some of the South African newspapers had written off the Lions and it was those headlines that Telfer gravitated towards. He'd heard all that bombast before. Every last word.

*Their weak point is the scrum*

*The Boks must exploit this weakness*

*The Boks must concentrate on the eight-man shove every scrum*

*Scrummaging will be the key*

*Their weakness is the scrum*

He surveyed the room. Straightened a chair and checked his watch. The forwards would be here soon. 'Everest,' he whispered. 'This is your fucking Everest . . .'

*

Across the city at the Cape Sun Hotel, Springbok head coach Carel du Plessis was preparing to give his own team talk to a group of players who'd already started having silent misgivings about him. Nice guy, but talked in riddles sometimes. A Springbok playing legend, but what did he know about going head-to-head with the McGeechans and the Telfers of this world? And what was that bullshit he said when appointed to the gig only a few short months ago? 'You don't need to have coached to be able to coach the Springboks. All you need is vision – and I have the vision.'

The vision that the Boks appreciated the most was that of an opponent bent double in a scrum or disorientated in a ruck, a man broken in body and mind by the relentless men in green and gold. They understood brute force and physical domination, some of the qualities that had made them world champions two years before. They had issues with their coach but they also had certainty about their ability to win regardless. They had too much power up front, too much class behind. To a man they were cocksure they had the artillery to put the Lions to sleep.

These uppity Lions travelling around the country beating up the provinces with their flowing rugby and their easy style. These tourists who thought they were something because they rolled over some weakened sides. Thirty-eight points against Western Province, forty-two points against Natal, fifty-one points against the Emerging Springboks, sixty-four points against Mpumalanga.

That was peace-time, though. This was war. Os du Randt, Naka Drotske and Adrian Garvey – the Lions had not scrummaged against such an awesome force before, not this summer, not ever. In behind them, Hannes Strydom and Mark Andrews – world champions, both. In the back row, Ruben Kruger, André Venter and Gary Teichmann – aggression, athleticism, class.

The Lions had shown they could play, but the Springboks weren't in any mood to let them. This was fifteen versus fifteen, but really it was eight versus eight. The series would be decided in the forward battle and the Boks had more beasts than any game reserve. 'I don't believe in false modesty,' Andrews had said. 'I can, without blushing, say that I'm the greatest forward in my position on the planet.'

Andrews was asked about Martin Johnson, the towering Lions captain. 'I've heard a lot about him,' he said. 'I just hope he can live up to what is written about him. He could get very demoralised if it doesn't work out.' That day in Cape Town was when Andrews and his band of bruisers intended to show Johnson and his Lions what Springbok rugby was all about.

# CHAPTER ONE

# THE DEATH OF DANIEL BONGANE

ON THE DOORNKOP farm in the conservative hotbed of Western Transvaal, Jan Tromp and his son Henry were judge and jury when it came to allegations of petty theft among the labourers on their payroll. Daniel Bongane was black and sixteen years old when he found himself accused of stealing seventy-five rand – about eleven quid – from a fellow worker. To the Tromps there was only one way to settle this. They produced a fan belt, got two other farmhands to hold the boy down and then took it in turns to use it as a lash on Bongane, Tromp Snr hitting the teenager five times, Tromp Jnr delivering twice as many blows, each one more savage than the next.

Bongane bled to death. The Tromps were brought up on a charge of manslaughter and were sentenced to two years apiece for assault with intent to cause grievous bodily harm. An appeal court cut the punishment in half. In the end they did four months and returned to their old life. For Henry Tromp, in his mid-twenties, that old life was part farmer, part rugby player. And not just any rugby player. Tromp was a hooker with a burgeoning reputation, a player of mighty strength, mobility and promise. It was 1993 and in two years' time South Africa would host the World Cup, their first appearance in the tournament since emerging from sporting isolation. Tromp was a live contender to make the squad, until that business with Bongane – an 'altercation' as one newspaper with apartheid-leaning tendencies put it at the time.

Kitch Christie, the shrewd Springbok coach, selected three hookers in his World Cup party, but Tromp wasn't one of them. He was talented, but toxic. Christie recognised the mood and ran a mile. When the Boks went on to beat the All Blacks in a final of spine-tingling drama and emotion, nobody gave so much as a passing thought to Henry Tromp. In these early glimpses of what everybody prayed could be a new and better South Africa, François Pienaar, the victorious captain, and Nelson Mandela, the great president, shared an unforgettable moment that symbolised hope and unity.

'I grew up in an Afrikaner community, went to an Afrikaner school, spoke only Afrikaans,' Pienaar said years later, when talking about the country of his youth. 'Children were seen and not heard and you believed the publicity of the day. I remember when I heard Nelson Mandela's name mentioned at barbecues or dinner parties, the words "terrorist" or "bad man" were an umbilical cord almost to his name. As a young kid I wish I'd questioned it, but I never did. I just thought that guy's maybe not a good guy, because sadly we didn't engage with our parents. You didn't ask questions like why black kids didn't go to school with you, why it was all just white. That's how you grew up, which is very wrong and very sad. I wish I'd had the courage of my convictions to ask questions, but I didn't. During those six weeks [of the World Cup], what happened in this country was incredible. I'm still gobsmacked when I think back to the profound change that happened.'

There were 60,000 people in Ellis Park for the final and 59,000 of them were white. After Joel Stransky's extra-time drop goal saw off one of the greatest All Black sides of them all, Mandela appeared in the green and gold Springbok jersey, for so long the symbol of apartheid, and walked out into an arena dominated by Afrikaners. He was now being celebrated by some people who had previously been content to see him rot in prison on Robben Island.

Looking back on one of the most famous scenes in rugby history, the captain now wishes he'd hugged Mandela on the podium. 'He handed the trophy to me and said: "François, thank you for what you have done for South Africa." I said to him: "No, Mr Mandela. Thank you for what you have done for South Africa."' When the final whistle went, said Pienaar, 'This country changed for ever.'

Maybe Pienaar said it more in hope than expectation because barely a year had passed before the name Henry Tromp came to the surface again and with it came ugliness, rancour and the kind of complexity that makes South Africa the most enduringly fascinating rugby country on the planet.

In August of 1996, the Springboks were preparing for a Tri Nations match followed by a three-Test series against the All Blacks in their citadels in Cape Town, Durban, Pretoria and Johannesburg – and a debate about Tromp raged all the while. Should he or shouldn't he be capped? The arguments, and the people making the arguments, illustrated with crystal clarity the labyrinthine nature of rugby politics in South Africa.

Steve Tshwete was sports minister in the African National Congress government. Born in Springs on the Witwatersrand in what was then Transvaal but is now Gauteng, Tshwete was a black activist. He joined the ANC in the late 1950s and when the organisation was banned he went underground and became leader of its military wing. Captured in 1963, he was sentenced to fifteen years on Robben Island where he became president of the prison rugby club. If anybody had cause to oppose Tromp's elevation to Springbok status it was Tshwete, but he didn't. By 1996, Tshwete was all about reconciliation. He felt that Tromp had done his time and deserved his chance.

So, too, did Mluleki George, another activist who was rounded up by apartheid forces and put away for five years from 1978. George was now vice president of the South African Rugby Football Union (Sarfu). 'Tromp deserved the sentence he got but I believe he has paid for his sins,' he said. A phone poll carried out by the *Star* newspaper, one of the nation's leading dailies, recorded seventy per cent opposition to Tromp's selection. Many of the callers were white South Africans. Some vowed that they would never again pay to watch the Springboks play if Tromp was given the nod. Two black icons of the struggle against apartheid expressing support for Tromp's inclusion and thousands of Afrikaners going the other way – Tromp became South Africa's perplexing mystery in microcosm.

The arrival of the Lions was less than a year away, but on the pitch and off it, South African rugby was unravelling. The waves of optimism that swept over the nation when François and Nelson had danced together at Ellis Park had now largely gone. Kitch Christie, the coach so beloved by the World Cup-winning Boks, had also left the scene. Christie had contracted leukaemia – he would die in 1998 – and had to step down, a horrible blow to the players who had come to look on him not just as a coach but also as a father figure. Christie was a disciplinarian but he was a brilliant man-manager. The Springboks won every single game under his leadership. His players would have run through walls for him.

André Markgraaff was his successor. Like Christie before him, Markgraaff had never played Test rugby but he had been a Junior Springbok lock, a successful businessman and had forged a strong reputation as an intelligent provincial coach with Griqualand West in Kimberly in the Northern Cape. He had also proved to be a popular figure during his brief time as Christie's assistant.

New Zealand arrived in Cape Town in August of 1996 already crowned Tri Nations champions, but the Springboks looked back to their best when they went into an 18–6 lead thanks to tries from prop Os du Randt and centre Japie Mulder along with two penalties and a conversion from Joel Stransky's boot. Shortly after half-time, however, Pienaar went to tackle Sean Fitzpatrick and took a knee to the side of the head. He was knocked out cold. He tried to play on but five minutes later he collapsed to the ground and was stretchered off.

Deep inside Newlands, Pienaar slowly came to his senses. Morné du Plessis, the team manager, came down to see how he was doing – and to break the news that in the subsequent minutes, the All Blacks had roared back into the game. When the full-time whistle blew, the Springboks had been defeated 29–18. Pienaar could barely believe his ears. To add salt to wound, he missed the entirety of the subsequent three-match series through injury.

'That was one of the hardest games of my career,' said scrum-half Joost van der Westhuizen later. 'I couldn't believe we lost. We lost a sense of direction when François left the field. That's no criticism of Gary [Teichmann, who took over the captaincy], but we'd got so used to François leading us over the previous few seasons and I think we would have held on if he hadn't been injured.'

With the Tri Nations now behind them, focus turned to the series. There was a different mentality when it came to an All Black tour. The Tri Nations was in its infancy; what was not was the rivalry between the Boks and the All Blacks. Despite nearly seventy years of trying, the All Blacks had never managed to win a series in South Africa, while the Boks still crowed about the legend of Boy Louw, Danie Craven, Ebbo Bastard and the mighty team of 1937 who had won their series in New Zealand.

With Pienaar ruled out with concussion, Teichmann was made Springbok captain. 'The captaincy was never something that I had aspired to – or even really wanted,' he reflects. 'But when François was ruled out and André asked me to step up, I had to accept. I had some encouraging words from my father and changed my mindset to embrace the challenge. But within hours of my appointment a storm blew up when some New Zealand journalists reported seeing James Small out at a nightclub at one in the morning on the Friday before the Test. James was initially dropped from the squad, then reinstated, summoned to a disciplinary hearing, hauled over the coals and then dropped again. At least, I think that was the sequence of events.'

Having sat as an unused substitute in Cape Town, Henry Tromp came into the starting line-up for his debut in the first Test of the series in Durban, packing down opposite Sean Fitzpatrick. The Boks lost again, 23–19.

'The series moved to Pretoria,' said Teichmann, 'and we were being hit by the press who said we were on the brink of ignominy, the first team in Springbok history to lose a home series to the All Blacks. Our backs were pinned to the wall.'

Tromp kept his place in the side for this mammoth occasion. The All Blacks were on the brink of rugby immortality; the Springboks on the cusp of disgrace. It proved to be one of the great encounters between the old rivals. All Black scrum-half Justin Marshall darted and probed, Jeff Wilson seared down the wing to score two tries, replacement scrum-half Jon Preston came off the bench to kick two long-range penalties under blistering pressure, and number eight Zinzan Brooke played like a man from another planet, his gargantuan workload topped off with a try and an audacious drop goal. In response, the Springboks scored tries through flanker Ruben

Kruger, lock Hannes Strydom and Joost van der Westhuizen with 11 points coming via Stranky's boot. As the score settled at 33–26 in New Zealand's favour, Teichmann's men battered the All Black line in an effort to score the converted try they needed to draw the match and take the series to the final game at Ellis Park. But they just couldn't break the All Black wall. At the final whistle players from both sides collapsed to the turf, utterly spent. Fitzpatrick thumped his fist on the ground in triumph.

'Exhaustion just flooded every cell of my body,' recalled Teichmann. 'I lay on my back, eyes closed, racked with pain. I heard nothing, saw nothing. Everything was screaming: my legs, my arms, my knees and the history books had just been rewritten. It was agony.'

The All Blacks, still hurting from the World Cup final, had their revenge. It didn't make up for what had happened the previous summer at Ellis Park, but routing the South Africans in their own back yard was glorious all the same.

The third Test was a dead rubber as far as the series went, but not for the Springboks who were determined to make amends. It may have been too little, too late, but they played some fantastic attacking rugby, scoring a sweeping opening try that was finished under the posts by Van der Westhuizen, who then turned provider when he darted for the line from a tapped penalty and slipped the ball to André Venter to score, while André Joubert added three penalties to his own try and Henry Honiball contributed a conversion and a penalty. The New Zealanders had been outmatched for most of it, two late tries from Walter Little and Justin Marshall just about taking the dirty look off the scoreline. The Springboks saved some face with a 32–22 victory. In terms of the series result it was immaterial; what was compelling, though, was the growing shift in mood among watchers of the Boks.

Like Tshwete and George, Trevor Manuel had been an ANC activist back in the day, regularly detained in his early years for his firebrand opposition to the way things were in his homeland. In 1994 he was elected as an ANC member of parliament and was soon given the brief of Minister for Trade and Industry by Nelson Mandela. By 1996, as Minister of Finance, he was a high-ranking figure in government.

Manuel made no bones about who he was supporting during the All Blacks trip to South Africa – he was, unreservedly and unapologetically, on New Zealand's side. The feelgood of Ellis Park 1995 seemed to wash right over Manuel, the notion that the Springboks were now a team for all South Africans and not just white South Africans cut no ice with him, not when there wasn't a single black player in the Springboks squad now that Chester Williams was injured, and not when Tromp was welcomed into the fold despite the brutal death of Daniel Bongane. During that series with the All Blacks, more and more home fans waved the old flag of the apartheid era. That wasn't lost on Manuel either.

That series defeat to the All Blacks was a bad enough beginning to his reign but there was worse – much worse – to come for André Markgraaff. Things had become strained between the coach and the captain François Pienaar. 'I could see that André was a clever man and his understanding of the game was beyond question,' said Pienaar, 'but I didn't think he was sure what he wanted to do tactics-wise. I took the decision to take a much stronger hand as captain.' It was a decision that wasn't welcomed by the coach.

At the end of 1996, Markgraaff named a squad for a tour to Argentina, France and Wales and though available again after missing the series against the All Blacks, the World Cup-winning captain was not in it. Troubled by Pienaar's totemic stature and constantly disagreeing with him about tactics and selection, Markgraaff cut him loose – and it was a sensation.

A media poll attracted tens of thousands of responses, ninety-six per cent of whom wanted Markgraaff sacked for his lack of respect towards one of South Africa's most beloved figures. The anger was raw. Henry Tromp, who had beaten a black man to death, was on the trip, but the heroic Pienaar, a powerful force for unity in a divided country, was not. He'd never play for the Springboks again. 'It's not the way I would have liked to finish my Test career . . . but there it is,' said Pienaar. 'It's well documented that I didn't really agree with certain things that happened around that time. If there was more honesty, I would have appreciated it. But there wasn't. I don't really want to talk about it anymore.'

The fallout was colossal. Markgraaff was inundated with hate mail, some of which even contained death threats. The newspapers went after him as well. 'The public hanging of a national hero impacts not just on the game, but on the nation,' wrote *The Mail & Guardian*. 'Outrage grows over the weekend sacking of charismatic Springbok captain François Pienaar, hero of the country's Rugby World Cup championship last year,' reported the South African Press Association. Even *The New York Times* got in on the story: 'It seems that South African rugby has much in common with American baseball. The two can't help but destroy themselves.' Writing in *Le Monde* in France, Frederic Chambon eloquently summarised the situation: 'The sidelining of the Springboks' captain, the most popular player in the country, has caused a national psychodrama.'

The next day, Springbok selector Ray Mordt and Sarfu executive committee member Keith Parkinson both quit their jobs in protest. 'I want nothing more to do with the national team,' raged Mordt. 'The coach gets the team he wants. I'm finished as a selector.'

'It is a sad day for South African rugby,' said Kitch Christie. 'How can you do that to a man who made this country so proud?'

**Gary Teichmann:** It caused outrage. This was just sixteen months after François led the Springboks to victory in the World Cup and now he was being left out of a squad of thirty-six players. The story was everywhere – all over the radio, on TV, in the newspapers.

**Os du Randt:** But no one was looking at the fact that François was struggling with form.

**Gary Teichmann:** He was only twenty-nine – he was hardly history.

**Os du Randt:** All the injuries he'd sustained during the preceding years were taking their toll and it reflected in his game. He'd had several concussions which affected his reactions and timing and he wasn't as good a defender as he'd been before. François was left out because he wouldn't make the team on his standard of play.

**Mark Andrews:** Markgraaff had a battle with François and there was lots of dissent and unhappiness within the group. But personally, I enjoyed being coached by Markgraaff. He was all about the players – they were his priority. With him, the team always came first.

**Joost van der Westhuizen:** François had been so close to Kitch Christie, it was always going to be awkward, but any team takes a strong cue from the relationship between the coach and the captain, and the players are usually the first to sense any lack of harmony. It wasn't easy, but I don't think either André or François was to blame. It was the situation. The players wanted everything to be the same as in 1995, but it wasn't working. The squad was starting to divide: you were either a Markgraaff man or a Pienaar man. I was trying to keep out of the whole situation because I respected both of them. Sometimes you can get the atmosphere right and other times just get it wrong.

**André Markgraaff:** It was one of those situations that develops when a person is revered by everyone for something he has done and he becomes almost untouchable, but sooner or later a change would have had to be made.

**Joost van der Westhuizen:** It seemed to us that André wanted to be in complete charge of the team and that wouldn't be the case while François was captain. There didn't seem to be a particularly healthy relationship between André and Morné du Plessis either. The management team had worked so well during the World Cup, it was quite a shock to sense the tension at training and around the hotels. The vibe wasn't good, but we were still a powerful team.

André Markgraaff also had other problems on his hands – playing contracts. After more than a century of staunch – and often draconian – protection of the game's amateur status, the International Rugby Board had finally bowed its head to modernity after the 1995 World Cup and announced that the sport was going to go professional. As giant television companies around the world vied for control of this new professional entity it became clear very quickly that the Springboks would play a massive role in determining the future direction of the sport. The Australian tycoon, Kerry Packer, began to pitch his vision for a fully professional version of the game, which he called the World Rugby Championship.

The WRC proposed a northern and southern hemisphere league, with the respective winners of each playing off for the title of World Club Champions. The WRC would pay the players' wages and offer the unions forty-nine per cent ownership of the franchises in exchange for using their existing stadiums. It was a bold, imaginative and innovative vision that could have borne significant fruit for all involved. And Louis Luyt was having none of it.

Luyt was the hectoring bully in charge of Sarfu, the president described by turns as a boorishly fractious individual with an unquenchable self-regard, or a bit of a sociopath with few redeeming graces. Nelson Mandela once called him a 'pitiless dictator'.

He was born Oswald Louis Petrus Poley. When his father was exposed as a polygamist and his mother annulled their marriage, he took the name of his grandfather and became Louis Luyt. He was a talented rugby player with the Free State, but not quite as talented as he claimed to be over the years. Luyt became a pillar of the Afrikaner world and regarded rugby as a white man's sport, their own personal fiefdom. He was close to the apartheid establishment and made little attempt to transform the game's racial profile. Throughout his presidency he was blighted by allegations of racism and nepotism.

There was always a feeling with Luyt that he was only in it for himself. One by one he pissed everybody off. When South Africa won the World Cup in 1995 he caused a walkout at the post-final function when he pompously claimed that if it hadn't been for isolation, South Africa would have won the previous two World Cups to boot.

Luyt manoeuvred his way from relative poverty to kingpin status in the Transvaal Rugby Union to the top job in 1989. He packed a lot of power into his giant frame and he wasn't giving any of it away to the likes of Kerry Packer.

Packer needed South Africa on board if his venture was to take flight, but Luyt headed it off at the pass. Just when it looked like François Pienaar was going to be the totem for the new WRC, there was a change of heart. Pienaar suddenly backed away. Captains and senior players from other countries were literally waiting for him at a meeting to move the project to the next level but Pienaar never showed. The Springboks withdrew from Packer's brave new world and the project died a death thereafter.

Luyt had committed to putting the World Cup-winning Boks on lucrative new deals. For the world champions, he pushed the boat out, albeit reluctantly. It cost the union a fortune – and Louis didn't like it. The repercussions were serious. In negotiating a better financial deal for his teammates, Pienaar had upset Luyt. That was one very powerful enemy. Some will always believe that Pienaar's sacking was belated revenge for forcing Luyt's hand.

The new contracts were welcomed with open arms by the heroes of 1995 but by the time the World Cup-winners were looked after there wasn't a whole lot left for the rest, the boys who had emerged in the wake of the great triumph against the All Blacks. Men like Gary Teichmann, the new captain in the post-Pienaar age.

**Gary Teichmann:** It is very difficult when you're supposed to play as one team but you have different players being paid vastly different amounts for essentially doing the same thing. Henry Honiball, André Venter and I weren't on World Cup contracts, so we got rawer deals than the guys who had them. I remember Louis Luyt said to me, 'You will get this much per game and this much per day and if you don't like it, I will get three other okes to do the job.' Because there were so few of us non-World Cup players, we knew he probably could have done just that. So I told Henry that we'd better just accept the offer, even though we weren't being paid anywhere near what the World Cup-winners were getting. They made up the bulk of the squad, so there wasn't that much unhappiness, but the situation started to change quite quickly. More and more new guys were coming in, replacing the

World Cup guys, and Henry was becoming a key player in the team. He started to get the shits. He wasn't being paid enough to justify being away from his farm.

One day in a meeting he told André Markgraaff that he could earn more money just sitting on his farm. Sarfu had a lot of money tied up in the contracted guys. It caused unhappiness and Markgraaff was the guy who had to find the money.

**Henry Honiball:** It felt as if Markgraaff was constantly discussing our contracts with us. We weren't asking for a lot of money, but they were playing hardball. I remember that, at one of those meetings, I was looking at my watch while Markgraaff was talking. He asked me what I was doing and I told him I was working out if I could get back to my farm in Winterton by nightfall. I said I was ready to go back because I could get more money from farming. The tactic must have worked, because Markgraaff got us the money we were asking for.

**Joost van der Westhuizen:** We tried to bond as a team but it was difficult when players were effectively being paid according to their status in 1995 rather than on current form. I know some people started to resent the World Cup players because their contracts guaranteed payments regardless of results or even whether they were playing. It was said some players didn't mind if they were picked or not, since they'd earn the same either way. I think it's true that some guys sat back and relaxed. For my part, I don't think my approach to the game changed. I still desperately wanted to play for the Boks. That was the way I was brought up. Money wasn't going to change that.

**Gary Teichmann:** At Natal we had Mark Andrews, André Joubert and James Small earning anything between six and ten times as much as their teammates. It was the same everywhere. Provincial players were invariably given one-year contracts loaded towards match fees rather than monthly salaries, but the World Cup Springboks, some of whom were on the brink of retirement, had been given three-year deals with the income guaranteed whether they played or not. It was absolutely catastrophic for team dynamics within the Test squad. There's no doubt in my mind that a lot of the problems we experienced in 1996 and 1997 were largely caused by that underlying issue. We spent far too much time talking, worrying and arguing about money. It was a shit show. Just one thing after another. We were wallowing in our problems.

**André Markgraaff:** Rugby seemed to be the last thing on anyone's mind.

# CHAPTER TWO

# IT'S THE KAFFIRS, MAN

ANDRÉ MARKGRAAFF HAD a turbulent start to his coaching reign, but after the victory in the final Test against the All Blacks he was determined to keep the momentum going on the end-of-year tour. Before they could leave South Africa, not only did he have to deal with the fallout of the François Pienaar affair, he also had to reconfigure his backroom staff.

Morné du Plessis stepped down from the manager's role in August, disturbed by the waving of apartheid-era flags during the Test against the Wallabies in Bloemfontein during the Tri Nations. Du Plessis issued a statement condemning the gesture. He himself then came under attack for his statement and was left hung out to dry by Sarfu. The lack of support from Louis Luyt was too much for the former Springbok captain and he tendered his resignation.

With Du Plesssis gone, Markgraaff assumed all the responsibilities for team management. He appointed three young coaches as his assistants for the tour – Nick Mallett came in to help with the forwards, Hugh Rees-Edwards with the backs and Carel du Plessis was appointed as a general technical advisor.

It was vital that the tour was a success for the players on and off the field – and, despite everything, it was. Markgraaff's new-look team recorded two thumping wins over the Pumas in Buenos Aires, then defeated France in Bordeaux and at the Parc des Princes (and in so doing became the first Springbok team to win a series on French soil), and then steamrollered Wales in Cardiff in the last Test to be played at the old Arms Park. 'At the end of the tour I was exhausted, relieved and proud of my team,' said Teichmann. 'The 1995 World Cup was history. This new squad were the real deal and we flew home looking forward to the twin challenges in 1997 of the British and Irish Lions tour and mounting a serious campaign in the Tri Nations.'

At the end of an intense and tumultuous thirteen-Test year, Markgraaff had won six in a row; after enduring severe criticism and scrutiny at the start of his time, his team were now beginning to purr. The Springboks were playing devastating, expansive rugby; their set piece was rock solid and their defence was dominant. 'We can look forward to the Lions tour with real confidence,' declared the head coach in the aftermath of the Cardiff victory.

But there was another storm brewing. A calamitous one.

In October 1996, Markgraaff met with André Bester, one of his former provincial players at Griqualand West. After a while the conversation turned to the dropping of François Pienaar and the intense flak Markgraaff had received from the English-speaking media, particulalry the TV channel, Top Sport. Markgraaff had no idea that Bester was recording the conversation.

'The whole fucking Pienaar thing is politics,' raged Markgraaff, 'the whole fucking country is behind him – in terms of the press. Top Sport is the media. TV is the government. Top Sport is the government. It is a kaffir station . . . it is for the kaffirs . . . it's the government, the whole fucking lot, it's the government. That guy [Pienaar] can be walking on fucking crutches, but they still fucking want him . . . it's the kaffirs, man . . . it's the fucking kaffirs.'

Bester was a former captain of the Griquas; he and his brother Piet, also a Griqua, had a simmering grudge against Markgraaff for failing to renew their contracts with the province when he had been president of the union. André Bester later claimed that he had recorded the conversation because Markgraaff had reneged on a promise to make him the director of coaching at the Griquas. 'I taped the meeting so that, if my agreement wasn't honoured, I could have used it,' said Bester. In February 1997, the Besters leaked their recording to the press.

It was 8.00 p.m. on 17 February when the SABC (South African Broadcasting Company) released a snippet of the recording. Markgraaff later claimed that the audio had been doctored and that he had paid Dr Len Jansen, an expert in voice recordings, a vast amount of money to prove it. He admitted that he may have been drawn to utter the word 'kaffir' once, but not the numerous times it appeared on the tape. As if it really mattered how many times he said it. Once was more than enough.

The fallout was seismic. Markgraaff called a press conference in his hometown of Kimberley. He was in tears as he spoke. 'I'm not making any excuses, but I was very emotional at the time,' he said. 'I apologise to the black people of this country and to the whites for causing them embarrassment. I've not acted in a spirit of reconciliation and I hope you will forgive me. This is not easy for me and I herewith tender my resignation as coach of the Springbok rugby team.'

'I admired the way Markgraaff handled the situation because he didn't deny anything,' said the Springbok hooker, James Dalton, years later. 'He took accountability, called a media conference and explained the context to what he said, why he said it and to whom it was said. He then resigned, knowing the scandal was too big to save him as the Springbok coach. I watched his conference and felt sorry for him as he wept. I knew the feeling of addressing the country and being reduced to tears because the emotion was overwhelming. It had happened to me after my suspension from the 1995 Rugby World Cup after a fight broke out in the game against Canada. I know Markgraaff wasn't everyone's kind of person, but I'd grown to understand him on the 1996 end-of-season tour to Europe and, from a rugby perspective, I thought he and Gary Teichmann had formed a strong partnership as coach and captain.'

Markgraaff had been confident that the Springboks were back on the road to becoming the best team in the world, but now everything was in tatters. Not only was he gone, but an internecine war was breaking out between Louis Luyt at Sarfu and Steve Tshwete, the South African Minister of Sport, who wanted a state investigation into issues of racism and suspected financial irregularities within rugby's governing body. Brian Van Rooyen, a lawyer and former Transvaal Rugby Union vice president, produced a 500-page dossier of alleged abuses and malpractices in Sarfu. Tshwete appointed a three-member task team to investigate Sarfu, a development which enraged Luyt and his son-in-law Rian Oberholzer, the Sarfu chief executive.

To add to the tumult, on 2 May 1997, it was announced that the Springbok lock, Johann Ackermann, and two Gauteng Lions players, Bennie Nortje and Stephan Bronkhorst, had tested positive for anabolic steroids. They were banned for two years. South African rugby was in freefall.

With Markgraaff gone, Sarfu needed to appoint a new head coach. With all the other pressures they were under, the executive committee decided that the easiest option was to simply promote one of Markgraaff's assistant coaches. It seemed obvious to many that it would be Nick Mallett who would make the step-up. 'Among the players,' said Teichmann, 'the consensus was that Nick would be named as the new Springbok coach. He'd been the dominant personality among the assistant coaches on tour and he appeared ready for the challenge.'

Having enjoyed a successful coaching stint in France, Mallett had returned to South Africa in 1995 to take charge of Boland – and transformed one of the country's weakest provincial teams into Currie Cup quarter-finalists. His work with the Springbok forwards on the end-of-year tour had been widely regarded as excellent. But while Mallett may have been lauded by pundits and fans, behind the scenes he was regarded with suspicion. Having fiercely criticised the Sarfu executive committee in a magazine article – and been dragged over the coals for it – he had made enemies. There was a school of thought within the corridors of power that he was too headstrong and too emotional for the top job. Mallett got bypassed. Instead, it was Carel du Plessis who was offered the role. It was a decision that stunned the country.

In the wake of the appointment, the journalist Donald McRae sat down with James Small at his home in Cape Town. 'Shit,' sighed Small when the conversation turned to the Springboks, 'we've had five coaches in the past four years. On the tour back in December we'd started to sort things out again. Everybody had found their place in the squad. Now with a new coach, Carel du Plessis, who hasn't done much coaching at all, there's a whole new ball game. Players don't like this kind of uncertainty because it kills your confidence. So, right now, it's very unsettled in South African rugby. We've got all this shit off the field and, on it, no one knows what the new coach is thinking or which players he might want to use. We're starting from a clean slate – again.'

Du Plessis was born in the Eastern Cape in June of 1960. He made his debut as the Springbok head coach against Tonga in

Cape Town on 10 June 1997, just two weeks before his thirty-seventh birthday. That Test with Tonga was the only game his Springboks played before they faced the Lions. Set against the ferocious backdrop of the Tromp, Markgraaff, Ackermann and Sarfu scandals, he faced a daunting start.

Du Plessis had never played against the Lions, but he had a long history with them. As a twelve year old boy he had stood with his father on the terraces at Boet Erasmus Stadium when the Lions clinched the 1974 series with victory in the third Test. He had been utterly entranced by the tourists and the image of Gordon Brown punching the air at full time had seared itself on his mind forever after. It was the audacious attacking talents of the Lions' backline that made the most lasting impression, though. 'To this day if you think about the '74 Lions, the names just trip off the tongue,' said Du Plessis in almost misty-eyed admiration. 'JPR Williams, Andy Irvine, Gerald Davies, JJ Williams, Ian McGeechan, Phil Bennett and Gareth Edwards. What a team.' He missed out the Irish centre, Dick Milliken, but there was no doubt that Du Plessis was entranced.

He forged a glittering career with Western Province, establishing a reputation as one of the all-time greats of South African rugby. People called him 'the Prince of Wings'. Because South Africa were in international isolation for the majority of his career he only played twelve Tests and never had the chance to face the Lions – he was too young to play against Bill Beaumont's class of 1980 and when it looked like he might finally have a chance against Colin Deans' 1986 team, the tour was cancelled. He retired in 1989 aged just twenty-nine, but with a heavily laden trophy cabinet. Du Plessis scored eighty-one tries in 108 games for Western Province, captained the side on fifty-seven occasions and won five Currie Cups alongside his brothers Willie and Michael. In his final season, he scored twenty-five tries, a Western Province record.

As a partner in a successful Cape Town financial services company he could have walked away from the game without a backwards glance, but he couldn't leave it behind. He became an assistant coach with the University of Western Cape and then, out of the blue, Markgraaff called him in late 1996 and asked him to join his Springbok staff as a technical adviser for the end-of-season tour.

When Markgraaff resigned in February 1997, Du Plessis was among those who expected Mallett to be offered the head coach position. He was as shocked as anyone when Sarfu offered him the gig. He had never been a head coach – at any level. In truth, he had hardly even been a coach. A lifetime of wanting to represent the Springboks had been reduced to a handful of appearances because of isolation. Now he had a chance to do as a coach what he had never done as a player – lead a team of world champions against the Lions, the team that had captured his imagination as a child.

In many ways you could see the logic of Sarfu's decision. In the aftermath of the Bester tapes, the understated Du Plessis was a safe option. The Prince of Wings was a clean-cut poster boy of South African rugby, the perfect antidote to the travails that had been continually befalling the Springboks since the turn of 1996. The appointment of a new black team manager, Arthob Petersen, also helped reinforce the sense of a fresh start.

'There have been questions raised about my suitability,' reflected Du Plessis ahead of the Lions' visit. 'I thought there would be a reaction as it's traditionally a position filled by someone with more experience. I accept that and now have to try and live up to the responsibility. If I didn't believe that I could make a difference and have some valuable input then I wouldn't have made myself available.'

Du Plessis decided against retaining Nick Mallett as assistant coach and instead appointed his former Stellenbosch, Western

Province and Springbok teammate Gert Smal as his number two. Smal had been a robust flanker whose career had been cut short by a knee injury. He had sealed his place in Springbok rugby folklore for knocking out All Black prop Gary Knight with a counter-punch during the New Zealand Cavaliers' rebel tour to South Africa in 1986.

**Gary Teichmann:** Carel phoned me a few days after his appointment and asked if I would meet with him and Gert. He flew up from Cape Town and we all had breakfast at the Elangeni Hotel on Durban's beachfront. Carel said he wanted me to remain as Springbok captain and was eager to hear what I believed the priorities were for the squad. I talked about the advantages of shorter and more intense training sessions, but I was much more intrigued to know which direction he wanted to take.

My impression was that he wanted to carry on where we left off in Wales. He seemed completely sincere and honest, young and enthusiastic. I left the meeting thinking that we could work successfully together, but there's no doubt that there was a nagging worry that he was inexperienced and we were moving forward on a bit of a wing and a prayer.

Du Plessis sounded like his own man when making his first state of the nation address. 'I want to develop a multifaceted style of attacking, winning rugby in which South Africa will be innovators rather than followers in the world game,' he said. 'I am excited by the challenge, particularly because we have so many exceptionally gifted players, and I would hope that I can encourage the team to play with flair and a bit of risk.'

These words were music to the ears of the Springbok fans – but the pressure was on. Untried, untested, Du Plessis was not only entering a political and administrative storm, but also a sporting one – he had to follow in the footsteps of Kitch Christie and the towering achievements of the 1995 World Cup winners but without the experience of François Pienaar and other Ellis Park immortals. And in the dugout opposite he would have a most formidable rival, one of the greatest minds the rugby world has ever known, a man steeped in Lions legend and one of Du Plessis' heroes from 1974 – Ian McGeechan.

# CHAPTER THREE

# EIGHT BOKS OF THE APOCALYPSE

GEECH STILL REMEMBERS the day the letter arrived, how he carefully sliced open the envelope, the first thing catching his eye being the embossed Lions badge on the top of the page. All these years later he can recall the sensation of standing in his hallway and staring at the words inviting him to be part of the 1974 Lions trip to South Africa. It still feels like it was yesterday.

That trip changed him. When he returned home his wife Judy said that he had a new confidence about him, a new belief in his own ability. He knew what it was to be a successful Lion and, as a coach, he desperately wanted that life-changing experience for his players. He was forty-two years old and only in his second season as head coach at Test level when he took charge of the Lions for the first time. It was 1989 and the Lions were in Australia. The visitors lost the first Test and won the next two to take the series. In his second spell, against New Zealand in 1993, the series went the other way, 2–1 to the All Blacks.

Those summers taught him much but he always said that 1974 was seminal. He had Ireland's Dick Milliken as a midfield partner in the Test series and they've been friends ever since. That tour, and the endless amounts of defending that had to be done in the face of waves of demonic Springbok attacking, is still fresh in his mind. He drew on those experiences when speaking to his players in 1997.

He spoke about the thirty-eight-minute Springbok bombardment in the third Test in Port Elizabeth, the unadulterated aggression of the Boks as they tried to save the series. The Lions had won the first two Tests and would win the third as well, but only after withstanding a battering the like of which McGeechan never experienced before or after.

Those minutes spent protecting his own try line lived with him, their relevance growing over time. 'The toughest thing I've ever been involved in,' he said. 'Dick and I were so under the cosh with these big men running at us time and time again that we never even had time to speak to each other. But we didn't have to. We just looked at each other and got on with it – we had to find a way to exist in those long minutes. The Lions chemistry, the communal feeling, it comes from respect. Many of my Lions feelings spring from that third Test. Sometimes you don't have to say anything to a fellow Lion, there's just a look.'

All of the big moments in Geech's rugby life happened after the death of his father. Bob McGeechan was brought up in Govan in sight of Ibrox, home of Glasgow Rangers. He was just five foot six inches tall; a useful boxer, a handy footballer, good enough to be a youth player at Rangers. But whatever dreams he might have had about becoming a professional footballer went before his twentieth birthday. He signed up for the Argyll and Sutherland Highlanders as a stretcher-bearer in the medical corps and went to war.

Bob's big mate was Ginger. Geech never knew the surname. On the odd occasion when Bob spoke about his army life he'd mention his pal and how close they were and what happened to him in the North African desert when their convoy came under fire from a low-flying Messerschmidt. Bob jumped out of the jeep to the left, Ginger jumped right. When the attack ceased, Bob crawled round the side of the vehicle to find Ginger lying dead.

His father's life was short but inspirational. Bob contracted cancer but never complained once. People talk about mental strength on a rugby field, but the character of his dad in coping with his disease was courage of an altogether different dimension. Bob McGeechan died in 1969 at the age of forty-eight. He missed his son's Scotland debut in 1972, missed him playing for the Lions in 1974 and 1977, missed him coaching his country to a Grand Slam in 1990. Geech tells a story about that famous day against England at Murrayfield. In the warm-up, Geech took a walk across the pitch. The Queen Victoria pipe band from Dunblane were getting ready to do their thing when the old pipe major approached Geech, told him that he'd gone to school with his father and that Bob would be very proud of him.

Geech was shocked and moved in equal measure. He said he didn't believe in the spirit world, but in that moment he wanted, and chose, to believe that this was no coincidence, that on some level Bob was with him. After missing his greatest days as a player, it gave him comfort to think that he was looking down on his greatest day as a coach.

After Scotland, Geech went on to coach Northampton. Although he had been out of international rugby for three years by the time Lions manager Fran Cotton approached him to lead the tour in 1997, Cotton knew that there was no better man. Geech had the passion and the knowledge. Having done it twice already, he knew all about the wonderful possibilities and the dangerous pitfalls of the job.

**Ian McGeechan:** We had a fantastic squad in 1989 and every single player was good enough to play in the Tests. They enjoyed themselves and kept each other honest and there wasn't a single player that we carried. In 1993 it was different. The squad had been chosen by committee and there were all sorts of trade-offs between countries and we ended up with six or seven players I wouldn't have taken had it been down to me. It had a huge impact on the tour. I said never again. When Fran asked me if I would come back as head coach in '97, I said I would, but on two conditions. Number one, I wanted to pick my own assistant coach; number two, I wanted myself, my assistant and Fran to pick the players – and nobody else. The tour was going to be hard enough without horse-trading. If I was going to fail then I was going to fail with the players I'd chosen. I blame myself for some of the things that went wrong in 1993. Towards the end of that tour some players lost heart as well as form and we allowed them to feel peripheral to what was happening. That was a mistake that I was determined to learn from.

In the summer of 1996, when the Springboks were hosting the All Blacks in that three-game series, he spent a week in camp with the New Zealanders. John Hart, the Kiwi coach, welcomed him in and gave him the benefit of his sometimes bitter experiences of touring South Africa. In those hours with Hart, Geech metamorphosed into a human sponge.

**Ian McGeechan:** John Hart was brilliant. New Zealand had learned from past tours that if they turned up for a training session at a rugby club, the scrum machine they had been promised would have mysteriously disappeared. There would be no rucking shields or tackle bags. They'd be given nothing. So they brought all their own equipment – they even brought their own scrum machine, which was unheard of at the time. We had to be self-sufficient and that was a first for the Lions.

The most important thing I learned was about the size of the squad and how to manage key positions. The All Blacks took an extra scrum-half and an extra hooker when they went to South Africa. We'd never done that before, but it was Sean Fitzpatrick who told me how important it was. It allowed him to get some rest through rotation. Without it, he'd have to start every game, or be on the bench, and he would have been knackered by the time it came to the Test series.

**Sean Fitzpatrick:** These were lessons that we'd learned over decades of touring there. The key to beating the Springboks is taking the game to them. They're so passionate about their rugby, you feel you're playing against the whole country. They don't lie down and you can't afford to let up for one minute. It's a physical and mental challenge. You've got to be superbly fit and lucky with injuries, but part of managing that is through squad rotation. A long tour to South Africa is a great test of a player's character. Anyone who plays in South Africa finds out a lot about themselves.

**Ian McGeechan:** John and I talked long and hard about what it took to beat the Springboks on their home patch. The All Blacks had thoroughly vetted every hotel and every training facility, so we did too – Fran went for a twelve-day reconnaissance mission to make sure that everything was just as we wanted it. We also had the biggest backup squad the Lions had ever taken. I produced a twenty page report on what I felt was needed to beat the Boks. I identified eight key players in their side. I got videos of every game those eight had played over the past two years. I wanted to know how they wanted to play so I could figure out a plan on how to stop them.

The eight players that McGeechan identified were a mixture of the old and the new, the familiar warriors from the 1995 glory team and the new brigade that had swept through in the years that followed. He made detailed notes on every one – the men at the heart of the Springboks.

### Os du Randt – *'On the rugby field it felt like I could crush anyone'*

Jacobus Petrus du Randt was born in 1972 in the small farming community of Elliot in the North Eastern Cape. The 260 hectares of land that made up the family farm, Marinus, was beautiful but rugged and it needed hard folk to tame it. 'It was a sheltered Afrikaans life,' Du Randt said of his early years. 'We didn't even have a television. When we were two or three my dad encouraged us to work on the land. So by the time I was six I was doing man's work. We'd be up at five in the morning and we'd plough the fields until late in the evening. I became very strong at a very young age. On the rugby field it felt like I could crush anyone.'

He thinks he was thirteen years old when people started calling him Os – Afrikaans for Ox. As part of his high school initiation some seniors tried to pin him down to shave his head, but he wrestled them away with ease. One of the seniors cried that he was as strong as an ox – and the nickname stuck.

It wasn't hard to see where he got it from. His grandfather was also Jacobus Petrus but everyone called him Oupa Koos. 'He was a huge man. He only had one hand – he lost the other in an accident with the bakkie [truck] on the farm – but it didn't stop him grabbing young oxen so tightly they could never escape. He also used to pick up an 80kg sacks of mealies [corn] with one arm, flip it onto his back and carry it like it weighed nothing at all.'

At six foot three inches and weighing somewhere between twenty and twenty-two stone – nobody was ever totally sure – Du Randt was a beast for a loose head prop, but what truly defined him was his dynamism. He could run and tackle and pass like a fourth back-rower. He had the bludgeon but he could play, too. 'As a kid my dad would sometimes scrum and wrestle with me and my brothers and he'd say, "Remember, the opposition isn't going to show you any mercy, so you shouldn't show him any." I remember my mother started crying one evening and said to my father, "You're turning my poor child into a murderer!" But I always remembered what he said. Whenever I played, I went in hard and I never showed any mercy.'

In 1994, having only just broken into the Free State team, Kitch Christie selected Du Randt for his Test debut against Argentina at the Boet Erasmus Stadium. He had only just turned twenty-two and had played just nine matches for his club, but Os nailed down the position and became a cornerstone of the World Cup-winning team.

Writing in *The Independent* ahead of the Lions tour, Chris Hewett graphically captured Du Randt's threat. 'Os is Springbok rugby's equivalent of Table Mountain. You cannot see over him – the official tale of the tape has him at six foot three inches but he looks three feet taller – and if you opt to go round him you are in for a detour of approximately four miles . . . Os on the hoof is a sight for sore eyes, the sort of African challenge Ernest Hemingway would have relished provided he was armed with a twelve-bore shotgun and a bottle of brandy.'

## Mark Andrews – *'I'm the greatest lock on the planet'*

Like Du Randt, Mark Andrews was born and raised in the little farming community of Elliot in the North Eastern Cape. At six foot seven inches tall, Andrews was rangy, but he was also hard – a trait so often found in South African forwards, but one that had been honed not just on the high veldt but also during his formative years in Europe. 'Not long after I finished school, I went to play club rugby for Aurillac in France. I was nineteen. I was supposed to be twenty-one so we lied about my age and there was a huge rumpus when the officials at Aurillac found out. I played and scored a try in my first game and started winning them lineout ball, so they were quite happy to let me stay.

'I tell you, playing in France toughened me up. I was playing with men – and they were rough men. My teammates were labourers, firemen and factory workers. It was no place to have a faint heart. The rivalry on the field was brutal and intense. My experience in France played a big role in turning me into the player I became.'

Andrews was one of the great leaders of the World Cup-winning team, not just as a lock but also as a number eight, where he played in the semi and the final. He was an immense natural talent no matter where he was picked and one of the most ferocious competitors of his era. He didn't believe in false modesty and was never slow to tell people of his pre-eminence in his position. His passion in playing for the Boks bordered on the scary. 'I'm often asked what it feels like to be a Springbok. It's almost impossible to explain. I've always been hugely competitive, I hate being second in anything and I think that helped drive me to the top. I won't play a pal at pool if I know he's better than me because I don't want to lose. I'd rather not play than finish second. I always had a massive fear of failure, which I think all great sportsmen have.

'When I was younger I'd go into a depression for two or three days if we lost even though rugby is a team game and it mightn't have been my fault. When I played for the Natal Sharks and we lost, I wouldn't go out and spend my money because I didn't think I'd earned it. But defeats made me train harder and be more focused. The hunger I had to win was incredible.'

### André Venter – *'I replaced Pienaar – no pressure!'*

Born half an hour away from Johannesburg in Vereeniging, where François Pienaar – his predecessor in the Springbok number six jersey – also hailed from, André Venter was a relentlessly physical back-row forward, a man who brought commitment to the cause to a whole new level.

'To me,' he once said, 'the Springbok shirt is representative of everything I believe in: my land, my fellow South Africans, my God. When I carry myself on to the field, I also carry the dreams of my country. We are all aware of this, everyone in the squad. It makes us hungry for victory.'

Lawrence Dallaglio first came across André Venter in 1994 when he toured South Africa with England. 'We played the Free State and I came up against this absolute wrecking ball in their back row. What a player. Fast, hard, totally uncompromising. And absolutely huge. I mean, they were all huge in South Africa, but he could shift as well. That tour made me realise that the game was already professional in South Africa, even if they didn't publicly admit it.

'The size of those guys, in every team, but particularly the Springboks, was unbelievable. Not just tall, but big – they were huge, huge men, all across the park; it was intimidating, scary. Really scary. You never wanted to admit you were scared when you came up against them, but you couldn't help it.'

Venter got his big break when Pienaar went down injured in the first Test of the 1996 All Blacks series. 'I replaced Pienaar – no pressure!' Unheralded on his first appearance, Venter got better and better with every Test. Tall, fast, tough and with a near hundred per cent record as an option at the back of the lineout, he was going to be a major thorn in the Lions' side. Added to that was an array of slick handling skills honed on the sevens circuit, where he had been close to being named as player of the tournament at the World Cup Sevens in Hong Kong in March 1997. Venter deserved his place on Geech's list.

### Gary Teichmann – 'François? My style was different'

When Gary Teichmann became Springboks captain in the wake of the Pienaar drama he had clear ideas about what kind of captain he was going to be. 'There was no way I was going to try to imitate François Pienaar. He was a one-in-a-million captain – a good speaker, a good motivator and a great player. My style was different. I believed in a total team game and I probably allowed the team to express themselves more than others might.'

The Springboks captain spent the first twelve years of his life in Zimbabwe. His parents were both originally from Natal, but had headed to Rhodesia, as it was then, shortly after they were married in 1957 and eventually settled in a small town between Harare and Bulawayo where his father worked as a stock auctioneer. Rugby was prohibited for anyone under the age of ten in Zimbabwe, so it wasn't until the Teichmanns moved back to South Africa in 1980 that young Gary took up the game. He was enrolled at one of the country's most prestigious schools, Hilton College in KwaZulu-Natal, and although his first sporting love was cricket, he broke into the Hilton under-14s as an outside centre before later being moved into the back row when he began playing for the senior team.

Teichmann was selected for Craven Week in 1984 and played in a Natal Schools team alongside Joel Stransky, but while Stransky went on to play for South African Schools, Teichmann missed out. He was much smaller than many of the hulking Afrikaner back-rowers on the scene and felt that he had maybe reached the peak of his playing career. After two years of national service, he worked for a time with his brother in Pietermaritzburg, but the business soon failed and he drifted listlessly before enrolling in a two-year farm-management course at an agricultural college. Although he was playing for both the Maritzburg University side and Natal under-21 team at the time, he still had no notion of what he was capable of on a rugby field.

'Any faint hope I might have nurtured of playing provincial rugby was blocked emphatically by the outstanding form of Andrew Aitken, who was playing number eight for Natal. Not only was he younger than me, but he was also mobile, strong and incredibly talented. Aitken was being hailed as one of the stars of the side that won the Currie Cup against Transvaal at Loftus Versfeld in 1990 – our first ever Currie Cup title. My introduction to the Natal squad the following season owed a great deal – if not everything – to Andrew's decision to go to university in Cape Town. If he'd stayed in Durban, it's almost certain that I'd have gone no further than the Maritzburg University club team.'

It was the breakthrough Teichmann needed. When Natal beat Transvaal in a famous 1990 Currie Cup final, Naas Botha, the Transvaal fly-half, had sourly proclaimed, 'It took them 100 years to win their first Currie Cup and it will probably take them another 100 years to win it again.' They were words that would come back to haunt Botha as Natal, with Teichmann to the fore, established themselves as one of the greatest provincial teams in South African rugby history. In fairness to Botha, Natal didn't win the Currie Cup in 1991 – but they did in 1992 and then, with Teichmann installed as captain, in 1995 and 1996. They took on the mantle as South Africa's leading provincial side. Teichmann's calm authority was at the heart of their success. His coach, Ian McIntosh, said that come 1996 his captain had become a giant. 'There was still an English versus Afrikaans issue in the squad back then, but Gary navigated it seamlessly,' said his team-mate Robbie Kempson. 'He drew all the guys together.'

The Springboks may have lost a global icon when Pienaar had been axed, but in many ways they gained a better leader for the collective. Teichmann was the kind of man who would always put the team before his own personal ambitions, who didn't crave the limelight or look to pave the way for his future career with smart quips or Churchillian pronouncements in press conferences. All he wanted was for the Springboks to succeed. Talk to his former players and you quickly form the impression that Teichmann was special.

## Joost van der Westhuizen – *'I just wanted the bloody ball'*

Joost Heystek van der Westhuizen played barefoot rugby at Laerskool Derdepoort in a poor area in the east of Pretoria. He started off as a wing, but hated how little he saw of the ball. He was then moved to prop and after that to the back row and he hated that even more. 'I said I wanted to play scrum-half, because they got lots of ball. I was only five or six years old, but I knew exactly what I wanted – I just wanted the bloody ball.'

For as long as he could remember, his father had taken him and his two brothers to watch the Bulls at Loftus Versfeld and at full time he would invade the field and try to touch his favourite players – Naas Botha and Thys Lourens. As he told his biographer, David Gemmell: 'Rugby was a way to express myself. Other kids would jump on their bikes or run or whatever. All I wanted to do was play rugby.'

He won his first cap for the Springboks in 1993 and set a new standard for modern, physical scrum-halves – rangy, powerful, more like a fourth back row forward than a diminutive link-player. He was strong and fast and tall and there was a steeliness behind the wolf-like green-blue eyes that spoke to his furious competitiveness.

Van der Westhuizen was a towering presence throughout the Springboks' World Cup campaign, but he truly showed his class in the final with his control around the set piece and his astonishing defensive performance. Early on, he made a critical intervention to bring down a rampaging Jonah Lomu. Three times during the game he brought the giant Kiwi winger crashing to earth and three times this act of bravery swelled the belief among his teammates. What was all the more remarkable was that Van der Westhuizen was making those tackles with a broken rib sustained in the semi-final against France. In the week building up to the final, he had to be given seven painkilling injections just to get him through.

In the aftermath of the series loss to the All Blacks in 1996, some critics began to question aspects of his game, identifying a weakness in his kicking and a tendency to take too much on himself around the fringes, but he shoved those words down their throats, first with a brilliant performance in the final Test victory against the All Blacks and then during the end-of-year tour. He was pivotal in the two victories over Argentina and another two victories over France in Bordeaux and Paris. In the win over Wales in Cardiff, Van der Westhuizen scored three tries.

'I'll never forget our game in Cardiff,' said Rob Howley, the Welshman opposite Van der Westhuizen. 'He was unbelievable. He was single-handedly the difference between the two sides. He had everything. He had speed over five, he had speed over ninety. He was six-foot two, but he had a low centre of gravity and a huge hand-off. He was a very smart rugby player as well. He was a lovely bloke off the field, but he was a bastard to play against. He was horrible, he was *horrible*.'

Geech studied Joost's game with the attention to detail of a scientist in a lab. 'He was the link between the two Natal players – Gary Teichmann at eight and Henry Honiball at ten – and the three of them had the ability to cause us all sorts of problems. The game had never seen anyone like him in a number nine shirt before. We knew that could be his Achilles heel as well. If we got up in his face, gave him no room, he might get frustrated and start to make mistakes. At the same time, if we didn't keep our concentration up, an angry Joost would make us pay.'

Ahead of the Lions tour, Van der Westhuizen was made captain of the South African team for the 1997 World Cup Sevens in Hong Kong at the end of March. They cruised through the pool stages, then beat France in the quarter-finals and New Zealand in the semis. They lost to Fiji in the final, a 24–21 thriller. He hadn't won a second World Cup but he returned home as sharp as a tack and ready for the arriving Lions.

## Henry Honiball – *'I grew up tackling'*

Henry Honiball, like Van der Westhuizen, redefined the physical specifications of a modern half-back. Where once the fly-half was one of the smallest players on the field – and certainly the cleanest when the full-time whistle blew – Honiball was different. At six-foot three he was huge for a number ten and contrary to every perceived stereotype of the position, he relished the physical stuff. 'I played rugby for a weaker school and all I used to do was tackle. I grew up tackling.'

Honiball was a conjuror with ball in hand and had an elegant running game. And he was brave, preferring to stand flat to the gain line and absorb punishment as he put the runners around him into space or exploded into the space himself.

'We called him the "Blade", which in Afrikaans is "Lem",' said Gary Teichmann.

'We also called him "Spook", because he just floated around, you never heard him,' said Joost van der Westhuizen. 'Even when he tackled me, he never said a word. He just smiled. His tackle was the hardest anyone ever made on me in my rugby career. He hit me so hard he cracked my sternum.'

Born in Estcourt in the Natal midlands in December 1965, Honiball was educated at Estcourt High School – a rugby backwater from where he became their one and only Springbok – and broke into the Free State provincial team while studying at the University of Free State. When he was only twenty-five, however, it looked like his rugby career might be over as he moved back home to work on his family dairy and cattle farm in Bergville.

'I played for Free State for a few years, but we were given just fifty rand a game,' he said. 'I had a farm that I had to keep going, so I couldn't afford to stay in Bloemfontein for just fifty rand a game. So I went back home and gave up rugby. That was in 1991. I remember getting a call from coach Ian McIntosh, who'd heard that I was back home. Mac asked me if I would consider playing for the Sharks. I said no. I wasn't interested.'

McIntosh persevered and eventually persuaded Honiball to come and play for Natal – quite the feat considering the round-trip from his home in Bergville to Kings Park was 280km and took five hours, a journey that Honiball undertook four times a week. 'I worked out that I covered about 7,000 kilometres a month in those years when I was playing for Natal and living on the farm. The Natal Rugby Union paid for the petrol, so that was good.'

As Natal's star soared, so too did Honiball's and when McIntosh became Springbok head coach in 1993 he handed the twenty-seven-year-old fly-half his first cap against Australia. Honiball had to bide his time, though. Joel Stransky became first choice. When the Springboks needed rebuilding after 1995, Honiball re-emerged.

Geech understood what the had to do. 'In our defensive strategy we needed to make sure that we were up very quickly on Honiball and also into the spaces around him. We did defensive drills with bags positioned across the field. It was about going hard into contact and then repositioning for the next play. There were three waves: the hit wave, the near defence group and then the wider group. It was all about line-speed. When we got at them we had to keep pushing through. We needed to make sure that every time Honiball looked for his runners all he would see were red Lions jerseys.'

### James Small – *'I could have ended up in prison'*

James Small was a winger, a box-office player that coaches, fans and commentators struggled to understand. He was fast, powerful and opinionated. A maverick, a bad boy, 'the Eric Cantona of rugby' as he was once described. His teammates nicknamed him 'No Rules'. He was rock 'n' roll but also vulnerable. He kept a piece of paper in his wallet with a quote from Cantona that read, 'To achieve happiness, sometimes you have to go through the worst depths of despair. Genius is about digging yourself out of the hole you have fallen, or been pushed, into. Failure makes you succeed.'

James Small came with very big complications. He developed a friendship with President Mandela, who told him he had a 'big job to do' in the minutes before the World Cup final. Small did as much as anyone to quell the threat of the mighty Jonah Lomu, but he was also the same James Small who was accused of racially abusing his teammate Chester Williams. The source of the allegation made it a compelling story – it was Chester Williams.

'You fucking kaffir, why do you want to play our game? You know you can't play it.' In his autobiography, that's what Williams claimed Small had said to him. Small would respond to the allegation through his lawyer, saying he had 'no independent recollection of the specific events to which Chester refers'. It was hardly the most robust of rebuttals, but according to Small, Williams later backtracked on some of his accusations, apologising in front of his former teammates for what he had written and conceding that there may have been some exaggerations in his book.

'I'm going to be honest with you, James was probably not the most liked player in the team,' said André Snyman, the Springbok centre/wing. 'Everybody wanted him on the team, but a lot of players just didn't understand his ways of doing things, things he said. It was just his behaviour off the pitch. I think some players couldn't understand why he was doing what he was doing.'

Small had always lived close to the edge, his tempestuous nature forever on the verge of violent expression. Rugby was the conduit that had helped keep these more self-destructive aspects of his personality under control – most of the time. 'I'm so fortunate,' he once mused. 'I was a hard guy, I could have ended up in prison. I used to go to those rough Johannesburg clubs late at night. I could easily have taken a bullet.'

Emotion was never far away. He sang the national anthem with more passion than anyone, tears rolling down his cheeks; when the Springboks made a trip to Robben Island in 1995, he openly wept in front of his teammates when he entered the tiny cell where Mandela had spent eighteen of his twenty-seven years in prison. 'That was where the sense really took hold of me that I belonged to the new South Africa and where I really got a sense of the responsibility to my position as a Springbok,' he said. 'There were prisoners still incarcerated on the island and they all cheered and sang for us and I burst into tears again. I was thinking about Mandela's cell and how he spent twenty-seven years in prison and came out with love and friendship. All that washed over me, that huge realisation and the tears just rolled down my face.'

He made his debut for the Springboks against New Zealand in 1992 in South Africa's first game after being readmitted to international sport after Mandela's release from prison. He scored four tries in his first eight Tests but then grabbed the headlines for all the wrong reasons when he became the first Springbok to be sent off – for swearing at the English referee, Ed Morrison, during a Test against Australia in Brisbane.

The transgression had no immediate effect on his Test career. He was back in the side the following week. A bar-room brawl after he'd starred against Argentina in October 1994 led to a ban from the end-of-year tour to Britain. Small had to make a public apology and look contrite before he was welcomed back into the fold for a pre-World Cup match against Samoa in April 1995, whereupon he went on to re-establish his place as a key component in the team.

Despite his importance to the Springboks, he had often felt marginalised in the rugby environment he had grown up in. He understood what it felt like to be the outsider. As an English-speaker, there was a clear division between himself and the Afrikaners.

'I know what it's like to be on the receiving end. I was an Englishman playing a Dutchman's game. When I began at provincial level I got fucked around badly by the Afrikaner players. I was made to feel unwelcome both by my own team and by the rival. Players in my own team tried to get their Afrikaner mates ahead of me in the selection. They ostracised me, and I was badly beaten too. At my Springbok initiation, they fucked me up so badly my dad wanted to report them to the police.

The point was that, for them, it was an Afrikaans game and there was no room for an Englishman. The Englishman was an interloper. But I used all that to spur me on and I got my way in the end. I became a Springbok. Yet the whole experience taught me an appreciation for the outsider, a sympathy for those in my country who didn't have the opportunities that I'd been so lucky to have.'

Becoming a Springbok had helped him quell some of his resentments. Lifting the World Cup had helped a little more. As 1997 loomed he was beginning to look forwards more than backwards, excited by the prospect of the new Super 12 season, the Tri Nations and a northern hemisphere tour at the end of the year. But most of all, he was excited about facing the Lions, a team deeply embedded in his rugby psyche.

'I was five years old when I first sat on my father's shoulders at the old Ellis Park. The Springboks against the Lions in 1974, the year they really fucked us up. It was the last Test and people were really screaming all around me. The Lions ripped us to pieces. That's my first rugby memory. I get goosebumps thinking of it. Gareth Edwards, JPR Williams, Phil Bennett . . . we used to be in awe of them. Y'know, I've never really been a student of the game but, man, some players stay with you.'

### André Joubert – *'The power of the mind is an incredible thing'*

In a time when Springbok rugby was ruthlessly effective but not necessarily the easiest on the eye, full back André Joubert brought a touch of elegance from the backfield. Whether it was scalpel-sharp running lines, space-creating passing or long spiralling punts, Joubert could rip apart the best defences on the planet. England coach Jack Rowell described him as 'the Rolls

-Royce of full backs' at the end of the 1995 World Cup season. Mostly he was called 'Juba'.

Born in Ladysmith in Natal in April 1964, he began his career playing for the Free State in 1986 and made his debut for the Springboks at the age of twenty-five against a World XV in 1989 before international rugby went into cold storage in South Africa.

In 1992, he moved back to Natal and, a year later, with the Springboks back from isolation, he restarted his Test career. In 1994, *Rugby World* magazine named him as their player of the year and *Midi Olympique* picked him at full back for their annual world XV. The following year he confirmed his status as the world's best full back with his performances at the World Cup. He also proved his bravery.

After breaking his hand in three places in the quarter-final against Western Samoa, he had an operation the next day to stabilise the bone with metal pins, spent time in a decompression chamber to reduce the swelling throughout the week and had a hurling glove flown down from Ireland to wear for protection. 'No problem,' he would smile whenever he was questioned if he would be able to play in the semi-final against France. In the aftermath, his coach Kitch Christie spoke in awe of his full back. 'The guy isn't human,' he said. 'I can't believe such bravery.'

More than just secure under the high ball in monsoon conditions, Joubert showed impressive pragmatism in the semi-final – as he did again in the final – suppressing his usual attacking instincts in favour of the more limited game plan that Christie had devised. 'Sometimes I could feel the bones moving, but there was no pain,' said Joubert nonchalantly. 'I've got a high pain threshold and maybe that helped. The power of the mind is an incredible thing.'

Although Joubert was entering what might be considered the autumn of his career, he was playing some of the best rugby of his life in 1996. He retained a whip-sharp ability to attack in open play, epitomised by the two electrifying tries he scored in the Currie Cup final as Natal defeated Transvaal 33–15 at Ellis Park. Later that year, in the aftermath of the Springboks' victory in the final Test of the All Blacks series, the defeated coach John Hart declared, 'Joubert's a sensational player. Sensational. Any coach would love to have him.'

His own coach was equally effusive. 'You see what a difference a fit Joubert makes to the Springbok side?' said André Markgraaff. 'Do you see? We've had to play without him for most of the winter. Now he's back and fully fit. Look at the impact he had on the game.'

That impact continued on the Springbok's end-of-year tour when Joubert once again enhanced his reputation in the victory over France in Bordeaux. He scored the match-winning try. 'He was the real difference between the sides,' said Joost van der Westhuizen.

Gary Teichmann said that Juba was the most relaxed person he'd ever met. 'Nothing seems to irritate him and nothing seems to upset him. Ever. I'd played so much rugby with him for Natal that I probably took him for granted but everything he did was executed with a touch of class, something that can't be coached, something the overwhelming majority of us have to accept is just granted at birth.'


From his time spent with the All Blacks in summer 1996, Geech knew what he'd be facing. Sure, there had been convulsions on and off the pitch in South African rugby almost from the moment they became world champions. Yes, they'd gone through coaches and assistant coaches at an alarming rate. Of course the aura of the Pienaar age had been heavily compromised by that series defeat to New Zealand.

Geech had a long memory, though. And nobody needed to tell him about the menace of a wounded Springbok, particularly when it was the Lions down the other end of the park. For this mission to beat all missions he started putting his backroom team in place. James Robson would again be the Lions doctor. His experience of being medic, confidant and father figure to the players on previous tours was invaluable. Andy Keast was appointed as an analyst, Dave Alred would coach the kickers, Dave McLean would be in charge of strength and conditioning.

Everybody knew how savage this was going to be, Geech most of all. There would be no escape from South Africa's intensity from first week to last and he needed somebody he trusted by his side, somebody with the hardest edge. There was one man and one man only he had in mind. Without hesitation he picked up the phone to an old friend in Galashiels.

# CHAPTER FOUR

# TELFER

EVER SINCE HIS youth, when his mother and father were in service to the Duke of this and the Lord of that in the Scottish Borders, Jim Telfer had a hatred of privilege that ran deep. His dad was a shepherd, his mum a servant in what he calls the 'big house' where the 'big people' lived, for part of the year at least, when they weren't living in one of their other estates in another part of Scotland – a country he believed they knew little of and cared for even less.

He was still a boy, confused and angry as to why some people in this world had so much and others had so little. He reckons now that the first stirrings of his socialism happened before he'd even reached his teenage years. Later, it manifested itself in so many different ways, but one of the examples he puts forward dates back to when he was a university student in Edinburgh, his daily walking route taking him past the front of George Heriot's private school. Telfer came to view that footpath as a battleground. When the uniformed kids came towards him he'd make a point of quickening his step and going straight at them. No way he was moving aside for this lot, no way was he kowtowing to the monied classes. If they didn't get out of his way, they got run over.

In everything he did, he brought a ferocious determination. When he made the Melrose first team at the age of seventeen, the old boys couldn't comprehend this new animal amongst them. Instead of supping pints in the clubhouse when the rain pissed down, Telfer would train and train and train. The worse the weather, the greater the pleasure he seemed to get from it. The sadist in him loved the fact that his rival for a place in the Melrose team or the Scotland team or the Lions team wouldn't be driven enough, or daft enough, to do the kinds of things he was prepared to do.

That meant putting his body on the line and suffering the consequences. That meant getting kicked and raked on a weekly basis. That meant going into games in the knowledge that he wasn't the most naturally talented back row forward but that he was one of the hardest. To understand what Jim Telfer became as a coach, you have to understand first what Jim Telfer was as a player.

In 1966, Telfer was part of Mike Campbell-Lamerton's Lions team that toured Australia and New Zealand. The tourists lost all four Tests against New Zealand, but Telfer's eyes were opened by what he witnessed down there.

He learned lessons on that tour which stuck with him for the rest of his rugby life. A seminal moment occurred in the tenth game of the New Zealand leg of the trip against a combined side drawn from South and Mid Canterbury and North Otago. The side was coached by Vic Cavanagh, a man regarded as a rugby genius. Cavanagh had turned Otago from bit-part players in the 1930s and 1940s into one of the powerhouse provinces in New Zealand primarily by taking the loose art of rucking and making a science of it. Under his guidance, Otago's small forwards – 'wiry little devils' as Telfer called them – would blast the breakdown with immaculate timing, perfect body height and clever angles. Soon his techniques were being copied around New Zealand.

That day in 1966 at Fraser Park in Timaru, Telfer witnessed it up close and personal for the first time. The hard man of the Scottish Borders thought he knew all about rucking. He was wrong. 'That was the day that made me think,' said Telfer. 'That was the moment that changed me.'

Telfer was a Lion again in 1968. The challenge of taking on the Springboks was almost as daunting as facing the All Blacks and the tour again exposed the weakness of British and Irish forwards. The colossal figures of Frik du Preez, Tiny Naude, Tommy Bedford and Jan Ellis dominated the series. While the Lions tours of 1966 and 1968 kick-started his fascination with coaching, the 1983 tour nearly ended it. Appointed as head coach for the trip to New Zealand, it was a devastating experience. The Lions lost 4–0 again and the torture almost broke him. Asked by a journalist what his future coaching plans were, he answered, 'Is there life after death?'

**Jim Telfer:** I was very close to giving it up. Losing 38–6 at Eden Park in the fourth Test: that was my worst moment ever. I was very disillusioned with coaching and I was also totally against the whole Lions concept by that stage. It was so difficult to get the team together and prepare properly before going into the biggest Test matches. I couldn't fault the players, because they'd given everything, but they'd come through a system that wasn't good enough to prepare them for the levels of excellence of that All Blacks team. For all that, I still felt that the fault lay with me because I'd failed to work around those deficiencies and differences, I'd failed to find a way for us to win – and there's always a way to win.

I remember getting home and walking along the street in Selkirk and not wanting to be there, in case folk pointed and laughed. But John Rutherford, Roy Laidlaw and Iain Milne, who had all been on the tour, came and saw me and they said, 'Let's keep going,' and I did. But it was touch-and-go. We pushed on and won the Grand Slam in 1984. That was incredible – but the scars from 1983 . . . they ran deep. Deep. They stayed with me. And even though I had more success with Scotland – winning the Grand Slam with Ian in 1990 was another great achievement – I thought my time with the Lions was done.

Every one of his forwards from those years could write a book about what Telfer meant to them. 'After ten minutes of a Test match, everybody's knackered,' he'd tell his players. 'You're up, you're down, you're making tackles, you're hitting rucks, you're scrummaging, you're out on your feet. Okay. Same for everyone, boys. You think and move slowly when you're tired. If the body is weak then so is the mind. That's a fact. But not us. No. What we do in training is we sharpen minds as well as bodies. We work and work and work like beasts and get you to a state of mental fitness where you can still make the right decisions even though you're blowing out your arse. Do you get me, boys? "Do I kick, do I pass, do I ruck, do I maul? I'm fucking exhausted but I know what I need to do because up here, I'm razor-fucking-sharp." Yes?'

To his Scotland players he was at times cruel and frightening and personal. David Sole, his captain in 1990, called him 'one of the scariest men alive'. Derek White, the number eight, was once asked, 'On a Richter scale of one-to-ten, how abusive could Telfer get?' 'Eleven,' he answered. There were many stories of Telfer in full rant mode, one of them from the dressing room in Paris. 'Jim was having a massive go at Damian Cronin just before we went out for the start of the match, calling him a big useless bastard, a lazy fucker,' recalled Chris Gray, the Grand Slam-winning lock. 'Damian was really chilled most of the time but he had a nasty streak buried deep within him. And when it came out, he was a bit scary.'

Telfer was about an inch from Cronin's face, screaming blue murder at a lock he felt needed regular doses of reality right between the eyes. 'Did Damian give him a shove? I'm not sure but the collar of Jim's jacket got stuck on a coat hook.' Along with the rest of the team, David Sole watched the madness unfold. 'I'd just seen the film *Midnight Express*,' said Sole. 'A prison guard gets impaled on a coat hook through the back of the neck.' Sole got to thinking that if Telfer wasn't careful he'd end up like that prison guard.

'Jim was in his element,' said Gray. 'The more furious Damian got the happier he was. He was on the hook shouting, "That's what we want, boys. Aggression!" We're all going, "Jesus Christ. Quick, let us out on the pitch to face the French. We'll take our chances against Carminati and Garuet rather than stay here with this madman."'

Telfer would tell the celebrated back row of Finlay Calder, John Jeffrey and Derek White that if they didn't work harder he'd go out on the street and find three others to replace them. There was a time when they decided they'd had enough of his relentless intensity and non-stop barracking. What sparked it was Telfer calling a back-row video session at seven the next morning. The lads were incensed and took a vow to ignore him.

*Are we going?*

*Are we fuck!*

*We snub him?*

*Yes!*

JJ got cold feet and walked into the meeting room at five to seven to find Calder and White already there. Why? 'Respect,' said JJ. 'And probably fear.'

And that was the thing about Telfer. His players might not have understood him at the time, but they respected him, respected his knowledge, respected the fact that he'd been there and had done it himself, respected that he wanted to get every last drop of talent out of them because he knew how good they were and how much they could achieve if they didn't 'fuck it up by being soft'.

Generations of Scottish players could have given the 1997 forwards the full lowdown on Telfer, but some experiences just have to be lived.

**Jim Telfer:** I had to think very carefully about taking up the offer when Ian contacted me in 1996. Could I go back into that environment? I was director of rugby at the SRU and I hadn't coached in four years and had never coached a professional pack of forwards. I was actually quite frightened when I thought of all these guys like Martin Johnson, Lawrence Dallaglio, Keith Wood, Jason Leonard and boys like that. They were professionals and I was an administrator – and I think they were a wee bit worried about my reputation as well.

**Ian McGeechan:** Tim Rodber was playing for me at Northampton and I remember him coming up to me before the tour and saying, 'What's Jim Telfer like?' and I said, 'You'll find out soon enough.'

**Gregor Townsend:** The guys at Northampton had heard stories about Jim and how he coached – they would have been exaggerated or even apocryphal stories – but the likes of Tim Rodber would say that there was no way anyone could do things like that with us. 'If he thinks we're going to be doing what you guys do up in Scotland, he's got another think coming – if he tries to do it, we're not taking any of that.' And Jim was obviously aware of this. He'd never coached these players and England were a dominant team and had some big characters. So he had to convince them that the hard work was the right way to go and he put it over in a way that got them engaged. Straight away it was like a love-fest.

**Jim Telfer:** It was early in the professional era – but they were professional. And I was lucky that the core of Englishmen in that team were rugby nuts, like Dallaglio, Johnson and Rodber. Eventually, I was dictatorial, but not initially – by the time I started shouting the odds I knew that they were with me. We cleared the air. Tom Smith, Keith Wood, Paul Wallace; Martin Johnson, Jeremy Davidson; Lawrence Dallaglio, Richard Hill, Tim Rodber. I got on very well with them. We had great players all across that squad. I knew what I had. I'd been around, you know. I wasn't coming into the thing without a reputation. Getting on a Lions tour when I was a player was just as difficult as it is now. I say that playing for the Lions is a higher honour than playing for my country. Some people don't see it that way, but I do. And I wasn't prepared to let them waste that opportunity by not working hard enough.

**Keith Wood:** Jim Telfer was tough, uncompromising, a little bit mad. His nickname was Creamy, because he would literally foam at the mouth. I really liked him because he had a fantastic energy and enthusiasm, almost on the point of being manic. You couldn't talk to Telfer for more than two minutes and not recognise that this guy was doing what he was born to do. It was clear that he just adored it. It was stressful and pressurised for him, but you looked at him and you realised: here's a man who's doing what he should be doing.

Technically, he was superb. I loved it when he would offer a little gem of advice: 'Actually, if you go on this angle, you're far more effective.' And you would do it and he would be right. I loved that. I liked Telfer a lot. I don't know whether he liked me particularly. He came up and said to me at one stage, 'I thought you were really loose and I wasn't quite sure about you at all,' and he said, 'But you're not,' and then walked off. He had a wicked sense of humour. He was a great man for a cutting remark or sledging. His tone was magnificent.

**Doddie Weir:** Today, coaches have a positive mental approach with the players. They tell them they're all great, they're amazing, they're the best thing out there. Jim didn't really do it that way. There was more honesty with Mr Telfer. The pit bull. The swearer. Couldn't care what was going on. Couldn't care who you were. Wasn't scared of anybody. He would say, 'Don't let yourself down, don't let your family down. Don't give me excuses.' He does not show any weaknesses, Jim Telfer. Very strong. Very organised. Very positive. He knows what's going on. To the forwards, when you were still allowed to ruck – and they still should be, by the way – he'd say: 'You're laying your body on the line.' And we did. And, sadomasochistically, I kind of enjoyed it.

**Jim Telfer:** My approach to begin with was to get back to basics, very simple drills, so that everyone knew what I was after. I kept notes of the drills we did each day, and also charted how often we did each one and how long we took to do them. My four essential principles – body position, tightness, leg drive and support from depth – were coached and if I had not ticked one off for a day or two, I made sure that it was covered soon after. I liked to have a balance and also a picture of what I was doing with technique.

**Dai Young:** The training with Jim was pretty basic stuff, just high intensity, and reinforce, reinforce, reinforce. He and I didn't really see eye-to-eye on tour, to be honest. Somebody kicked the ball and it hit Jim straight on the back of the head. Jim whips around with his glasses all askew like something from Benny Hill and he looks at me. I've buckled up laughing. I couldn't help myself. To this day I still think he thinks it was me. I couldn't get the words out to explain it wasn't. He held it against me for the first couple of days. I feel I'm a pretty serious guy when I crossed the whitewash and I trained as hard as anyone else, but I do like to have a bit of a giggle to lighten the spirits. That didn't go down well at all with Jim. It seemed like every time he turned round he saw me having a laugh with one of the players. I wouldn't take away from his influence on that tour, the speeches, and his methods. They may have been basic, but they were effective. He got us all working together and everybody knew their role. I've seen him since and we've had a laugh about it.

**Ian McGeechan:** Jim took a couple of early scrummage sessions and only rated the performance as three out of ten. I wasn't too worried. The scrum and lineout are all about coordination and timing and it takes a while for players to get used to each other. I knew they'd improve. Jim would take care of it.

# CHAPTER FIVE

# IT HAD TO BE JOHNNO

THE LIONS NEEDED a captain and as confident as Geech was about his selection of Jim Telfer as his man to drive the forwards, he was every bit as sure about who he wanted as his on-field leader. There was talk about Ieuan Evans of Wales, Keith Wood of Ireland and Rob Wainwright of Scotland, but none of them were chosen.

Geech selected a guy with little experience of captaincy and with a questionable track record in keeping his cool in hothouse environments. In a few high-profile incidents, he'd thrown a punch in a Test match against Argentina and incurred the wrath of Jack Rowell, his England coach, then stiff-armed a poor unfortunate against Wales. Geech was fully aware of his reputation but he went with him anyway, without a scintilla of doubt.

**Ian McGeechan:** I knew a year before the tour that Martin Johnson was the guy to lead us. As Northampton coach I'd seen how influential he was for Leicester and I'd heard about it from other players. He wasn't Leicester's captain but he was a massive presence. Jim said to me, 'Are you sure?' And I'd say, 'I am.' He'd say it again, 'Are you certain?' I'd say, 'Jim, I've never been more certain about anything.'

**Martin Johnson:** I wouldn't have been massively comfortable with it. I never strove to be captain of anything. The England captaincy thing was big, Will Carling had retired and there was a drama about who was going to replace him and Phil de Glanville was given the job. My name had been mentioned very, very occasionally – and I didn't care. I didn't care. People were like, 'Oh, he dreamed of being the captain of England and captain of the Lions.' Well, playing's good enough and, actually, the captaincy is a bit of a burden. It's quite nice just being one of the boys. You can sit in the back and giggle in team meetings and take the piss. You can't do that when you're captain. We went to a shopping mall during the tour at one stage, about three or four of us. It was an arranged autograph session. There was hundreds of people there and they had a mic and started asking questions, a few rugby questions and then: 'Martin, Martin, you're captain of the Lions. How do we solve our political problems in South Africa?' 'Uh, what do you want me to say? I'm twenty-seven years old!'

**Fran Cotton:** I asked two questions when we were looking at the options: how was each player going to cope with severe pressure and was he going to be on the front foot or the back foot? Character was a vital part of the selection process. Johnno fitted the bill in every category.

**Martin Johnson:** Fran phoned my mother, who's sadly passed away since, but he spoke with my mum before asking me to become captain. It was a character conversation. He's not asking my mum how good a second row I am, it was about my character.

**Fran Cotton:** His selection was a message to the South Africans. When the captains were called for the toss, we wanted the giant shadow of a guy who would make it into a world XV to fall across the home dressing room.

**Martin Johnson:** Yeah, Fran always said that they'd gone for me because they wanted someone big to knock on the Springbok dressing-room door and intimidate them. I think there was a little kidology going on there. I'm pretty sure the South African players wouldn't have been bothered by how tall the Lions captain was – but they certainly bit at it, saying things like, 'Well, we've got Kobus Wiese. We'll send him to knock on *your* door.'

My discipline had become a bit of a thing. I'll tell you an absolutely true story. That year, 1997, we played Wales in Cardiff. They were all pumped up and I got into a bit of a row with Scott Quinnell and he started launching punches at me and I'm holding him and I look at the touchy and he puts his flag out, so I think, 'We've got a penalty here.' So I get rid of Scott and carry on playing. The whistle goes. Great, here comes the penalty. And then I look round and see that the touchy has taken his flag down. So I go over to him and I say, 'What are you doing?' I can see that he's dropped his flag because the crowd are shouting at him. You know what it's like in Cardiff, it's absolute bedlam and they're screaming at him for putting out his flag. And Will Carling had to pull me away because I was starting to go berserk. Scott Quinnell had just thrown three or four punches at me and I'd not thrown any back. So later in the game, right at the end, I get into a ruck, and I clean out a Welshman with an arm across his chest, just to get him out the way. The touch judge puts his flag up. Tim Stimpson gets the ball and breaks clear and I have to watch him run sixty yards at the Arms Park to score a try knowing that it's not going to count and a penalty's coming against me for a personal gripe I've got with that touch judge who's put his flag up to say to me, 'Don't ever cross me.' In the aftermath it became a big story: 'Johnson costs a try', blah-blah-blah. But it wasn't exactly like that. That's the honest story.

**Lawrence Dallaglio:** We grew up in an era when the game was more violent, incidents happened and everything was fair game. From about 1995 that began to change. What was previously acceptable became unacceptable. There were more cameras in the ground, a greater chance of getting caught, and, yes, it took a few people a little longer to cotton on to this. People were also looking out for Johnno, in the same way they used to look out for Roy Keane. One little incident and you're in big trouble. Johnno would serve his one- or two-match ban and newspapers would say he was a disgrace, but it only added to his aura. Eventually the message got through to Johnno that he was no good to us sitting in the dressing room.

This would be Johnson's second Lions tour. His first had come four years earlier when he was parachuted into the trip to New Zealand after Wade Dooley had to return home following the sad death of his father. He may have been a nervous rookie going there, but he made an instant impression, making the starting line-up for the second and third Tests. If folk back in the UK were surprised by his quality then wise old Kiwis were not.

At the age of nineteen Johnson had had a sojourn in New Zealand, first with Tihoi, a tiny club near Taopu in King Country, then with King Country itself and later with New Zealand Under-21s. 'At Tihoi, most of the players were either farmers or bushmen who felled trees for a living,' he said. 'Some guy would turn up that you hadn't seen before and he'd put his kit on and go out and smash people for eighty minutes. We had guys who would play prop one week and in the centre the next. They would get stuck into each other. It was physical work.'

All of this opened Johnson's eyes. After just a few games, he received an invitation from the great Colin Meads, chairman of King Country, to train with the provincial side – and within ten days he had forced his way into the team.

'My first game for King Country was against Auckland B. Frank Bunce ripped us to pieces. I'd never seen anything like it. He was better than Will Carling, better than Jeremy Guscott. I said, "Who's that guy?" They said, "Oh, that's Frank Bunce . . . he's getting on a bit now. Can't get in the Auckland team." I thought, "Jesus Christ! A player like that can't get a game!"'

Johnson was impressed, but soon it was his performances that were turning heads. He played throughout the season for King Country and was then selected to train with the New Zealand Under-21s. The following season he lined up alongside several future All Blacks, including the fearsome wing Va'aiga Tuigamala, full back John Timu, flanker Blair Larsen and prop Craig Dowd.

**Colin Meads:** I remember when the New Zealand Under-21 selectors first contacted me to say they were interested in picking Martin they asked, 'Is the boy going to stay here or is he going back to England?' I'd talked with Martin and I told the selectors that, as far as I knew he planned to spend the rest of his rugby career in New Zealand. There's nothing surer than he would have been an All Black. Martin was a young beanpole, slightly ungainly but he had all the courage in the world. I think he genuinely planned to stay, but in the end we lost him over a twist of fate.

**Martin Johnson:** I needed a shoulder operation. There was a specialist recommended to me back home, so that's who I went to see. Once the op was done and I was recovering, I was back in the Leicester set-up and the New Zealand side of things felt like it was done.

**Graham Rowntree:** How do you describe Johnno? He just had a presence, didn't he? Any team he played in, he ran the team.

**Keith Wood:** He had a great strength to him. I mean, the guy's the most annoying prick you could ever play against because he'd be strangling you and he'd somehow be suggesting to the referee that this is well within the laws of the game. It's very funny how you can dislike a guy one week and love him the next.

**Tim Stimpson:** The number of times Johnno's protected the likes of me. He'd literally crawl on top of me when I was getting my back ripped open in the old-fashioned world of rucking. He'd lie on top of me, have *his* back ripped open and then giggle through it. Then he'd rub his knuckles into the back of my head and say, 'Go on, Stimmo. Good lad.' And then he'd run off with his shirt ripped open and blood pouring everywhere. I'm not bullshitting, he literally put his body between me and pain.

**Graham Rowntree:** He was never the loudest of characters, never said too much, but what he *did* say was always intelligent and everybody listened to him. I think that's the mark of a good leader – knowing what to say and when. And you knew that he'd be giving 110 per cent in every moment of the game. You just knew it. He was very much a 'follow me' kind of leader. Demanded standards. Hated losing. Hated losing at *everything* – hated losing at tiddlywinks. He hated losing at touch rugby. I remember being an eighteen-year-old running around an athletics track on a Tuesday lunchtime trying to keep up with the bugger, but he wouldn't lose, wouldn't let me come close. He wouldn't have it. Then he went off to New Zealand – and came back a monster. Came back a Test animal. Ah, he was special.

**Rob Howley:** His team talks were very simple, and very direct, but they were hugely motivating. He was made from the same mould as Willie John McBride. He's very dour. He's a very private person, but he understood the Lions, the importance of four countries coming together. The opposition knew if they were ever going to beat the Lions pack, they had to beat Martin Johnson. He was a winner. You'd want him in your trenches every day. He was an outstanding second row. He was obviously technically and tactically outstanding, but his presence was immense. That's why they had to look after him so much with all his niggles. It didn't matter if he didn't train – even if he hated missing it – the important thing was getting on the pitch for the matches.

**Martin Johnson:** At first, you probably try and do too much as captain. You worry about things. You have to find a comfort with it.

**Scott Gibbs:** I'm starry-eyed about Johnno. I always looked up to him as a player. As a captain, I like a guy who says it as it is, doesn't have to say too much, delivers on the field. He's a guy that you don't want to let down and who doesn't take a backward step. All the cliched stuff, but it's true. You'd follow him anywhere.

**Tim Stimpson:** For someone who looks like he should be a bit of a Neanderthal he's someone who geekishly, analytically, loves the game. When I played with him for Leicester, we'd walk off the field at half-time and in the space of thirty seconds he'd go: 'This is what's happening. We're winning there. So-and-so's tired. They're coming up on the short side, we've got to work on that. Is that right, Stimmo?' And I'd say, 'Yes, Johnno.' His ability to read a game was unbelievable. Legends like him and

Willie John McBride, they did a lot of their leadership without opening their mouths.

**Matt Dawson:** There is an aura about Johnno and I don't think he's aware of it. It's not just his presence on the rugby field, which was huge, but his persona off it. He's just a lovely guy, a true friend. As hard as nails on the field but as honest as the day is long.

The Lions met up in Weybridge in Surrey for team-building. Integral to the process was booze – and plenty of it. There was a pub near their camp called the Bull Inn and the boys horsed into the drink, the big characters holding court, the quieter ones growing more comfortable with their new surroundings. It was all about making friends and drawing closer together as a group.

Johnno's Lions were an eclectic bunch, some gregarious, some shy, some superstars, some real surprise packets. 'The selection was phenomenal when you think about it,' said Johnson. 'Geech picked guys who weren't even playing in the Five Nations. England's scrum-half in 1997 was Andy Gomarsall. We had three England scrum-halves on that tour and none of them was Andy Gomarsall. England's first choice centres in the Five Nations were Phil de Glanville and Will Carling. We ended up with three England centres in South Africa but Phil and Will didn't make it. Nick Beal wasn't in the England team that year, but he was still picked for the Lions. So, Geech and Telfer trusted in themselves to find the players they wanted.'

From the outset, some appeared nailed-on for the Test side, but never made it. Others looked like mere back-up players, but they came steaming through to play the biggest games of their lives. There were four Irishmen, five Scots, eight Welshmen and eighteen from England. Everywhere you looked, there was a story to tell.

## Neil Jenkins – *'I broke my arm, I could feel it mulching'*

I'd played all the 1997 Five Nations games at full back, which I didn't like – I'm not going to lie. I didn't like playing full back for Wales at all, but it gave me a chance to go on a Lions tour. Then I bust my forearm early on during my fiftieth cap against England. I only lasted about five or ten minutes. I was going down on a loose ball with Richard Hill when I felt a sharp pain and thought, 'Crikey, that doesn't sound right.' Carcass [Mark Davies, the Wales physio] came on, and had a look at me and I played on. But while I was playing, I could feel it mulching – I could feel it moving and that. Jon Humphreys asked me to take a kick at goal. I did, and it dropped short because I couldn't raise my left arm. I couldn't get it up and it was starting to hurt a bit. Turned out I'd suffered a clean break of my forearm.

I had an operation the following day, and was ruled out for ten weeks. It was nip and tuck whether I'd be fit for the tour. I used a magnetic coil to help with the healing. A guy from Pontypridd called Don, bless him he's passed away now, used to drive me around everywhere because I couldn't drive. He'd drive me to this place near Hawthorn in Rhydfelin for my treatment. When my arm was a bit better, we'd end up going to Snooker World in Treforest in between appointments because I'd be going a couple of times a day. Realistically the op I had was a twelve-weeker, but I was desperate, absolutely desperate to get on that plane. I don't tend to find I'm a lucky person, but I certainly had a stroke of luck there. Things went my way for a change.

The day I got picked, I was at home with my wife in Efail Isaf, and we were planning on going to the Ideal Home exhibition. It was one of them: 'Do we leave now and not wait for the mail, to find out, or do we just wait for the mail?' I did think at the start, 'Let's not worry about it and just go.' But then, I thought, 'Bugger this, I need to sit here and wait for the mail,' and that's what we did. She opened the letter. It's difficult to put into words. Your first cap for Wales is unreal, it's like a drug. And then to be picked for this was an incredible achievement. I'll never forget that day. I was in a very good mood going round the Ideal Home exhibition.

## Scott Gibbs – 'A little bit of Halifax, a little bit of St Helens, a little bit of Widnes'

One of the big things from that tour was the number of former rugby league players that were picked. There was a big rugby league influence in our squad. We brought a little bit of Halifax, a little bit of St Helens, a little bit of Widnes and a little bit of Leeds with us. When we were given time off in the afternoon and were encouraged to put our feet up, Taity [Alan Tait] and I would sneak off and do a boxing session in the gym. We had similar sorts of backgrounds and those sessions were great for my mentality. And then Dai Young came and trained with us as well. Suddenly the three turned to six, the six to twelve, and before long we were all going. It was just an infectious habit. All the exciting things like going on a wine tour, going out to the bush, playing golf, all those things were encouraged and laid on, and the guys did them, but I think that slowly over time more and more guys got switched into doing the extras in the gym. That's where our influence as guys who'd experienced a fully professional environment in league came to the fore. 'Wine tour? No, thanks, we're gonna punch bags for an hour. Nothing crazy. Come with us if you fancy it.' And before you know it there's a bit of a movement, you know? Everyone felt a little more empowered about their own training standards and thought, 'Yeah, this is the right thing to do.'

**Tom Smith – *'Suddenly, I was in a different world'***

Looking back, I can't believe how ignorant I was of the tour and what it meant. It was my first season of international rugby and the year before the tour I was playing second XV rugby in Dundee. The thought of playing at the highest level just wasn't on the radar at all. I don't think I was even aware that there was an announcement being made. I was ninety-six kilos when I went on the tour. Nowadays that would barely get you in the backs never mind the front row.

I'd only toured once before, with Scotland to New Zealand as an uncapped player the previous year. In South Africa, I was suddenly in a different world – greeting ceremonies at airports, receptions at the High Commissioner's place, rooms in the grandest hotels. It was quite a jolt for a young player who'd only known a Travelodge on the outskirts of Hamilton. I knew what the Lions were, of course, but I don't think I understood for a moment what it meant to be chosen.

**Jeremy Davidson – *'You fucking arse, Bentley'***

It was pretty intimidating coming into the room and seeing all these legends of the game in one place, but you get over it pretty quickly – you have to. Then I got roomed with John Bentley. He starts talking and talking and talking. He pulled the curtains closed – it was quite an old hotel, big heavy curtains that let no light in – and I said, 'Will you set an alarm?' and he goes, 'Oh, no, no, I'm up every day at half-six, don't worry, I've got kids, I'll be awake at half-six.' So, good old naïve Irishman, I believed him. I woke up and it was like one minute past nine and we had a team meeting at nine: 'You fucking arse, Bentley.'

Trainers on, clothes on, out the gate, down the corridor, boom-boom-boom, into the team room. If I'd been a bit cuter I'd have let Bentos go in first but I ran in. Late for the first ever meeting. Fran Cotton goes, 'Well, boys, this is not acceptable; this is not the way we want to start the tour, Jeremy and John, I hope we don't see this again.' I was like, 'Fuck, how can this happen to me?'

### Peter Clohessy – *'What do I do, Woody? What do I do?'*

This is Keith Wood and I'm going to speak for the Claw because the Claw wouldn't be a great man for speaking about himself. The Claw lasted one day of the Lions tour. It was almost entertaining. He turned up at the training session and couldn't run. His back wasn't great, he thought he'd be fine but he kept falling over.

We were doing a warm-up defensive drill where we were running in lines – running forward ten yards, back-pedalling five yards and then running forward ten yards again. Repeating it over and over and making sure you kept in line with the guys next to you. Well, the Claw would run forward okay, but when we back-pedalled you just heard this shout of 'FUCK!' and he would keel over. I'm not kidding, it was like something from a cartoon. He just keeled over flat on his back and lies in a heap on the ground. He does this two or three times and then he gets yanked off by McGeechan and Telfer.

So we get back from training and I go and see him because I'm worried about him. And I said, 'Claw, what the fuck was going on?' and he said, 'They've taken me for a scan and I'm out.' 'You're out? You've done nothing.' He said, 'I've a disc problem, I thought it wasn't too bad.' He was fine going forward, but he couldn't put any weight on his leg going backwards. It was hitting a nerve and he was collapsing. Poor fucker. He said, 'I'm out, I'm having to go away, I think they're bringing Wally [Paul Wallace] on the trip.' About two hours later, I get a knock on my door and it's Bob Weighill [a member of the Home Unions committee], and he says, 'Mr Wood?' He was particularly proper and posh, a lovely man, a really lovely man, but absolutely clipped. 'Mr Wood,' he said, 'we're having a small issue with Mr Clohessy and I wondered if you might be able to facilitate resolving the situation?' And I said, 'What's the problem, Bob?' and he said, 'Well, as you know, Mr Clohessy is injured and he is going home.' And I said, 'I do know that, it's very sad.' He said, 'He's refusing to give back his gear.' And I said, 'Okay, I'll go and talk to him.'

I go in to see the Claw and I was going to tell him, 'Give back the gear,' but he's sitting there absolutely distraught. The Claw doesn't do low; this was a moment of rare vulnerability. He said, 'All I've ever wanted to do is play on this fucking tour, it's all I've ever wanted to do and they've got my name all over the bloody kit.' He was nearly crying, he was so emotional. I couldn't get over it. For a guy who doesn't ever show that kind of emotion, he was overwhelmed by it, and he was saying, 'What do I do, Woody, what do I do? What do I do?' And I said, 'Sure, tell him to shove it, like. Tell him to shove it.'

Bob walked in immediately afterwards, and said, 'Mr Clohessy, about—'

'You can fuck off, Bob!' cried the Claw.

And I remember thinking, 'For fuck sake, this is real. The emotion here is so raw.'

It just shows you how important it was; how much he wanted it. It had 'PC' written on every piece of kit, so to be honest it couldn't be used again. And do you know what he did when he went home? He gave all the kit to the underage players at Young Munster. I don't know whether he's ever told that story publicly, but it's a lovely thing he did. He needed the time to process his grief at going home and then he passed it on to the young kids. I tell you, Claw's one of the toughest that you'll ever meet and he's one of the softest you'll ever meet. I love the guy.

## Paul Wallace – *'I wasn't supposed to be anything other than a dirt-tracker'*

My form for Saracens was good and I'd got a kind of unofficial nod that I'd be going on the tour – but then we lost to Scotland in our final game in the Five Nations and that was a big blow. I didn't play particularly badly – or particularly well – but final games in the Five or Six Nations always weigh heavily whenever it comes to Lions selections. I was all set to go on the Irish development tour to New Zealand and Samoa. I was pretty upset. I felt I was playing better than Peter, but when Peter got injured I had a point to prove.

I crossed paths with him at the airport. We'd always had a competitive element between us, but I did feel sorry for him. To an extent. We were on opposite sides of the glass going on an escalator and we just waved to one another. We couldn't speak, so I just gave a kind of sympathetic nod. There was no pressure on me. I was very young still for a prop, Jason had had the tight head shirt for the Lions in New Zealand in '93 and Dai had had the shirt for the tour to Australia in 1989. There was no expectation that I would be anything other than a dirt-tracker.

## Lawrence Dallaglio – *'I was driven by a higher purpose'*

My sister Francesca was an amazingly talented girl. She got into the Royal Ballet School aged eight after about five lessons and she embarked on a career where she worked so hard – she got honours in every single exam, Spanish, jazz, classical, whatever it was. Although she was away at ballet school for the majority of her schooling, when we got together we were a very close-knit family. We spent a lot of time together – as you would expect in an Italian-Irish household. We wrote letters to each other, which is rather lovely. Typical boy, I probably wrote one letter for every four of hers.

When I was sixteen, we were both invited to a party on the *Marchioness*, a riverboat on the Thames. We all sat down as a family and had dinner together before the party but I started not to feel very well and decided not to go. She went, I didn't – and she didn't come back.

The next morning my mum woke me in a terrible panic and said, 'Have you heard the news? The *Marchioness* has sunk and they haven't found your sister yet.' I knew at that moment that she had died. She was only nineteen but very mature for her age and so responsible and there was no way she wouldn't have called or come home. It was incredibly traumatic. It took them four days before they found her body. It blew me away. And it blew my family apart. It was horrific.

My parents grieved very differently – my father tried to be stoic and strong while my mother was overcome with anger with the injustice of what happened and campaigned for years for a public inquiry into the truth behind the accident. I was left in a kind of lonely place and there was just this massive hole in my life.

I drifted for two years, not playing any sport, not really doing anything, I had no real purpose in life. When I eventually came round, I realised that I needed a bit more stability, something to give me a bit more structure. I decided to join a rugby club so I literally picked up a newspaper and Wasps happened to be at the top of the table in England at the time – in 1989/90. I could have joined any number of clubs, but I thought, 'I'll go there.' I walked in and it had a real working-men's club kind of feel to it and I really enjoyed the environment. No one knew me, no one asked any questions about what had happened to me, they just accepted whoever joined for who they were – and that's what appealed to me. Little did I know that five years later, the game would turn professional and rugby would come to completely dominate my life. I was just enjoying being somewhere that put a smile on my face. My parents used to come and watch me play – as all of our teammates' parents did, supporting us through everything – and it put a smile on their faces, and that was kind of it, really.

I've always felt throughout my rugby career that I was driven by something a bit more than just wanting to play the sport. I was driven by a higher purpose of wanting to honour my sister and to do something that would really help bring my parents together again. It made it very emotional for me.

I became a man on a mission after I lost my sister. Part of that might have just been me growing up. It's very hard for me to understand. Was I successful as a result of the fact I decided to grow up, or as a result of the fact my sister died? I'll never know the answer to that.

If you find the right emotional touch-points, the power of what you can achieve is phenomenal. In every game I ever played, I always thought about my sister at some point. When you get all philosophical about it, you look back and you just have to be grateful for the nineteen years we had her for. She was wonderful, beautiful, talented.

I come from relatively humble beginnings – my father is an Italian immigrant who came to England in the 1950s and my mother is English-Irish, brought up in the East End of London. I went to Ampleforth, a traditional rugby school, but I never thought I'd be a rugby player, if I'm honest. I think, like most kids in this country, I wanted to be a Premier League footballer. But when you realise that you're not very good or you get too big, you play rugby. But rugby was never a big thing at home when I was growing up. We were in a small flat in Barnes and my parents worked incredibly hard to provide for my sister and me.

If you're half Italian, half Irish, it makes you a pretty dangerous Englishman because it makes you an Englishman who's not afraid to show his emotion.

### Keith Wood – 'The surgeons said it was time to retire; I was twenty-three'

I sat on the bench for Ireland when I was twenty and a week later I dislocated my shoulder playing for Garryowen against Dungannon. I had surgery and I was out for a year. I came back and it still wasn't right. It went again in '95 in the World Cup and I had a posterior dislocation, which is very rare. A really nasty injury. It took me fifteen, sixteen months to get back to play after that. It was a kind of triple surgery. A couple of surgeons said it was time to retire. I was twenty-three. Then I met a great surgeon in London, Ian Bayley, and he said, 'Ah, no, you'll play, you'll be fine. It'll hurt, though.' He was my guru for the rest of my career – and I had a few other operations. In total I've had eleven on my shoulder and one on my elbow. It was difficult at times. I had two operations, twelve weeks and six weeks before going on that tour. I remember waking up after the second operation to remove the pin that had been stabilising everything and realising that most of the pain was gone. It was amazing, actually. It was just gone. I was so happy. I had a huge scar, though. I mean, maybe a six- to eight-inch scar, it was quite crazy. We used to call it the shark bite.

I played four weeks later. I played three matches in ten days or twelve days, to prove that I could go. It was probably a bit foolhardy, in retrospect. I remember being told by the Lions, 'Look, you don't have to: you're on the trip.' It was a great call to get, but I wanted to prove to myself that I could go. A Lions trip is every player's ambition, but I wouldn't have contemplated going if I'd had the slightest, remotest thought that I might not be up to it. At that stage, I'd had two operations on my left shoulder and three operations on my right shoulder, but I wouldn't have got on the plane if I didn't think I could do it.

### Alan Tait – *'My dad was everything'*

I lost my dad years ago, but he was massive to me. My dad was everything. I talked to him all the time. He would pull me down more than push me up, to be honest, but I didn't mind that. Just to hear his voice say, 'You should have done this, I wouldn't have done that.' Every word he said, I listened to. It wasn't always right, but that's it. He played union and league like me. We were both building trade workers, I grafted with him a lot before I left it to go professional; we worked together on the building sites, aye. He was Alan. Even the same name.

He never came to a stadium to watch me, ever. Well, actually, that's not true. Him and his pal went to Wembley to watch me play once. He didn't tell us he was going. He went to Murrayfield for my last ever game and I had to twist his arm to bloody do it. Maybe he was nervous about going. He never said. He was an honest Kelso man. No nonsense. You see a lot of dads will travel everywhere now and it's good to see and they'll give them a hug after a game, but he never, ever done that to me. He would never give us a hug. I think it's just the way they were, like. Old school. But what an influence he was. What an influence.

## Ieuan Evans – *'Just go, you daft idiot'*

Believe it or not, I was uncertain about going. By that point I was thirty-three years of age and I was coming towards the back-end of my career. We'd just had a baby girl and there was a degree of uncertainty about whether I wanted to go on a third tour. Even though professionalism had come in, we hadn't really got a grasp of it. Professionalism then was about cashing a cheque rather than anything else.

I'd been on two tours and loved everything about the Lions, but this time I had a family and we were getting married after I came back later on in the summer. We'd just had a baby girl, just bought a house, so the conversation at the time was: 'Do I really want to?' But as soon as I sat down and considered it, I realised there wasn't any doubt. I said to myself, 'Don't be so bloody daft, it's a Lions tour!' Because I'd loved the previous tours so much, and done well on them, I thought, 'It's perfect, going on a third tour, there aren't many people who've done that,' and the uncertainty just vanished fairly quickly. I thought, 'What are you doing, you daft idiot? You've got to go.'

## Will Greenwood – *'An uncapped Lion and all the cameras on me'*

I hadn't yet been capped by England. Phil de Glanville, Will Carling, Jerry Guscott and Mike Catt were the centres that season but there were rumours going round that I might get the nod for the tour. I was sharing a flat with Austin Healey. Aus tells it like this: 'I remember making it down-stairs the day the selection letters arrived. There were a couple of bills . . . and two Lions letters. I put Will's in my pocket and shouted: "Yes! I got in!" as he was walking downstairs into our lounge. Will thought he hadn't got one. "Ah, mate," I said. "I can't believe it. I'll make you a cup of tea. There's a press conference in Leicester today to announce Martin Johnson as the tour captain, though. Can you give me a lift in? I quite fancy getting pissed with the lads to celebrate." He agreed, but was gutted. "You should have got in, pal," I said. "Particularly because your dad is Fran Cotton's best mate.'"

So I give him a lift to Welford Road in my little mini Metro and I pull in and Graham Simmons from Sky is there. I wind the window down as I go in and he says, 'Well done, Will!' And Aus is going, 'Oh that's nasty of him, why would he say that to you?' We park up and as I step out the car, all the cameras are suddenly on me and they all say, 'Congratulations! An uncapped player, that's very rare.' And I go, 'What?' I turned around to see Aus holding my letter. Little shit.

### Barry Williams – *'Shut up, you're third choice for Wales'*

I only had one cap when I was selected. There were a lot of rumours in the press that I was in the mix for the Lions but at the time I was third choice hooker in Wales. I played out in France for the old 'B' team or 'A' team, whatever. This game in France was probably March time, and fair dos, Fran actually introduced himself to me, told me I'd had an outstanding game and we shook hands.

There was still another couple of months before selection. I was due to get married during the Lions tour and I told my wife, 'My agent's telling me I've got a chance to go with the Lions.' 'Shut up,' she said, 'you're not even in the Welsh team, you're third choice.' I said, 'Yeah, you're right enough, you're right enough.' That was it really, then the morning of the selection, my agent rang me up and said, 'You're going.' I said, 'I doubt it.' It was the old-fashioned way then, we had a letter sent to us with a stamp and all that. I'm sure the whole of Llandovery knew before me that something was going on. The postman – you know what they're like in the sorting office. Llandovery's a small little town. That morning, the guy – instead of just posting it, he knocked on the door to hand me the letters, and he made sure that one was on top. That's village mentality for you, isn't it?

Off he went then, and I opened it. I was like, 'Wow'. I couldn't believe it. My wife works in Barclays bank in the same town, so I went down to see her and she looked at it and started crying. She said, 'But we're getting married.' I said, 'Uh, no. I'm going to South Africa.' That evening after work, my father came around, my mother came down. Little party, wasn't it. And my father went to her, 'Diane,' he said, 'a little word of advice. I wouldn't fight it, because the boy is going, and if you want to get married, he can get married to you when he comes home.'

While I was away, my wife was reorganising our wedding. I came home on a Wednesday, got married on the Saturday. She was planning all that while I was away.

### John Bentley – *'The Lions wasn't for the likes of me'*

My first cap for England was in the one-off inaugural Millennium Trophy match against Ireland in 1988. We won 21–11 but afterwards, I felt depressed. It was an anti-climax. Don't forget, in 1988 a winger got the ball almost as a last resort, especially a winger in an England shirt. But I'd hyped myself up so far that I became a lame passenger.

I played against Australia on tour a month or so later and we lost 22–16, although I was pleased with how I played and I scored a try. The problem was that they were playing me on the wing and I wanted to play in the centre, but Will Carling was coming through and I wasn't going to shift him. I wasn't courting a move to league, but when you play in the heartlands of Lancashire and Yorkshire, offers weren't ever far away. I was twenty-one when I made the decision to sign for Leeds in the November of '88.

To play rugby union again was a huge step and I never expected to be called up to play for the Lions – it was a different world. To play for the Lions was never even a dream. It was a place where legends existed, not the likes of me. I'd signed for Newcastle in September. My year was going to be spent playing eight months for Newcastle and four months for Halifax in the Super League.

Fran Cotton rang me in the January and said they needed to look at me playing against slightly better opposition. He said he'd contact England and see if they could get me a game for the second string. He rang back and said, 'The news won't come as a surprise but they won't touch you.' So when I got selected for the tour, I think the majority of people had never heard of me.

I sat down with my wife, Sandy, and we puzzled over how we would cover the direct debits while I was away. If I'd played rugby league that summer I'd have earned more than twice what I did with the Lions. But there are some things in life that money can't buy.

# CHAPTER SIX

# WE DOUBLED DOWN, REMORTGAGED THE HOUSE

IN THE SPRING of 1997, John Taylor, the former Wales back row and Lions tourist in 1968 and 1971, approached Fran Cotton about making a behind-the-scenes documentary of the tour. It had been a great decade for sports filmmaking with the release of *Hoop Dreams*, the study of two schoolboy basketball prospects in Chicago, *An Impossible Job*, the revealing feature on Graham Taylor's England football team with its unforgettable catchphrase 'Can we not knock it!' and the award-winning *When We Were Kings*, the brilliant account of the Rumble in the Jungle between Muhammad Ali and George Foreman.

The rugby project was nowhere near as grandiose as those three, but it turned into something very special. Cotton's interest was piqued. Aware that he had to raise as much money as he could for a trek that would cost an unprecedented amount for a northern hemisphere team, Cotton saw a chance. The deal was done. Taylor and his associates – cameraman and director Duncan Humphreys and director/producer Clive Rees and his sons Fred and Adam plus soundman David Brill handed over

£30,000 of their own money for the rights. They had no notion as to what was about to unfold, no concept that their film, *Living with Lions*, would become one of the most beloved fly-on-the-wall sports documentaries ever made.

**Duncan Humphreys:** Fred and I had been making commercials – cheap as chips things, all quite frustrating. There was no satisfaction in what we were doing. We were looking for something else and one day we went for lunch in a pub in Poland Street in London and after about three pints, maybe four, he said, 'You've moaned enough: what are you going to do?' and I just went, 'I'm going to try and make a documentary about the Lions.' And he said, 'I'm up for that.' And I said, 'Well, okay, let's see if we can do it.'

**Fred Rees:** My father ran a production company and we decided we'd take the risk because we were told by Fran and everyone else that once we had the rights then the BBC or ITV would come on board and give us the money to actually make it. So we paid the money and went to the BBC and ITV and instead they all said: 'You're mad, the Lions are never going to win, no one's going to want to watch this film, we won't give you any money.'

We were terrified. What do we do now? We're on the edge of a cliff. Either we've lost all this money or we have to find a whole load more to make the film. So, in our great stupidity or wisdom, we doubled down and remortgaged the house. The whole thing ended up costing around 350 grand, so the house, everything, was on the line.

**Duncan Humphreys:** Clive, Fred's father, got excited about it and was prepared to finance it – although I don't think he probably wanted to finance it as much as he actually ended up doing – and then we verbally agreed it all with Fran. There were some legals involved but the agreement was really just done on the back of a fag packet; 'Yeah, you'll make a video, yeah, fine, great, and we'll have right of approval,' and that was kind of it. Really and truly, it was basically just done on a handshake between us all and Fran Cotton. And next thing you know, we were making the film.

**John Taylor:** I said to Fran early on, 'You realise, of course, if this thing goes belly-up then you can't suddenly shut us out, tell us what we can and can't film.' Fran acknowledged that and I believe that if the tour had fallen apart he would have been true to his word.

**Fred Rees:** To begin with the players were pretty wary of us being there and it was quite difficult breaking the ice with them.

**Martin Johnson:** I wasn't particularly keen on the idea of them poking a lens into everything and I could see a lot of potential problems if things started to go wrong.

**Duncan Humphreys:** We all got full Lions training kit, so straight away we started blending into the background. It had never been agreed that we could put microphones on Telfer and McGeechan. But we just did it, every day. And they assumed it must have been in the contract, which it wasn't.

**Martin Johnson:** I said to the boys, 'Look, I'll go down and look at the edit when they're finished and make sure there's nothing on there that we don't want to be there, so no one gets embarrassed.' I went down to see them and they started showing me this footage of the changing room before the first Test and I said to them, 'You weren't in the first Test changing room.' But they were. They were in the corner. They had a massive big camera, a massive big sound boom most of the time, lights, couldn't be more obtrusive, but you just got totally used to them being there.

**Fred Rees:** We lived in a limbo. We weren't the journalists and we weren't the team. We lived in a place inbetween. We were ignored most of the time, which was great for the film. You don't want people conscious you're filming them. John Bentley played a big role in its success.

**Ian McGeechan:** People were surprised when Bentos made the squad. I don't really know why. He had so many of the qualities we were looking for. He was a hard runner on the pitch and a terrific bloke off it. Fran knew him from years before, but we also spoke to those around him who confirmed that he was a great asset in a large group. He was popular but also very professional. Like all the ex-league players he was a real talker, always communicating. Those league guys all had a magnificent attitude to training. They were very, very professional in everything they did.

**Dai Young:** Bentos is crazy, absolutely mad as a hatter. He was the star of the show. Constantly up to mischief and playing pranks. He kept everybody laughing and terrorised me for a couple of weeks. He was obsessed with table tennis, always hassling me to play him at all hours of the day. He once knocked on my door at quarter to one in the morning wanting to play and I refused. He was as strong as an ox though and he physically wrestled me out of the room and insisted I play him. In the middle of the bloody night. I was playing table tennis at one o'clock in the morning just to shut him up. I wanted to strangle him on occasion, but he made my trip.

**Fred Rees:** At the beginning, at the team-building event, we explained to Bentos what we were doing and he said, 'Guys, there's no way you can make a fly-on-the-wall film about a rugby tour, the boys won't let you.' He suggested that some of the boys do some of the filming which worked really well because he was a real character and he was pretty funny. He recorded some magical stuff and added humour. He helped capture another side to the tour that maybe we couldn't have done. Because it all felt so very real, that's the reason why people really like it – we didn't recreate anything and it was completely genuine. We handed out a few videocams and told the players to go off and film what they liked. Most of it was the usual mucking around but Bentos was particularly brilliant. He would just bare his soul.

**Graham Rowntree:** They handed out mini-cams that were the size of your fist. Christ, some of the footage. I hope it never sees the light of day again. It was like giving lunatics machine guns. They handed out these cameras across the squad, so they're getting footage of all sorts. And then they had cameras in all the main meetings. But remember they were a group of guys who had pumped their life savings into it. It was a gamble. And thankfully it paid off for them. They were good, good guys.

**Fred Rees:** There was a moment when we were in Soweto and the Lions were giving a sort of training camp for the local kids. It was one of those things that they're obliged to do, and some of them liked doing it and others viewed it as a bit of a pain in the arse in some ways, but Rob Howley, to his credit, he was there for longer than anyone else, he was being lovely with all these kids and really put a lot of himself into it. Once we'd finished, I was walking off with him and he began asking about the film, who was going to broadcast it and I explained to him that no one was going to broadcast it and we had basically risked everything we had to be there. You could see the penny dropping and him suddenly realising that, bloody hell, in many ways we had a lot more to lose than they did. Win, lose or draw, they were getting paid. But if the film bombed, we were losing everything.

There was a meal in South Africa in the first week and we sat down and there was me and Duncan and my father, and then

Dallaglio and Guscott sat down and then they realised they were stuck at this table with us, and basically one of them said, 'We're not sitting here eating with this journo scum,' and they got up and just walked off and went and sat somewhere else.

**Duncan Humphreys:** Look, Guscott was the most naturally talented English back, certainly since David Duckham, perhaps ever. But there's no doubt he took a lot of crap over the years from journalists and he didn't give away his trust easily. Dallaglio would also have been cautious because I think they saw us as journalists in their midst, which we weren't, of course. Not in the sense of looking for newspaper headlines. We weren't there looking to shaft them – but they didn't know that.

Humility might not be a word many fans would associate with Jerry Guscott, but to cast him in the role of the stereotypical arrogant Englishman would be to completely misunderstand him. He had a titanium confidence in his ability, of that there was no doubt, but it was a confidence earned through hard work allied to freakish natural talent, not some kind of ingrained upper-class sense of privilege. To accuse him of that was to be ignorant of who he was.

Born and raised in Bath, he had risen through the club's ranks to become the star player in a star-studded team that blew away all comers in Bath's glory days of the 1980s and 1990s. A former bricklayer and briefly Bath Badgerline bus driver (which had earned him the unwelcome nickname of 'Buscott' from his clubmates), he was a rare and brilliant talent. But he also had an edge.

To really know the man, you needed to know his family. Stuart Barnes knew both. 'His mother, Sue, sadly now gone, was the daughter of a military man,' said Barnes, who played fly-half for Bath, England and the Lions alongside Guscott for nearly a decade. 'She took no shit. Great sense of humour, sharp tongue.

Like mother like son. As for his father, Henry was Jamaican. Very elegant, very suave. A proud man. A sharp-eyed man who could identify an insult in the blink of an eye. In my first few years with the *Daily Telegraph*, just before the '97 tour, I picked Jerry out as a player past his prime. Henry was unhappy. He let me know over a pint in the Bath clubhouse. I didn't mind. That's what fathers are for. Chastised, I staggered, drunk with insults, from the public to the members' bar. Walked straight into Sue. "Ah, there you are . . . I want a word with you . . . thank God, somebody can tell my son he's not perfect." We shared a gin or two. Jerry had Henry's spike, a point to prove to the world on the field. Off it he had his late mother's straight-talking integrity.

'Jerry's mum and dad gave him the perfect mindset to become a great player. All that was needed to go with the mental strength and determination was the natural talent. And that was extraordinary. Whenever we played together, I would fire flat, hard passes into his channel and he'd glide onto the ball and just ghost past defenders. It was almost impossible to realise the speed and timing of his runs. To feel the throaty roar of his filthy laugh, a face that could freak out in horror like something by Bacon, was to remember that this bloke who played rugby like a god was very much human; flawed, imperfect, deliberately arrogant but warm, generous and impulsively fun at the same time.'

Guscott made his debut for England against Romania in May 1989 – and scored a hat-trick. A few months later, he was the catalyst that hauled the Lions back from 1–0 down in the series against Australia. When the Lions returned home from the tour victorious, Guscott was on his way to creating a reputation that would see him anointed as the 'Prince of Centres'.

With ten cup and six championship trophies for Bath and three Grand Slams and a Five Nations championship for England under his belt along with a second tour with the Lions in 1993, his star was, as Barnes intimated in his *Telegraph* article, at last beginning to wane in 1997. 'Although she was pleased for me, deep down my wife Jayne must have felt a bit disappointed when I was named on the tour because she knew I was going to be away for the birth of our daughter, Saskia,' said Guscott. 'We'd discussed in great depth what we would do if I was selected and we'd decided that I would go, but she must have been hoping that I wouldn't be picked.'

**Gregor Townsend:** Jerry brought a confidence to everything he did. He'd played on Lions tours before and always played very well. He'd swung the series in '89 with a brilliant individual try and he had similar moments of genius countless times for England and for that great Bath side. There was just a class about him on the field. He wasn't starting for England that year, but the Lions were his domain. There was a sense of, 'I don't care what [England coach] Jack Rowell thinks, the Lions is my environment and Geech appreciates me.' There was an arrogance about him which, if you took it the right way, could be really positive for those around him.

**Alan Tait:** We didn't always see eye-to-eye but his ability was undeniable. When he opened up in training he was really quick. Like Martin Offiah, in fact, but able to use his hands and feet as well. He was so much more than a finisher.

**Martin Johnson:** A lot of people have this impression of Jerry as arrogant and a bit aloof, but that's not really him. I think he just had confidence in his own ability and opinions. He'd been around the top echelons of the game for a long time and had some very good ideas. He was such a good player that you couldn't ignore him or his opinions.

**Jeremy Guscott:** The basis of my confidence was: I know I can catch and pass, I know I can kick the ball fairly well, I know

I can read and understand the game pretty well, I've worked fucking hard to be fit. I did a lot more training than most people will ever know. I had a good foundation and a good basis to be confident in what I could do. I had very little doubt. I had nobody tapping me on the shoulder; I had no doubts. I didn't let demons play in my mind.

The Lions flew into Johannesburg's Jan Smuts Airport to a relatively low-key welcome, but the words of Steve Tshwete, the Minister of Sport, that greeted them off the plane were significant. 'When the Lions came here in 1974 and I was a prisoner on Robben Island we very much wanted them to beat the Springboks,' said Tshwete. 'It is different now. The whole country is united behind the national team, for rugby is destined to become a unifying force for our people. The potential is great and while we are not looking at a miracle where everything mushrooms overnight, we are deep in the process of making the sport accessible to all. The tour will play a part in that process. It is a great event.'

**Ian McGeechan:** The '74 tour had a profound effect on me for so many reasons, but it was only when I came back in '97 that I really understood how much of an impact that tour also had on South Africa. In Cape Town, before the first Test, a black man came to me with a huge album stuffed full of cuttings from 1974. He said the Lions gave him something to believe in during a brutal time and he thanked me and introduced me to his family. That was very poignant.

And then Steve Tshwete asked to meet Fran Cotton and myself privately after his speech. As soon as we walked in he said, 'Fran Cotton, four Tests, prop. Ian McGeechan, four Tests, centre. You dropped a goal in the third Test.' He said he didn't miss a minute of those Tests on the radio while he was imprisoned on Robben Island with Nelson Mandela. The hairs went up on the back of my neck and I felt humbled that these men, who had suffered terribly, found such hope in the Lions.

**Jim Telfer:** Fran Cotton, 1974 undefeated Lion. Sitting next to him, Ian McGeechan, 1974 undefeated Lion. You could see how much that meant to the South Africans. They couldn't seem to get away from the fact that they had been beaten by the Lions in 1974 and the victors were there in front of them. They really respected that pair – so they were great choices as manager and coach. It was important psychology.

**Martin Johnson:** When Steve Tshwete told us the story about him and the other political prisoners on Robben Island listening to all the 1974 Test matches on the radio and cheering each time the Lions won, the enormity of that story . . . it made you realise the impact of the Springbok badge on the non-white South Africans – and it was amazing in many ways that they still played under it. But that was all part of the Rainbow Nation, wasn't it? Mandela wanted to change what the Springbok meant as a symbol, but to guys like Tshwete, well, Geech and Fran were these legendary figures.

**Fran Cotton:** It was a lovely welcome from Tshwete, but we were written off from the moment our plane landed. They were world champions and the Super 12 was perceived as a vastly superior and more professional competition to anything in the north. That new generation of Bok players had possibly forgotten, or just didn't know, how big a deal an incoming Lions tour was. It had been seventeen years since the last tour in South Africa.

**John Bentley:** They were the current world champions so they gave us no chance. Absolutely no chance. I don't think many people back home gave us much chance, either. Louis Luyt made a speech where he made a joke about tampering with our food, like the All Blacks claimed had happened to them before the 1995 World Cup final. It wasn't the funniest, to be honest.

**Jeremy Guscott:** Luyt gave an awful speech. 'Thanks for coming, but we're going to stuff you 3–0.' It was fantastic for us. We knew we were better than that. They could write us off all they wanted. It really pissed people off. I looked around at the squad and thought, that's a little bit arrogant, because to actually look at the calibre of this squad, the coaches and the management and say 'thanks for coming and being a bit of cannon fodder for our great Springbok team', that was incredibly disrespectful. The fact they thought we were just here to make up the numbers, and to allow the Springboks and the provincial teams to run over us . . . I just thought it was pretty poor form. It wasn't very gracious.

Louis Luyt was aware that the Springboks had a few injuries. Mark Andrews and Kobus Wiese, the locks, were struggling. Japie Mulder, perhaps the finest defensive centre in the world at the time, was touch and go. Chester Williams, the great symbol of multi-racial Rainbow Nation rugby, had been ruled out of the series with knee trouble. Luyt made light of it. 'We have a million rugby players in this country,' he said. 'I think we'll get fifteen on the field to take on the Lions.'

If Luyt's welcome had been disparaging, the press previews in South Africa were equally withering. Very few could even countenance the possibility of the Lions coming close in the Test series. Some were steadfast in their belief that the tourists would get whitewashed and could lose as many as four of their provincial matches. 'There's no doubting that we had a mutual bonding around one fact,' said Richard Hill. 'Not only did the South African players, media, and public think we didn't have the ability to win the Test series, many people in Britain and Ireland didn't think we could win it either.'

## CHAPTER SEVEN

# KOBUS WIESE IS ANGRY

THE TEAM FOR the first tour match was announced late morning on Wednesday 21 May, but first they had to go through a gruelling two-hour training session at Kings Park. Even in the dead of winter, Durban enjoys a gentle climate. For the players entering Telfer's torture chamber, the temperature of eighty degrees must have felt like more than a hundred in next to no time.

**Neil Back:** Part of those sessions was about making us mentally tough enough to cope with the physicality that the South Africans bring to rugby. Jim was very old school with the cargo net out which we all had to go under. It was easy for me because I'm small but the bigger guys, he used to smack them on the head with a stick.

**Doddie Weir:** Ah, the old broom handle! Yeah, I'm not sure if anyone outside the Scotland players expected that old boy to come out. 'If you're too high, you die,' was one of his favourite expressions. I'd been used to it since I first played under Jim at

Melrose. He used to crack you on the head if you were too high. I'm not entirely sure what boys like Johnno and Dallaglio made of that, but to be fair to them they didn't say anything – and they learnt pretty quickly not to go too high.

**Dai Young:** When we were doing rucks, Jim was doing it with you. All his body was going with it. He was the driving force. Sometimes we make the game harder than it needs to be. Jim wanted to make it as simple as possible so that everybody knew their roles.

Amid the luxurious surroundings on the Beverley Hills Hotel in Umhlanga Rocks, Fran Cotton announced the team to face the Eastern Province Invitational XV: Neil Jenkins, Ieuan Evans, Jerry Guscott, Will Greenwood, Nick Beal, Gregor Townsend, Rob Howley, Tom Smith, Keith Wood, Jason Leonard (captain), Doddie Weir, Simon Shaw, Lawrence Dallaglio, Richard Hill, Tim Rodber.

For Rodber, it was a return to the scene of one of his most gruesome rugby memories. England had toured South Africa three summers before and in the first Test against the Boks Rodber had produced one of the outstanding performances of his career in a magnificent England victory at Loftus Versfeld. The next midweek he was asked to double up and sit on the bench against Eastern Province, but was called into action when Dean Ryan broke his hand during an early altercation. Twenty-nine minutes into what would later be dubbed 'The Battle of Boet Erasmus', England were attacking the Eastern Province line when Steve Ojomoh was stopped just short. As players from both sides flew into the ruck, Rodber was hauled out and pinned to the ground before being punched in the face by flanker Simon Tremain – the son of All Black legend, Kel. Rodber – normally the epitome of discipline as an officer in the Green Howards –

exploded off the turf and began to batter Tremain in retaliation, sparking a mass brawl. As the players were pulled apart, out came the referee's red card and Rodber became only the second player in English rugby history to be sent off, following in the ignominious footsteps of Mike Burton against Australia in 1975.

**Tim Rodber:** I was stupid taking the retaliation as far as I did, in hitting Tremain so many times. But the red mist came down and you had to be on that pitch to appreciate the kind of things that were going on.

**Graham Rowntree:** It was one of the most violent games I've ever been involved in.

**Tim Rodber:** Jon Callard had been stamped on his head just a few minutes earlier and had to have twenty-five stitches. He could have lost an eye. Graham Rowntree got knocked clean out. Nobody was safe and you had to have eyes in the back of your head. I just reacted.

**Lawrence Dallaglio:** It was always very hostile over there, but that Eastern Province game got out of hand because the referee was so out of his depth. That was my first England tour and I learnt a huge amount from it – but above all else I learnt just how physical the rugby in South Africa was. I've still got the scars on my back from some of the rucking.

**Graham Rowntree:** It was World War Three. It was just running battles all through the game. So I'd had a taste of South African provincial rugby. I knew what was coming.

**Tim Rodber:** You know, it took me about three years to get over it. For three years I held back in games, frightened to push myself to the limits in really physical situations because I didn't want to go through all that shame again. As a player, I was someone who needed to live on the very edge. I needed that aggression to fire me up to play well, but deep down the memories of what happened at Boet Erasmus put a block on my game.

It finally changed when we played Ireland in Dublin in the '97 Five Nations and that earned me the chance to go to South Africa with the Lions. Nick Popplewell whacked me at a lineout – and I whacked him back. And I knew then what had been missing. I hadn't had that edge for a long time. Violence is too strong a word for it because I'd never describe myself as violent, but in a game like rugby you have to look after yourself, show people they can't take liberties. That little flare-up in Dublin was just what I needed.

Going into that first tour game, I knew what to expect from Eastern Province, especially when they brought in guys like Kobus Wiese and Hennie le Roux, who were out to make a point. South Africans tend to see rugby and physical confrontation as a test of their manhood. Fran said beforehand that we couldn't be seen to take a single step back – we had to stand up for ourselves and, if necessary, be prepared to show them that we weren't going to be punched around. Had the tour happened a year earlier, I'm not sure if I'd have been ready for that.

As it transpired, Rodber would have to wait a little longer before getting a taste of the South African welcome. A stomach bug ruled him out. The Lions would have to tame Kobus Wiese, the fierce World Cup-winning lock, and Hennie le Roux, the ferocious World Cup-winning centre, without him.

Wiese was a hero to rugby fans in South Africa. He had won eighteen caps since his debut in 1993 and had only lost twice. He had been a significant presence in the '95 World Cup engine room and was the team's enforcer – quite the accolade when you consider some of the other characters in that side.

Raised in the remote diamond-mining town of Oranjemund, Wiese had been educated at the famous Paarl Gymnasium alongside fellow World Cup-winner Balie Swart. While Swart went on to play for Stellenbosch University and then Western Province, Wiese had stayed in the hard-man Afrikaans game, plying his trade for Boland, Western Transvaal and then Transvaal on his way to the pinnacle of South African rugby.

Wiese was outspoken and popular among his teammates, but there was a darkness to him, too. In South Africa's first Test after lifting the Webb Ellis Cup, he was lucky to avoid a red card after just five minutes against Wales when he threw a huge haymaker that poleaxed his opposite number, Derwyn Jones. Afterwards, Wiese claimed that he had just been too hyped before the match and it had been an unfortunate incident.

He had performed magnificently on the Springbok end-of-year tour in 1996, playing some of the best rugby of his life. On his return he was handed the captaincy of Transvaal. Wiese was a cult hero to his own people but at thirty-three there were some who felt that his time at the top was gone. Unfortunately for the player, one of those people was Carel du Plessis.

When Du Plessis announced his first Springbok squad just before the Lions' arrival, he left both Wiese and Le Roux out. Both of them had been outraged by their omission and angrily declared to the press that they might follow François Pienaar and Joel Stransky overseas.

'I was disappointed by their reaction,' said Du Plessis at a press conference shortly after they'd gone thermonuclear. 'I told both players before the announcement that they were going to be left out and I hoped to talk to both of them in more detail some time in the future . . . They must concentrate on working on their strengths.'

Wiese and Le Roux were adamant that they were still more than good enough to do a job for the Springboks – and they now had two shots to prove themselves against the Lions ahead of the Test series: once for Eastern Province, who they had been invited to join as guest players, and once for the Gauteng Lions. Both made no secret of their desire to take their fury out on the Lions.

**Kobus Weise:** I was dropped from the Bok squad and I hope I'm not being arrogant in saying that I was very surprised to be dropped. New coaches had come in. Carel du Plessis was the head coach and Gert Smal was his assistant but even though everything was new in the Springbok management I had no idea in the build-up to that series that I wouldn't be part of it.

I had just come back from an unbeaten Bok tour under André Markgraaff and he'd named me as the player of the tour. I thought I'd played really well in Argentina, France and Wales. So to be left out came as a massive shock and it was interesting to read in Kitch Christie's book that he thought it was one of the weirdest selection decisions he had ever witnessed in rugby. To this day neither Carel nor Gert have told me why I was dropped. I was dropped at the same time as Hennie le Roux, another Transvaal player. That led to speculation at the time that it was an anti-Transvaal selection, but nothing was ever verified.

So ja, I was an angry guy coming into that game. I wanted to prove a point, do some damage. I didn't care who these guys were, I just wanted to take them on and show that I was still more than good enough to be a Bok.

**Mark Andrews:** The key to beating the Lions in a Test series is to beat them early on in the tour, while they are still trying to forge their team loyalty, so that the squad might fragment and divide up into the Irish, Welsh, Scottish and English cliques. Having a guy like Kobus playing them early was great for us in the Springbok camp. He was the kind of guy you wanted in a game like that – angry and wanting to prove a point. If anyone was going to soften the Lions up, it was Kobus Wiese.

**Doddie Weir:** I was going up against him. Big laddie, that one. He was like a bull. And he was hungry to make an impression. He had a bit of a reputation with his fists and his boots. Anything, really. It was going to be fun.

**Dai Young:** There was never an out-and-out incident where somebody punches you straight in the chops, but there were plenty of incidents where they'd drop a knee into your back, push your head into the ground or stick an elbow into the face as they fall on you, stamp on your ankles if they can. Always a little bit of afters. I don't think they wanted any bad publicity, for people to consider it a terrible tour with loads of scrapping. They wanted to create the impression that those days were in the past. But you always had to keep your wits about you.

**Ian McGeechan:** Port Elizabeth stirs all sorts of good memories for me. It was where we clinched the series in 1974 and had a famous wild night afterwards. It was peculiar to go back to the Boet Erasmus stadium for the first time since. The ground was only a ten-minute walk from our hotel, so Jim and I took a walk down there in the morning to check out the pitch, the changing rooms and so on. It hadn't changed much since I'd played there – it still had the big bank of steel terracing and a gangway down from the changing rooms to the field. When we got back to the hotel, you could sense the edge building among the players. We did a few lineout drills on the hotel lawn then went in for our final team meeting before the game.

The Lions gathered in their team room at their hotel in Port Elizabeth and Fran Cotton stationed himself behind a table where the match jerseys were handed out. 'The first game on tour's always special,' began Cotton. 'I think for all of us there's going to be a little tingle through the spine when we see those red shirts trot out onto the rugby playing fields of South Africa for the first time.'

Geech moved to the front of the room. He waited a few moments for everybody to settle before he began to speak. The speech, captured in all its glory by the *Living with Lions* filmmakers, became one of the iconic moments from the tour.

'Well boys, I said from the word go that there are teams within teams. You've got the jerseys – you carry the responsibility. You carry the challenge. What you've got now is four countries playing as one. I think Jim and I both feel privileged, and to a certain extent humble, about coming together with the most talented players in the British Isles. The mantle you carry, and the challenge that you have, is to put a marker down in South Africa about the way we can play rugby . . . If somebody goes into contact, there has to be three, four, five behind him. There *has* to be. There *has* to be that commitment to get behind the ball. There *has* to be that commitment to knock them away. And then there *has* to be the commitment to get in behind them and make the second wave.

'I want the marker down today. But I'll tell you, as Fran says, the fucking hairs on the back of my neck will be up when you run on that field. A Lion in South Africa is special. The Lions are special, the legends go with it. You're making it – you're making history; you're putting a marker down – you, this afternoon, are saying what the '97 Lions are all about.'

**Keith Wood:** I remember each of those speeches from '97 because every one of them struck a chord. You sit down either the day before or the day of a match and Geech and Jim would start speaking and it just started to join the dots. They understood the philosophical approach involved with the Lions – and you can see that all these years later.

At the time you were thinking, 'Wow this makes sense, I get that and I believe in that.' Both of them were besotted with preparation, not just for a training session but for a speech. They would put in huge hours to get it right. So, yeah, there was emotion and venom in some of the things they said, but it was still thoughtful. I would say that in those original speeches they made it clear what it meant to be a Lion. It was phenomenal to be in the same room. Yes, you'd already been wearing your tour kit and training together but suddenly, when they spoke, you really felt like a Lion.

**Jason Leonard:** Johnno was rested for the first few games of the tour and I was chosen as captain against Eastern Province because of my previous Lions experience. I think Jim had made some noises in the press about it not being hugely important if we didn't win and it was more about bedding in combinations and getting the boys playing together, but I'm not sure how serious he actually was about that. I think we all knew it was important to get the tour off to a good start and I knew I'd been selected because they needed someone who understood what they were doing, because for new guys pulling on the Lions shirt for the first time, it can be a bit overwhelming. So I was made captain to try and give a steady hand. I'd been there and done it, but even though it was the first game of a long tour, I knew it was vital that we came away with a victory.

**Keith Wood:** Jase is right about that moment you pull on the jersey for the first time. It's massive. You can lose sight of the basics of playing because of all the emotion. And for me, the Lions badge meant an awful lot. My earliest memories of the Lions was seeing my father [Gordon, a prop] in his tour blazer from 1959. He wore it all the time. He was very, very proud of it. He was buried in that blazer. There was an aura all over our house in relation to what the Lions meant to him. When I started playing rugby, I wanted to have the same commitment to that jersey and to that blazer.

**Scott Quinnell:** So we're getting ready to play Eastern Province and there it is – your Lions jersey. It was the reason I came back from rugby league. My father had toured with the Lions in New Zealand in '71 and '77 and South Africa in 1980. My godfather, the Swerve [Mervyn Davies], toured in '71 and to South Africa in '74. My uncle [Barry John] toured in 1968 to South Africa and to New Zealand in '71. To follow in their footsteps was very special.

**Will Greenwood:** Geech said that the challenge ahead of us was like ten Five Nations matches and three World Cup finals in the space of eight weeks. That gave you some perspective. I'd been called into the side to face Eastern Province at the last minute for Gibbsy. It was quite good that way because it meant that I didn't spend too long getting nervous about playing – although I still remember what a weird feeling it was to pull on a Lions jersey before I'd ever pulled on an England one. I was obviously shitting myself – but I tell you one thing that made me feel better and that was seeing Neil Jenkins pacing around the dressing room and retching his guts out. He sounded like a bloody walrus trying to hump its way up a beach to mate.

**Neil Jenkins:** Ach, it's always been the same. I was always very nervous when I was younger before I played. It was the lead-up I hated, the dead time. That's what used to get to me – the waiting. The changing rooms and stuff.

**Ieuan Evans:** That's one thing a bit of experience taught me – never change next to Neil Jenkins. It's not very nice when you're running out to play and you're flicking bits of Neil Jenkins' vomit off your jersey.

**Dai Young:** It was unbelievable how he could go from that to doing what he did on the field.

**Neil Jenkins:** The playing I always found easy. Once you got on the pitch and did the anthems, you kicked off and you were playing and everything was fine then. I wish I could have just turned up half an hour before the game, got strapped, got stretched and gone and played.

**Duncan Humphreys:** We were standing in the changing room before that first match and we were filming and filming and filming, and then Jason looked round and said, 'Right, time for you boys to get out.' And I kind of went, 'Oh, bugger . . .' I knew that if we got kicked out of that changing room, we'd get kicked out of every single one for the rest of the tour.' So I went and spoke to Fran and said, 'Look, if we're not in this dressing room, it'll become a thing – and this whole film relies on us being in moments with the team.' And Fran thought about it for a moment and then went, 'Okay, fine.' And he just went and had a word with Jase, and Jase said, 'Oh, alright then, no problem.' Jason wasn't bothered at all, but it was huge for us. After that, we were all-access.

The sun beat down from a clear winter's sky as the two teams ran out. There was barely a breath of wind. Two weeks of training was all that the Lions had had together and it was now time to start seeing how some of the new combinations were going to work.

**Ian McGeechan:** I wanted to get Rob Howley and Gregor Townsend together as soon as possible. It would have been crazy to wait too long to see what sort of partnership might evolve. It was a mouth-watering prospect.

**Rob Howley:** During the first five weeks, Geech engaged a lot with me and Gregor, encouraging us to work together in training, to get to know one another. He didn't say we were going to be involved in the Test matches, but that was the unspoken understanding. Gregor was an impulsive and off the cuff kind of player. He was very intuitive. High risk, high reward.

**Gregor Townsend:** I loved playing with Rob. I very nearly signed for Cardiff after the tour because I wanted to carry on playing with him. He was so sharp, had a great pass, an electric break. He was so talented. It was pretty clear that with us in the Saturday team together they wanted to build our partnership for the Tests.

**Neil Jenkins:** I knew I was going to play in the first game against Eastern Province, because I knew they'd want to find out about me, find out if I was fit and if my arm was okay. Gregor was at ten, I was at fifteen. Guscott was playing. We had a good backline. Rob Howley was at nine. I hadn't played for eleven or twelve weeks, but I was ready for it mentally.

**Scott Gibbs:** It was a hostile crowd. Everyone was keyed up and the spectators had been drinking. At one point a massive fight broke out on the railway side of the ground and some of the crowd were climbing onto the caboose of a train and fighting there. It was some afternoon.

**Ian McGeechan:** The first twenty minutes were almost perfect, it was as if we'd been playing together for years. Take Jerry's try –

it was a beauty. It had everything in it – a back-row move, inter-passing, recycling at the breakdown, quick ball, a long cut-out pass and Jerry drifting off his man.

Worryingly, they suffered a dip in the second quarter and allowed Eastern Province to build momentum. Kobus Wiese was beginning to do damage. At half-time, the Lions' lead was just 10–6. Up in the stand, Carel du Plessis was taking notes. He had an idea that the Lions were vulnerable at fifteen, that Jenkins was not a full back and could be exploited if Geech persisted in playing him there. 'I think that's where the Lions might have a weakness,' he said. 'I'd like to see him put under pressure.'

On the hour-mark, Jenkins was exposed both for his positioning and for his pace when Eastern Province winger Deon Keyser raced through the midfield and left the Lions' full back for dead on his way to scoring a wonder try that gave his side an 11–10 lead.

**Neil Jenkins:** Yeah, he did me, and I suppose I struggled a bit with my positioning, especially at first – but, you know, I was never a fifteen. I can tell you straight, I was never, ever a fifteen. I'd been a ten all my life and I know a lot of tens now play like a second full-back – and I probably did a little bit of that back then – but I wasn't a fifteen. Keyser did me, but I didn't let it bother me.

**Jeremy Davidson:** I came on as a sub, and I was running around like a headless chicken. I was on in the back row, I came flying off a scrum, they passed the ball inside, I got white line fever and suddenly dropped the ball right in front of the line: a thing I will never, ever let myself forget. I'd been on the field fifteen seconds of the flipping Lions tour, you've got the line in front of you, nobody there to catch you, and you drop the ball. Nightmare.

**Jason Leonard:** It had been a bit sticky for a while, but we'd stuck to our guns and played the sort of rugby that we'd wanted to – the sort of rugby that we believed would beat South Africa in the series. We won 39-11. One of the best moments for me was when Kobus Wiese took a short ball from their scrum-half and Scott Quinnell absolutely halfed him. I don't think that happened to Kobus many times in his career.

**Martin Johnson:** Scotty smashed him right on his arse, which was a huge psychological blow for them, seeing their hard man taken down like that.

**Scott Quinnell:** I was twenty-four when I went on that tour. When I was a rugby player, I wasn't the person I am now. I was a lot quieter. I just wanted to get on with it. Didn't do too much talking. I did the talking on the field. There wasn't much need at that time for talking off the field. It was very much a case of leading from the front and leading with actions.

**Jeremy Guscott:** He says he was quiet on that tour? I don't think so.

**Gregor Townsend:** The thing that helped us in the early games was that we were all fit. We came through to win a lot of matches in the last fifteen to twenty minutes. And that Eastern Province game was one where I thought if we'd played another ten minutes we could have scored another five tries. In the last ten minutes of that game, every time we got the ball someone was busting through the defence with somebody else on their shoulder. So it was a nice feeling. We all had things to work on, but to see some things come off that we'd worked on at training must have pleased the coaches.

The Eastern Province captain, Jaco Kirsten, wasn't quite so generous with his praise. He admitted that his side had underestimated the Lions but that the Springboks would have no problem taking them up front. 'At 11–10, we thought we would definitely win,' said the hooker. 'The front five of the Lions are vulnerable, particularly in their physical strength. You can definitely take them on up front.' He even suggested that the Super 12 champions, the Auckland Blues, could defeat the full Lions Test side. What hope, then, would the Lions have against the world champions? Kirsten's smile and rueful shake of the head suggested that, as far as he was concerned, there was only one possible outcome.

There were clearly some early jitters in the Lions' performance – Wood had struggled a few times with the accuracy of his throwing, Townsend had put his side under pressure with some poor kicking and Jenkins had also missed a couple of relatively straightforward efforts in front of goal (albeit striking the post on both occasions) as well as his defensive frailty when Keyser scored – but by and large the experience had been positive. The back row and second row had performed superbly, with Weir outplaying Wiese. Howley had looked exceptional at scrum-half, and the centre pairing of Guscott and Greenwood had looked dazzlingly slick.

**Neil Jenkins:** I was just happy to get through the game to be honest. Tim Stimpson was probably the number one full back on tour and rightly so – Tim was an exceptional player and had had a good season for England and Leicester, so I always thought, 'I need to make the most of every chance I can, hopefully get a chance at ten in one of the games, and just try to do what I do, really. Do the simple things well, play well and kick well.' That's what I did.

The media analysis varied depending on which part of the world you were in. 'The Lions emerge from the bloodstained bullring of Boet Erasmus with a clean bill of health, Doddie Weir takes Kobus Wiese to the cleaners at the lineout and the only fight involves half a dozen drunks and a streaker on the roof of a train overlooking the ground,' wrote Chris Hewett in *The Independent*. 'Port Elizabeth just ain't what it used to be.' Meanwhile, the South African *Cape Argus*, was decidedly underwhelmed by the favourites. Projecting forward and assessing how the visitors would fare against the Republic's biggest guns, they came to a straightforward conclusion: 'These Lions look like pussycats'.

# CHAPTER EIGHT

# HE KEPT HIS DEAFNESS SECRET

ON THE SUNDAY afternoon, the Lions took a short flight from Port Elizabeth to East London. Almost as soon as they stepped off the plane, the thick bank of dark clouds that was gathered overhead opened and it began to rain. And rain. All through the night and into the next day it poured down. The ground where they were due to have their Monday morning training session was waterlogged so they moved their session to the Basil Kenyon Stadium, where they would be facing Border on Wednesday afternoon.

After the struggles in the scrum against Eastern Province, Telfer was keen to have a live scrummaging session. There was nothing particularly newsworthy about that in itself, but it soon hit the headlines.

**Fran Cotton:** There was a flare-up between Mark Regan and Barry Williams. A lot was made of it in the press and it's captured on the video, but there wasn't much to it.

**Mark Regan:** It happens in club training most weeks, so there was nothing to get in a sweat about.

**Barry Williams:** Every training session where there was contact was like a game, because you wanted to wear that jersey. Didn't matter whether it was on a Wednesday or a Saturday, you wanted to wear that jersey. It was live scrummaging, we went down hard on the scrum and he didn't go down. He kind of kneed me in the face, and there was a punch-up. Fair dos to the English boys, they let it go, they thought he deserved it. Then after the training session we went back to the hotel, and Jim Telfer pulled us together. It was lunchtime and they had arranged a table for two for us to have lunch together. Bit of banter, like. But hey – what happens on a training field or on a rugby pitch, it happens. It's just the way life is. Nothing changes. Obviously, we were in the same position. We were always looking for it.

**Fran Cotton:** When you get a scrummaging session as ferocious as that, tensions run high. There is a lot of personal pride amongst the players and you get the occasional incident, but Rob Wainwright was the captain that week and he dealt with it.

**Simon Shaw:** Ronnie [Mark Regan] always had this thing about earning your stripes. I think he felt particularly aggrieved that Barry had come out of nowhere to make the tour and there was a joke going around the Welsh boys with them calling him 'Barry Three Tours' because he was talking like a man with a wealth of experience behind him. I think it all rubbed Ronnie up the wrong way. He always made things very personal against his opposite number and would have seen getting on with his rival as a sign of weakness.

**Scott Quinnell:** I remember thinking, 'Yeah, that's what we need. That's what it's going to take.' When I played for Llanelli, Simon Easterby and Mike Phillips used to fight all the time, and if they weren't, you used to orchestrate a fight just to get them into the right mindset. It was what was needed. In South Africa, you need to be bold, you need to be brave, and you need to be on the edge. That's the atmosphere the coaches created. It was just two teammates fighting. It happens week in, week out up and down the country. That just shows the passion that both players and everybody had for it. You always want to make a statement in training, you want to hit people hard and make sure you get into that Test team. When there's fighting in training, you know the intensity is there already.

**Paul Wallace:** What was funny was that it was Jim, of all people, who came in and broke it up and was scolding everyone for giving the South African media something to write about.

Regan was competitive, loud, chopsy and often acted the clown, much to the delight of his teammates and, often, to the chagrin of his coaches. It was all part of his combative and gregarious nature, but it was also a mask he put up to hide a disability that none of his teammates knew about. Having suffered from a severe bout of measles as a child, his hearing had been permanently damaged. Mark Regan was profoundly deaf.

**Mark Regan:** My mum said to me, 'You'll have to get hearing aids,' but I said, 'I'm not wearing hearing aids to school, I'll get absolutely torn apart. I can't be dealing with it, Mum.' So I didn't have them. My grades suffered, so my parents sent me to Clarke's Grammar, a private school in Bristol. It really helped because the classes were small. You weren't forgotten about and they really focused on me.

Despite his hearing problems, he embraced rugby, playing for the Bristol under-11s all the way up to the first team at the age of nineteen. He won his first cap for England in 1995 in a Test career that would see him win forty-seven caps and a World Cup and play as a pro until 2009, but throughout this entire period he kept his deafness a secret from his teammates and coaches, only publicly addressing it in 2020.

**Mark Regan:** I was too worried to say anything to the players or coaches because I thought the piss-take would be relentless. I was good at giving it out, but not too good at taking it. It's only been in the last ten years that I've been more comfortable with it.

In 2019 he saw an audiologist and was fitted with hearing aids for the first time. It was like a whole new world to him.

**Mark Regan:** I was able to engage in conversation like never before because I could actually hear what the other person was saying. Before, I would mishear and feel quite self-conscious about looking stupid for asking them to repeat themselves. I'm not actually stupid – I just couldn't hear.

I learned to lip read early on and that's how I managed. At lineouts, I'd be looking at the caller's mouth rather than listening to what they were saying. It took a lot more concentration than most other hookers had to put in, but I still had some of the best throwing averages. Luckily, I had twenty-twenty vision and could see their lips moving. I also memorised the movements for each call and that helped a lot.

I look back in anger now, really, and think, 'Why didn't you tell people?' People would have understood more about me then, the way I was, what sort of character I actually was. But I didn't feel comfortable with it.

Shortly after the training session ended, the team to face Border was unveiled: Tim Stimpson, John Bentley, Allan Bateman, Scott Gibbs, Tony Underwood, Paul Grayson, Austin Healey, Graham Rowntree, Mark Regan, Dai Young, Doddie Weir, Jeremy Davidson, Rob Wainwright (captain), Neil Back and Eric Miller.

It was a surprise to see the continued omission of Martin Johnson. Cotton reiterated the party line – that Johnson was merely being given a chance to freshen up after a long and arduous season, but there was growing disquiet in the press that Johnno was struggling. It was already well-known that he would be having surgery on a groin issue when he returned from the tour. Was there a chance he might not be fit at all? Cotton dismissed it out of hand. They were managing him for that exact reason – so that he would be fit for the Test series – and he assured the press pack that Johnson would be leading the team out on Saturday against Western Province.

**Martin Johnson:** I had a groin issue that was going to need an op, but our doc, James Robson, reckoned that it would be okay to manage it throughout the tour. If it flared up badly, I'd just have to have a cortisone injection. It wasn't that bad. After the first couple of training sessions, it was giving me some grief, so it was decided that I'd sit out the first two games. It was weird not leading the team out, but there was nothing I could do. I then damaged the AC joint in my left shoulder in training, which was another headache. It was hard to watch the first couple of games, but actually the hardest thing was sitting out the training. I was watching Jim flogging the boys and I couldn't join in properly. I hated it.

On the Tuesday morning, the headline on the front page of the local paper in East London read: 'Muddy Field Awaits the Lions'.

Tucked away in the bottom corner was another story: 'Plot to Kill Mandela Suspected'. It was clear where all the attention was focused.

Border was the least glamorous of the Lions' fixtures. They had a proud tradition of playing the tourists and had famously defeated the Lions in 1955, but they were in a rebuilding phase under New Zealand coach Ian Snook. Eastern Province, who the Lions had just dispatched, had finished ahead of Border in the 1996 Currie Cup and Snook's side had endured an even tougher start to the 1997 season.

Snook knew several of the Lions players fairly well having coached at Bedford and then at Old Wesley in Dublin. Although he had lost some senior men that season, he had a few secret weapons up his sleeve in his bid to run the legs off the Lions – not least a young back-three player by the name of Russell Bennett.

**Russell Bennett:** My route to the Springboks was a bit different in that I was selected out of Border, which was a less fashionable province. I had made my Natal debut in 1993, but didn't make much progress. Then Border came on the phone. The money offered was half of what I was earning in Durban, where I was working for the Dunlop tyre company. So I phoned my father and asked him what I should do. He said, 'I can't make up your mind for you. You must decide, but if rugby is what you want, then you must take a risk.' So I did. I put all my possessions into my 1.2 Corolla and moved to East London.

**Rob Wainwright:** I was captain for that game and, God, I was nervous. How do you deliver a pre-match speech to those players? I'd had a great season with Scotland the year before, but in '97 I'd been struggling to get back from an injury and then we had a difficult Five Nations. I think I scraped into the Lions squad by the skin of my teeth. So, bizarrely, I was kind of scared by the whole idea of captaining the Lions. There's a certain element of inferiority in the Scottish psyche and the idea of having to be in charge of all these big guns from England, Wales and Ireland was very daunting.

But I was over-thinking it because when a team is so full of experience the captain's role is only the odd wee touch on the tiller. All the roles that a captain and a coach would usually fulfil are in the team already: you have your motivators, your tacticians, it's all there.

The rain beat down relentlessly and a blustery wind blew in hard from the Indian Ocean. A huge amount of surface water still lay on the pitch at the kick-off and it was evident from the start that it would be a very different type of game to the first match in Durban.

John Bentley announced himself on tour by scoring after just two minutes, but after that the conditions dictated play and the match became a slog. Paul Grayson, who had not played in over two and a half months because of injury, began to toil. His normally reliable radar in front of the posts was malfunctioning and he was at fault for winger André Claassen's try shortly after half-time that gave Border a shock 11–10 lead.

**Jeremy Davidson:** For the Border guys, playing against the Lions was the game of their life and it poured out of the heavens, so it was a leveller. It was a mud-bath. It was kind of every man for himself in those conditions.

**Ian McGeechan:** Grays was struggling, but I didn't want to dent his confidence by bringing him off. I decided to switch the focal point of attack by subbing on Matt Dawson for Austin Healey. Austin's game was all about speed and flick passing, which wasn't suited to the conditions, whereas Matt was good at getting the forwards on the move and bringing in the midfield runners. I figured Matt might take some of the pressure off Paul – and it worked.

**Martin Johnson:** It was tough on Grays. He hadn't played a competitive match for ages and the conditions were horrible. He missed five kicks at goal and he didn't look anywhere near match fit. I think it had been in the back of his mind that he wasn't fully fit since we had first met up for the tour, but he must have been holding on to the hope that a bit of rest and the good weather in South Africa might aid his recovery. It's something that you do as a sportsman. You cling on to hope. Rest, extra training, whatever. You'll try anything. I've lost count of the number of times I felt virtually crippled on a Thursday and then, come Saturday and the match, the adrenaline kicks in and that got me through the game. I was worried about the effect Grays's fitness problem would have on team selection during the rest of the tour too. Tim Stimpson was the best full back we had at that particular point, but he wasn't a noted goal-kicker. With Grays out of the reckoning, that would mean there was only one kicker of real note in the entire squad: Neil Jenkins.

**Ian McGeechan:** We finally got it all together in the last twenty minutes. Doddie led a great lineout drive and Rob Wainwright went over to score, then Tim Stimpson made it safe with a last-minute penalty to make it 18–14.

'The Lions front row had a dreadful day against two feisty young props,' wrote Peter Bills in *Rugby News*. 'Paul Grayson, the Lions' fly-half was even worse than his props. With Gregor Townsend almost as unconvincing at fly-half in the first match, the Lions are in deep trouble. They will regret leaving Jonathan

Davies at home . . . In the end, the Lions only won because of two remarkably generous decisions by the referee. He gave Mark Regan a try even though there was a double movement and he gave Rob Wainwright a try when it was more than doubtful that the ball had been grounded.'

In the aftermath, Border captain Ruhan van Zyl echoed the sentiments of Eastern Province captain Jaco Kirsten when he said that the Lions' main weakness was up front. The Springboks, he was sure, would destroy the Lions' pack.

**Russell Bennett:** I actually watched the Lions game on video the other day. They tried to run the ball in atrocious conditions. It was crazy. For a team that had been struggling, we did pretty well and I was pleased with how I played. That game probably helped me get selected to play for the Boks a few weeks later.

**Martin Johnson:** We shouldn't have made such hard work of a team only rated eleventh in South Africa.

**Eric Miller:** Border was my first game of the tour and I remember being so nervous. What I don't remember is getting a bang on the face – it was probably the adrenaline and the speed of the game that meant I didn't notice, but it was all swollen up after the game. I was taken to hospital as a precaution, but when the doctor saw it he instantly knew I'd broken my cheekbone. Hearing those words was just the worst nightmare because you know, deep down, that's it. You're gone and heading home.

My cheek felt numb but nothing compared to what you're feeling when you're told your tour's over. Fortunately for me the Lions doctors were experienced and they were used to dealing with those types of injury all the time. They decided I should get a second opinion and that saved my tour. It was in the same hospital but it was a different doctor and they said that it was in an area which wasn't serious enough to deem me unfit to play and I was given the all-clear. These are the injuries that happen on tour that you don't hear about. I was very nearly on the next plane home.

**Scott Gibbs:** I took a bang. We went to the Boland general emergency room for an x-ray on my ankle and the attendant radiologist was delighted to see me because he recognised that I'd had the same injury four years earlier, when his son was born, and he'd named his son after me. Imagine that. What are the chances of me landing in a Boland emergency room for an ankle injury and the radiographer's son was named after me four years earlier? Incredible. It had been an identical injury but just on the other ankle. Luckily there was nothing major wrong, I just had to strap it up and rest it for a while – but it meant I didn't have to worry about being sent home.

**Ian McGeechan:** We weren't so lucky with Paul Grayson. It was hugely disappointing for him and the rest of us when we realised on the Friday that he had no chance of recovery and had to be sent home. Mike Catt was called up from the England tour in Argentina to replace him.

**Paul Grayson:** It's like winning something and then losing it. When I felt the muscle pull in training on the Tuesday, I put it down to fatigue: to my mind, I was fit enough to last the game. To fly home . . . ah, it was very hard to take.

**Martin Johnson:** I was gutted for Grays, but Catty was a good guy to come in as a replacement – and I'd actually been surprised he hadn't been named in the original squad. He'd grown up in South Africa, knew the country and the style of rugby they played.

**Mike Catt:** I don't know why, but I never stopped believing that I'd join the Lions tour at some point and so I'd flown out to Argentina with England in a really positive frame of mind – and actually had the most fantastic trip, one of the best I'd ever been on. I was playing really well and knowing how incredibly physical South African rugby is, I felt sure the Lions were going to need reinforcements. I had a blinder against Argentina, scoring a try and landing seven kicks as we thrashed the Pumas 46–20. The next day, Jack got the call saying that Grays was out and they wanted me to come to South Africa.

**Martin Johnson:** Jack Rowell was a bit awkward about releasing Catty to us.

**Mike Catt:** Jack was desperate for me to stay. 'You can go after the Test on Saturday,' he told me. I replied, 'Look, Jack, I'm sorry, but I can't do that. This is a once-in-a-lifetime opportunity.' A Lions tour is the ultimate for any rugby player and the senior players all agreed I was doing the right thing in going, but nevertheless I felt bad. England had never won a series in Argentina before and the following weekend they got hammered 33–13. But what else could I do? I couldn't turn down the chance to be a Lion.

**Martin Johnson:** The whole aim of the Border game as far as I was concerned was to get in and out with a win in our pockets and no injuries – and we hadn't really managed it. Grays was out of the tour and Scott Gibbs had been stretchered off early in the second half with suspected damaged ankle ligaments that we thought might be pretty serious and Tom Smith was still suffering with a stiff neck that he'd picked up against Eastern Province. The only real positives from the game were that we'd picked up a win and both Alan Tait and John Bentley had played well.

The following day, the *Cape Times* let the tourists have it: 'Lions starting to look like pussycats'. In the match report, Border scrum-half, John Bradbrook, fired into their perceived deficiencies up front. 'They were soft,' said Bradbrook. 'Both going into the tackle and in the tackle situation. South Africa will be making a big mistake if they don't take these guys on up front. I tried to hassle their back row and scrum-half a bit. It seemed to intimidate them and, even on the occasions I took the tackle, it never felt like I had been pumped back in the contact. They appeared to shy away from head-on contact. That, more than anything, surprised me.'

# CHAPTER NINE

# ONE-ALL, WANKER!

AFTER A WEEK of torrential rain, the sun shone brightly as the Lions left their East London hotel and headed for the airport. Their next stop was Cape Town for game number three and the first of the major examinations of the tour: Western Province in front of 50,000 fans at Newlands.

Western Province, although not in the Super 12 that year, were on an unbeaten run and their side was full of Springboks past, present and future. The pack was fearsome, with grizzled battlers Fritz van Heerden, Gary Pagel, Keith Andrews and Robbie Brink alongside future Boks Corné Krige, Andrew Aitken and the fast-rising superstar of South African rugby, Bobby Skinstad, on the bench. They were all champing at the bit to launch themselves at the underbelly of the Lions.

James Small was in the backline. A desperate man, Small was wired to the moon to prove to Carel du Plessis that he was still good enough for a place on the Springbok wing. Alongside him in the back-three was fellow Springbok Justin Swart while another Springbok, Dick Muir, captained the side in the centre alongside future Bok Robbie Fleck. Among the lesser-known names was a young utility back by the name of Percy Montgomery.

Golden boy Percy had been born and raised in South West Africa (now Namibia), but had the blue and white stripes of Western Province in his blood. He'd been sent to board at the prestigious South African College School (SACS) in Cape Town, just a stone's throw away from Newlands stadium, when he was eight years old.

**Percy Montgomery:** I used to love going to Newlands, watching the rugby and getting lost in my own world where I was playing for Western Province and wasn't just a schoolboy on the side of the field. Those were great days, taking the walk down from SACS to Newlands to watch Province play. I wanted to make it so badly, my teachers used to say my favourite subjects were first and second break because it meant that I could go on the field and practise my kicking. I became obsessed. I used to run Newlands Forest most mornings before the other guys in the boarding house were awake, get back, sneak a carton of milk, down it, have a shower and be ready for first break's kicking. If they'd given grades for sport, for getting up early and for dreaming big about being a Springbok, then I would have been top of the class.

**James Dalton:** He was just a kid when he came into the Bok set-up and he formed an instant connection with James Small. The two had played together at Western Province earlier in the season and, in many ways, 1997 was the year in which James, the glamour boy of the Bok backs, passed on the baton to his successor. Both James and Monty were like moths to a lightbulb when it came to media attention. They were the pretty boys of Springbok rugby, and, on the field, they were lethal in attack.

Montgomery realised his dream when he made his Province debut in 1996, but it took another season before he established himself in the team, impressing new coach, Harry Viljoen, so much on a pre-season tour to Argentina that he declared Montgomery to be the most exciting backline player in South Africa with a game-breaking x-factor. 'He will play for the Springboks this year,' Viljoen told the *Cape Times* ahead of the 1997 season. 'You should have seen how good he was in Argentina, playing at outside centre and fly-half. He has power and pace and he's getting bigger all the time. He also gives any backline another attacking option because of the distance he gets on his kicks and he's eager to learn.'

Ahead of the Lions' arrival, the twenty-one-year-old Montgomery wowed domestic fans in the Nite Series (the forerunner to the Vodacom Cup), combining explosive attack with bone-jarring defence that belied his slight frame – and soon it was more than just Viljoen calling for his elevation to the national team.

When the Lions' team was announced, Martin Johnson was in. 'At last, Lions reveal their most valuable asset,' read the headline in South Africa's *Mail & Guardian*. 'Johnson's absence from the first two tour games has been the cause for more than one eyebrow to be lifted,' reported the newspaper. 'He is perhaps the greatest asset the Lions have right now, given the problems Springbok coach Carel du Plessis has with assembling a physically and match fit second-row . . . It is not a bad thing that Cotton and McGeechan want to save their best for the most important matches. Now we can sit back and see how good a player Johnson really is.'

The captain had a strong core of his England teammates selected around him as Cotton read out the side: Stimpson, Evans, Guscott, Tait, Bentley, Townsend, Howley, Rowntree, Williams, Leonard, Johnson (captain), Shaw, Dallaglio, Hill and Rodber.

**Martin Johnson:** The hotel was only five minutes away from the ground and you could feel it hanging over the boys in the build-up. The atmosphere was pretty tense. This was the first proper test of the tour. You could see the lift that being in Cape Town gave the players.

**Rob Howley:** Newlands was where the tour began for real.

**Scott Gibbs:** Cape Town, to this day, is my spiritual home. There is something about that city that gives you energy. It's easy to say that, because we all appreciate how wet and awful UK weather can be, but it's not just the climate – it's the people, it's the landscape, it's the food, it's everything. I went to live there from 2010 to 2016, I thought to myself, 'God, if I could start over again now, and play rugby in the southern hemisphere, and play in Cape Town, it would be an enormous thrill.' It left an indelible mark on me.

**Ian McGeechan:** It was one of the absolute heartlands of South African rugby and they had several players who were wanting to push for a Test place – not least James Small.

In a video session before the match, Andy Keast highlighted some clips of Small in action. Keast had worked with the winger when they had both been at Natal and he knew his attitude as well as he knew his game.

'You see here,' said Keast, standing in front of a paused clip of Small in action during a team meeting captured on *Living with Lions*. '[Small's] actually waiting and he's trying to pull the inside defenders across. When he plays for the Boks, especially early on, and in big games, he does the opposite early. He wants to fly in because he's very . . .' Keast pauses. 'Messed-up in the head, basically. And he likes to prove a point.'

'As far as James Small's concerned, he's going to want to make it the "James Small show" tomorrow,' said Geech. 'He'll want to prove to South Africa that he's the best winger in South Africa. He'll want to run it and get involved. In that respect, his rugby will be very indisciplined – he'll be trying to get involved in everything.'

Speaking to Donald McRae ahead of the tour, Small was laser-like in his focus on the Lions. 'This is going to be a huge season for South Africa and, hopefully, for me too,' he said. 'To play against the Lions would be one of the highlights of my career. I'd put it on a par with playing the All Blacks. It's that momentous.'

Small had missed the 1997 Super Rugby season because his Western Province team had failed to qualify as one of the top four Currie Cup sides in 1996, which was the way South Africa chose its Super 12 representatives at the time. But he was confident that the rest would do him good and that he could add to his haul of thirty-six Springbok caps when the Test series against the Lions kicked off.

**Ian McGeechan:** We spent quite a bit of time analysing Small. And the back row discussed how they were going to defend against him with Bentos off the set-piece because we knew that he'd be looking for the ball a lot and would want to make an impact on the game. We knew he was desperate to play against us for the Boks and this was going to be his main chance to show that he was good enough.

**John Bentley:** He was the biggest name in South African rugby. I'd been warned about him back in England by my Newcastle teammate Inga Tuigamala who said Small was the best player he'd ever played against – but very mouthy. He was passionate, hot-headed at times. People said we were very much alike. It seemed we were destined to meet.

**Martin Johnson:** It was a hot day and the pace of the game was expected to be fast and I was a bit worried about whether I'd last the pace. I was itching to get out there – it felt like I'd been in South Africa forever without doing the one thing I'd gone there to do. But if I'd thought the game was going to be tough, nothing could have prepared me for the reality of it. I was absolutely knackered after twenty minutes. I thought their initial onslaught would blow itself out, but they kept on coming. There was no doubt about it, we were shell-shocked by the power of Western Province's game. They dominated the scrum, wheeling us at will, and scored two early tries. We needed to regroup and change our game plan.

**Graham Rowntree:** The forward pack had been getting a bit of a slagging from the media and from some of the local coaches. They were getting stuck into us. Of course they were. And in the Western Province game we struggled in the set piece again. It was ferocious. They were getting the wheel on the scrum and launching their backline off it. I remember one particularly painful video session after the game, where we reviewed one of their line breaks for a try and it was from a wheel on the scrum. It was my end of the scrum, which I didn't keep up. It was brutal. And quite rightly, we were getting some grief.

**Percy Montgomery:** The sideshow was between James Small and John Bentley. They were at each other all game – I'd never heard two guys going at one another like that before. Or since. They were calling each other every name in the book and neither was prepared to back down. And when they were too far apart to hear each other, they'd carry on throwing out signs like wanker and up-yours. James accused Bentley of eye-gouging him and each guy was trying to outdo the other in showmanship. I'm sure the crowd loved it, but it was all a bit over the top for me. I was never one to swear at opponents or get psyched up that way, but

James was always very vocal and would see that kind of verbal sparring as part of a battle within a battle. I can't remember an opponent who seemed to love that approach as much as Bentley did. It was something else watching the two of them go at it – and while some of the stuff they said was pretty crude, other stuff was bloody funny.

**John Bentley:** Geech moved me to the left wing so that we'd be in each other's faces, which obviously wound Small up. He thought we were making a big thing of it – and he was right. It was our chance to try and undermine him before the first Test. I knew I had to play well to get a place in the Test team, but I also had to play well to undermine his confidence.

In the game within a game, Bentley was the first to get the upper hand. It was his break off the wing that took the Lions deep into Western Province territory and it was Bentley again who was on the end of Jerry Guscott's pass moments later to finish of a sublime piece of attacking rugby.

**Tim Stimpson:** I remember getting caught with a cheap shot in the first half and I heard my ribs go ding, ding, ding. I couldn't really breathe and at half-time I said to Geech, 'I think I'm in trouble, mate. I think I'm going to have to come off.' And he said, 'Okay. Have a bottle of water, let's go and have a little chat.' And I'll never forget this – it still makes the hairs on the back of my neck stand up when I think about it – he said, 'Where are we?' I said, 'Newlands.' He said, 'Who are you playing for?' 'The Lions.' And he said, 'Okay. It would mean a lot to me personally if you could try and play on for a few more minutes. I think it might be really important. Do you think you could try, for me?' And I was like, 'Yeah, yeah, yeah, yeah, yeah.' Ian McGeechan is asking me to play on for this shirt. Of course I can.

I can honestly say that that's one of the most influential moments of my life. You realise the body's a carcass. It's just a vehicle. It's all about your will. You can give up or you can push on. He knew exactly how to manage me, and I carried on playing the rest of the tour with that mindset.

The heat appeared as if it might be draining the Lions midway through the match, but when the sun dipped behind the mountains the tourists upped the tempo again. Province needed a response – and they very nearly got one from Small who burnt Bentley on the outside, chipped ahead and was only just beaten to his kick ahead by a covering Guscott. On the way back into position for the twenty-two drop-out, Small shouted in Bentley's face: 'One-all, wanker!'

**John Bentley:** It was a battle within a battle. The worst moment came when he rounded me – he caught me flat-footed, kicked ahead and nearly scored. Thank God for Jerry. As Small ran back past me, he had his finger circling the air, swearing at me and saying, 'I've got you in my pocket.' The supporters were giving me heaps of stick.

Stimpson added a penalty a few minutes later and then Small was up against Bentley again. This time, the Lion scragged him into touch and as they crossed the line, Small hurled the ball at Bentley's head, which sparked a wrestle between them. As they were pulled apart, Bentley pushed his hand into Small's face. The Western Province winger grinned as he walked away.

**John Bentley:** I really had to dig in for the rest of the game. He took a high ball at one point and I was all over him. He later alleged that I gouged his eye, which is nonsense. He was just furious that I was getting the upper hand.

**Doddie Weir:** That, in many ways, showed the way of the tour. John Bentley, a bit of an unknown, was up against James Small – and made him very small. He got the better of him mentally and physically. And that shows you sometimes what the game's about.

**Martin Johnson:** We were still behind early in the second half, but then showed we could do what a lot of people claimed we couldn't. We began to compete with them physically and then tore them apart with our running and handling game.

**Jim Telfer:** Rob Howley was outstanding in that game. He made a beautiful cut and break through the midfield and then put in a lovely long pass to his right to put Ieuan Evans in for a try in the corner. It was an absolute beauty.

**Scott Gibbs:** Rob's speed at the breakdown and his speed of pass was giving the guys an edge. It was giving the guys a metre and a half of space. In the midweek games, in the provincial games, that was what was giving us our flow and our freedom. He was playing magnificently. He looked more controlled and composed in that position as the tour went on, and it was like, 'Wow. This guy is *tearing* people apart.'

Before the end, Bentos landed a metaphorical punch to Small's solar plexus when he cantered in for his second score of the day to seal a 38–21 victory. Province had hit them with three tries, the Lions had scored four.

**John Bentley:** It was job done. The defence had creaked a little but we'd scored some great tries ourselves. I was pleased from a personal point of view as well. James Small refused to shake hands with me after the game, even though I offered my hand to him, and the South African press made a massive thing about the way I'd psyched him out. He got slaughtered in the press for saying he'd allowed himself to be intimidated. Two days afterwards he alleged that I'd gouged his eye, which I hadn't. I wasn't allowed to comment on it.

As important as the win and the cowing of James Small had been, another positive was that the tour captain had at last played – and lasted the distance. 'That,' he gasped at full time, 'was harder than any Five Nations match I've played. Ever. Full stop.'

Beside him in the boiler-house, Simon Shaw had been outstanding, as had Richard Hill at openside. The half-backs Howley and Townsend were inspired while Alan Tait in midfield and Tim Stimpson at full back were buzzing and busy throughout their time on the field. Stimpson had helped himself to a haul of eighteen points and was considered by many to be in pole position for a Test spot. It was clear that Neil Jenkins had a serious fight on his hands at fifteen.

**Jim Telfer:** I remember a comment from Johnno afterwards, when he was asked at the press conference why the Lions hadn't closed the game up after going ahead and he said, 'The modern game we play doesn't allow us to stop playing rugby. We won because we kept playing.'

**Martin Johnson:** Dick Muir, the Western Province captain, said that he was surprised and impressed by the speed and ambition of our game. Some of their players actually came into our changing room after the game to congratulate us and tell us to ignore some of the criticism we were receiving in the press.

'It's beginning to dawn on the South African rugby fraternity that the cutting edge of Martin Johnson's party is a whole lot sharper than they imagined,' wrote Chris Hewett in *The Independent*, 'and the manner of the visitors' 38–21 victory on a Cape afternoon of scorching heat and scalding pace left good local judges reaching for a stiff drink or ten before sundown . . . After witnessing the brilliance of Rob Howley and Gregor Townsend at half-back, the no-nonsense aggression of Alan Tait in midfield, the undiminished finishing prowess of Ieuan Evans and Tim Stimpson's cucumber-cool progress as a front-line goal kicker, not even the most myopic Western Province die-hard could dismiss the Lions out of hand.'

'There are still flaws and glaring weaknesses in the scrum,' caveated Mick Cleary in *The Observer*. 'From the very first locking of the two packs it was obvious that the Lions' front row was having a torrid afternoon. They were never secure on their own ball, the scrum either shunting backwards or slewing sideways.'

'They've got to get that scrummage sorted out,' said Andrew Aitken, who impressed in the Western Province back row. 'If they try to run ball in retreat against the Springboks they'll find themselves in real strife.' For all that Aitken was now repeating a standard post-match criticism of the Lions' scrum, he was also emphatic in his praise for the rapier-sharp Lions backs. 'Their lines of running were extremely good, as were their ball skills. It wouldn't surprise me one bit if the Lions reached the first Test unbeaten. The scrum is the key area for them now. They can do most other things far better than we thought.'

# CHAPTER TEN

# WE NEEDED TO SUFFER

AFTER THE WIN against Western Province the boys hit the town, arriving at a Mexican place called Cantina Tequila for a proper booze-up. Gregor Townsend remembers it well. 'Keith Wood's got the girl who's got the tequila, he's lying on the ground – now, you couldn't do it nowadays because everyone would be taking photos of it. You'd be in the tabloids, you'd be destroyed. There was one night we got warned – remember *Loaded* magazine? We had a meeting to say that a *Loaded* journalist was coming out with a photographer, so we had to make sure we didn't do anything silly. There was a group of us came back, probably at like two in the morning after the Western Province game, and this journalist and photographer from *Loaded* were sitting in the reception. We were lucky that nothing happened – there was no story for them. I remember reading the article in the next month's magazine and it was mainly about Lions supporters and South Africa and had some interviews with players, but they were obviously waiting to trip someone up with a scandalous story.

**Barry Williams:** Social media is the fucking killer for everyone. Every sportsman. You could be innocently having a chat with someone and the next thing you see so-and-so is in the paper. It's spoiling things. That '97 tour was the crossover tour before things got stupid, before they were selling rights for everything and they wanted their pound of flesh.

**Rob Howley:** As a player you're very mindful that drinking alcohol affects your ability to train, but there's a balancing act because you need to get to know the other players. Especially as a nine – it's really important that you get to know your forwards because you're the one shouting and screaming at them in the game. Sometimes the language you use on the field is different to what you'd use in the bar. You have to be honest and direct. Having a beer with them and getting to know them socially accelerates the friendship and makes it easier for you to bark orders at them on the pitch.

**Dai Young:** After every game we all went out together and had a couple of beers and a meal and a lot of the times it would be where the supporters were as well, which was great. It was a fantastic atmosphere, and you realised pretty quickly how important it was and how many people were out there. You can easily become trapped in a bubble and not realise how important it is outside of that.

**Alan Tait:** Geech had thrown me in at twelve against Province because Gibbsy was injured and on the night out in that Mexican place, Dai and Gibbsy were having a few beers and Dai called me over and he says, 'You've just got Gibbsy his ticket home after that performance.' I'd played well. Gibbsy was pretty down because he'd done his ankle in and Dai had no sympathy at all. He said, 'That's your ticket now, Scotty boy. They're going to be flying you home after Taity's performance.' And I could see Gibbsy's face, and honest to God, he was absolutely broken. I said, 'Hey, Gibbsy, come on, man, you'll be alright, pal.' He went, 'Oh, God, you reckon they'll send me home?' and Dai was just rubbing it in and rubbing it in. I said to Gibbsy, 'Look, mate, don't be ridiculous. I'm not a twelve. I won't be playing twelve in the Test matches. I'm telling you: you're the twelve, so get your head on.' It was a position I could play, but I wasn't comfortable there – certainly not for a Test match for the Lions. I was a thirteen or even a winger, but twelve was kind of strange to me. Gibbsy was clearly going to be the man. He just needed to get his ankle right and the coaches were going to give him every opportunity to do that, but it's bloody funny looking back on the way Dai was winding him up. No mercy at all.

The following morning, bleary-eyed and dying from hangovers, the Lions flew to Pretoria. The newspapers were full of reports of the spat between Bentley and Small including Small's allegation that his opposite number had gouged him during Saturday's game. Fran Cotton addressed it at the next press conference. 'We're here to talk about rugby, not massage James Small's ego. As far as we're concerned, the allegation is nonsense. I suspect the motivation is really to deflect the attention away from the fact that he had a pretty average game and Bentley put two tries past him.'

Small responded by saying, 'It annoys me that people are always prepared to judge my actions without knowing the full story. What he did was not in the rules. He fingered me in the eye when I was defenceless.'

**John Bentley:** It was a total fabrication.

**Ian McGeechan:** It was an accusation that we treated with the contempt it deserved.

**Fran Cotton:** The whole thing was totally unnecessary. Small was a very good player but he was obviously into the psychology bit too. He wanted to unsettle us and get some payback after John had got the better of him.

**John Bentley:** The South African management seemed to find it all a bit embarrassing. Carel du Plessis said, 'At this level you have to be able to stay in control and James allowed himself to be weak.' The South African rugby union decided not to cite me, so they obviously believed my side of the story.

**Ian McGeechan:** We had to move on quickly from the incident – and Jim didn't hang around. We'd scrummed poorly against Western Province and Jim was furious – which was bad news for the forwards.

Jim Telfer had reached the end of his tether right enough. He gathered his players together and gave it to them straight. He thought they were docile against Western Province – 'tip toeing through everything', as he put it. He felt some were either in the comfort zone or were knocking on the door of the comfort zone. It was time for him to send them a reminder of what they were going to be dealing with down the line and how tough they were going to have to be in order to meet what was coming their way. Captured for posterity by the film crew, it was another classic Telfer address.

'There are two types of rugby players, boys,' he said. 'There's honest ones, and there's the rest. The honest player gets up in the morning, looks himself in the fucking mirror and sets his standard, sets his stall out, and says: "I'm going to get better, I'm going to get better, I'm going to get better." He doesnae complain about the food, or the beds, or the referees, or all these sorts of things. They're just peripheral things that weak players are always complaining about. The dishonest player.

'If I tell a player he's too high or he's no' tight enough – he's too fucking high, he's not tight enough and that's it and I'm the judge and not the player. And we accept that. And we do something about it.

'I've coached Lions teams before and we've complained and carped about this, that and the next thing. And I liken it a bit to the British and Irish going abroad on holiday. The first thing they look for is a fucking English pub; the second thing they look for is a pint of Guinness and the third thing they look for is a fish and chip shop. The only thing they accept is the sun. They don't take on anything that's good or decent or different abroad. If we do that, we're sunk. Because we don't go back bitching, we don't go back carping: "Oh, if we'd done this at Twickenham or the Arms Park or Lansdowne Road or Murrayfield . . ." No, no, these days are past. What's accepted over there is *not* accepted over here. And it's not accepted by us – me and you.

'So from now on, the page has turned. We're on a new book. Different attitudes. We're honest with ourselves. And in many respects in the forward play – and let's be fucking honest – we've been second best. We can match them. But only if we get it right here [a finger rises to his head] – and right here [he points to his heart]. Two weeks. There're battles all along the way. There's a battle on Wednesday. There's a battle on Saturday. There's a battle next Wednesday and there's a battle the following Saturday; there's a battle the following Tuesday; until we're fucking into the big arena. The one we were there on Saturday. And by that time the fucking Lions have to make them fucking roar for us. Because they'll be baying for blood. And let's hope it's fucking Springbok blood. We're focused. From now on, the kid gloves are off. It's bare knuckle fucking stuff. And only at the end of the day will the man who's standing on his feet win the fucking battle.'

**Keith Wood:** I could probably recite you that whole speech right now, more than twenty years later.

**Tom Smith:** Jim is very articulate and I think it's his background as a teacher, he's a very good communicator and what he was saying to everybody was pretty stark: we weren't going to succeed if we didn't address this problem. I remember the intensity of that meeting: it was just deadly silence. You look at the forwards on that tour – you've got Jason Leonard, Keith Wood, Martin Johnson, Lawrence Dallaglio – all guys that are vocal, but there was just total silence as Jim spoke.

**Rob Wainwright:** The hairs on the back of your neck were standing up after that.

**Martin Johnson:** He was right. We'd been a distant second in the scrums.

**Jim Telfer:** The basic principle of what I was saying was that the players had to be honest with themselves. They had to look in the mirror and understand what was required. From now on, we'd be taking no prisoners and we wouldn't pick anyone who wasn't prepared to work. We had to adapt to the conditions. No whinging; all positivity.

**Keith Wood:** I heard a lot of strange talk about Jim Telfer before I went on that tour. It was good to see it was all true. He drove us to the absolute edge of our ability and it was about weeding out any possible flaws in the squad so you were left with this team that had the mental toughness to get through the Test series. I've said it before, if we were on tour for another day we'd have killed him. We were all falling apart by the very end of it. We hit a level of effort and training that, to be honest, we weren't fit enough for. We pushed ourselves beyond the limit. It was both technical and mental – and we loved it.

The Lions were preparing to play their fourth game on tour against the bruisers of Mpumalanga in midweek but first they were having a forwards training session that none of them will ever forget, even if they live to be a hundred.

**Ian McGeechan:** It was forty scrums in forty-five minutes.

**Matt Dawson:** It was fifty or sixty.

**Neil Back:** A normal scrum session at club level would involve you doing four sets of three, maybe at a push five sets of three, on the machine. But we did twenty sets of three – so sixty scrums.

**Keith Wood:** We did forty-three scrums. These numbers etched on my brain. Forty-three scrums in forty minutes.

**Gregor Townsend:** That was the hundred-odd scrum session, wasn't it?

**Graham Rowntree:** Jim knew how to drive a pack. No bullshit; drive us hard; lots of physical contact. We were training hard and fast every day and then we did fifty scrums in that session. Fifty scrums! It may have even been sixty or more. It felt like two hundred.

**Gregor Townsend:** They got killed. It was just: scrum, do some tackles, come back and scrum, get up and sprint to the posts, do some mauling, come back and scrum.

**Tom Smith:** Jim loved that machine, it was his toy. It was a piece of torture equipment. They dug the stakes about a metre into the ground and the pads had hydraulics built in that Jim could control with a lever. You'd hit the scrum and the pads would move under the pressure but because the machine itself was dug into the ground, it wouldn't move. Then Jim would pull on the lever, the hydraulics would kick in and the pads would start to push back at you. So you had the weight of your pack pushing from behind you and the hydraulics pushing from in front of you. And you had to hold, hold, hold – and then it was up and sprint sixty metres, sprint back, and on again, and on again, and on again.

**Keith Wood:** It was a stupid bit of kit, actually, because they had worked out that you can get up to two and a half tons of pressure across the front row's neck in a scrum, and so that's what the hydraulics were built to do. In a scrum you might have that pressure of two and a half tons – but not the entire time. Something always gives after a second or two. Either my opponent gives or I give – something happens, someone goes up, someone goes down. Well, a hydraulic machine doesn't give and so our job was to hit the scrum and hold it for thirty seconds. And the only thing that could give was us, because the machine was unrelenting. I put a disc out on that Lions tour. Actually, I tore my groin as well, which I think was exacerbated by our scrummaging sessions.

**Paul Wallace:** It was like a punishment. But what Jim was great at was getting the extra few per cent out of you. You thought you were doing everything you physically could, but he would demand more – and you found that you could give it.

**Jeremy Davidson:** It was fucking horrible, but he had our total buy-in.

**Keith Wood:** I remember Telfer's line, when we broke from the scrum, which was: 'Run as fast as you can and then accelerate.' One of those lines of magic, right? You just had to put yourself into another place, mentally. It was just horrendous. You'd hit the machine, the pressure would come on, you'd bind as tight as you could, you did everything you could, and you went to another place. That was all, it was just . . . It was horrible. It was white-hot and it was horrible. But we learned that our well was pretty deep, that is one thing for certain. So I don't begrudge the session. I hated the machine, but I don't begrudge it at all. I think it's a kind of mark of pride that we did that session.

**Jim Telfer:** That was the most concentrated session I ever did on a scrum machine. We probably did about sixty scrums in thirty minutes but not one player complained, not one player bitched. We actually had a lot of the press watching – they'd heard about this mammoth session we'd planned and had come to see it. It was designed to be as much a mental exercise as a physical one because I knew that we were moving into the toughest part of the provincial tour. We were due to play against three of the most famous provinces in South Africa – Northern Transvaal, Gauteng and the then top province, Natal – in eight days. Fran Cotton called it 'the Bermuda Triangle' because any players who didn't stand up there would disappear. I know I nearly broke them and I'm sure a few ended up a bit shorter. But they responded.

**Martin Johnson:** One of Jim's main strengths was that he talked with complete conviction. He sometimes got so intense that he started frothing at the mouth. If a coach gets the tone wrong, everyone can switch off. But with Jim, everyone switched on and improved. And, to be honest, we needed to. The scrum wasn't going well but after that we really went for it in the sessions. They became a lot more aggressive and very hard work.

**Tom Smith:** We needed to suffer as a team to bring us together. Sometimes there's something to be said for just going through a collective experience like that to make everybody concentrate on what they need to do to fix any problems. And once you've been through an experience like that together, you always have each other's back. It binds you.

**Jim Telfer:** I was convinced that the key to success was the front row and I told the players that there was no way we would annihilate the Springbok pack – very few teams have ever done that in South Africa – but if we got parity, we had a chance. The point about that scrummaging session was that it could be regarded as money in the bank; those players involved now knew that they could reach that level again if necessary. A number of doubts will have been erased from their minds.

**Richard Hill:** You live people's experiences. You live their pain and you live their joy when it's over. You knew that the guys around you had the capacity levels for hard work. You knew that everybody that was there was prepared to go to the last breath, because you'd seen it. You knew how far they could go and you also knew that if you weren't putting it in, you were letting them down. It was a session that still gives me nightmares, but it was such an important moment in the tour.

**Scott Gibbs:** He knew what he wanted. He wanted them rucking two inches off the floor, so the body height was very important. It sounds ridiculous, but whether it was a broom handle or a cane, he wanted the guys lower so they could create quicker ball, and cause a bit of damage along the way. You'd watch them trampling on each other in training, Jim bellowing away. It was brutal, man.

**Jeremy Davidson:** Looking back and having gone into coaching myself, you realise that Jim was a lot more astute than you would have given him credit for back in those days. You kind of thought of him as a bit of a grumbly growler kind of coach who got you motivated by shouting at you and intimidating you, but there was a lot of method and thought behind what he did. Jim knew best. The South Africans were just men mountains. No matter what team you came across, you were looking up. You came to a lineout, you were looking up at the guy opposite or you were looking at him and thinking, 'God, he's twice the width of me and twice the depth of me'.

**Martin Johnson:** My shoulder was giving me grief, so I couldn't train a hundred per cent. The session that morning was brutal and everyone worked very, very hard, doing everything Jim asked of them – but I felt a bit of a fake, just sitting watching the lads while Jim shouted at them. I could see their legs getting tired, I could see them going through the pain . . . and I was sitting there twiddling my thumbs. I hated it. Sometimes you knew you had to rest and that was one of those days, but it was difficult at the time because I wanted to be out there doing it. Not just because I was the captain, but because I *wanted* to do it.

*

Witbank was in the heart of the coal mining region, with over twenty collieries still in operation. It was a stark, industrial town blanketed in smog and was home to the Mpumalanga Pumas, formerly known as South East Transvaal. They were a big side – surprise, surprise. Big and proud and nasty. Two years earlier they'd beaten Wales 47–6, a testament to their ability and their aggression. The game against the Lions came to be known as the Battle of the Wild Cats. The locals had their braais fired up as early as ten in the morning on match day. This was looking like another savage physical confrontation in the making.

**Tim Stimpson:** Every hotel we stayed in there'd be someone saying, 'Wait 'til you get to Witbank,' or 'Wait 'til you get to Bloemfontein' – and that would be the cleaner, just threatening you. Their attitude was, 'Yeah, yeah, you've had a good start but just wait 'til you see the true Bokke. We're going to kick your heads in.'

**Jeremy Guscott:** The Afrikaners are very supportive of their country, their men, their players. It's very macho, but it's quite blinkered. Some of the Afrikaners that I met were quite open, and knew their rugby, and realised that there were two teams in a game of rugby. In general, we were very well greeted, very well received and very well liked. That wouldn't be the perception, but the reality was we'd go into schools, we'd do some coaching, we'd go to rugby clubs, we'd see men, women, boys, girls, grandparents, most elements of South African society and the hospitality was very good. I enjoyed how we were looked after.

After Louis Luyt's welcome in Joburg, I expected it to be quite partisan. When you went to Pretoria, it was like going to Gloucester but on a larger scale. Durban, bang on the coast was quite partisan. It's hardcore, but nothing I didn't expect. It wasn't uncivil, it was just very one-sided. If you played well or did something well, it wasn't applauded, not that it should be. That's what happens away from home. You have to play against it. The best thing you can do on tour is to silence a crowd, or to get them to have a go at you. If they're having a go at you, you know you're playing well. There are two ways of having a go at you. They can rub your face in it because their team's doing well or they can have a go at you to try to put you off. Most of what we got over there was the latter.

The press were pretty relentless in beating us down. Despite the results and the performances against the provincial sides, it was very much 'Don't worry, come the Tests, the Boks will sort this lot out.' But in the different areas of South Africa, the different cities, we were always well looked after. Apart from Witbank, that was proper hicksville.

**Martin Johnson:** Joel Stransky was with me at Leicester at this point. He said, 'Never mind beating Western Province – Mpumalanga, that's a tough, tough match.'

The team to face Mpumalanga: Nick Beal, Ieuan Evans, Allan Bateman, Will Greenwood, Tony Underwood, Neil Jenkins, Matt Dawson, Tom Smith, Keith Wood, Paul Wallace, Doddie Weir, Jeremy Davidson, Rob Wainwright, Neil Back and Tim Rodber. The Northampton number eight became the fourth different Lions captain of the trip.

**Neil Jenkins:** I'd been involved against Mpumalanga with Wales two years before, and they absolutely smashed us. They gave us a few verbals, a few sly digs. So when I got picked for this game, I was like, 'Happy days – there's a chance for a bit of payback here.'

**Rob Wainwright:** The ground was exceedingly hard and it was covered in smoke because they were all braai-ing around the pitch. It was a really weird atmosphere when we arrived because we were literally warming up in a cloud of smoke. I mean, most of the other stadia, the bigger stadia, there was a lot of braai-ing going on but it was behind stands and out of the way, but this was right by the pitch.

**Ian McGeechan:** Everyone kept telling us that we would be in for a tough time up front. They'd drawn with the All Blacks the previous year and put over forty points on Wales before that. The province is about an hour's drive east of Pretoria, in farming and coal-mining country. We expected a very physical game, especially as they had drafted in some Northern Transvaal players to boost the squad.

**Dai Young:** There was a lot more trash talking going on from the South Africans. There were little things happening off the ball. You knew that they were going to try to soften up anyone in a Lions shirt, which would be a moral victory. Every game you played in, there was going to be a big scrum. Half the time, the props would be bigger in the midweek games because they don't need to get around the field as well. When you go down a little bit in levels, some of them just scrummage. That's all they want to do. And some of the guys we came up against were big guys. They were wearing the jersey like a badge of honour. It meant so much to them and they really wanted to get one over on a Lion. They felt that if they did damage, it would make a big dent in the Lions' hopes.

**Scott Gibbs:** I wasn't at all conscious of South Africa's reputation as being the hardest, most uncompromising rugby nation before I went there, but Geech told us the tour would be incredibly physical – that they were out to hurt us, that nobody was giving us a chance. It was only really when we started to kit up and face opposition that you understood how abrasive and how vicious it could be. It was right in my sweet spot. I revelled in it. It gave me a lot of energy and confidence. It was fantastic for me, for a player of my mindset.

**Neil Jenkins:** Just as in '95, there were quite a few verbals from the Mpumalanga players, a lot of swearing, calling people this, that and the other. Typical Afrikaans. That's the nature of them.

They really give it to you. I always remember coming off the field and saying to one of their players, 'Who's the fucking pussy now?'

**Rob Howley:** Geech wanted the ball in and out of contact, to move the point of attack. That was a theme we worked on throughout the tour, going down these channels and offloading prior to, or at the point of, contact. We were comfortable with that as players. Don't take them on at their strengths, but make their size a weakness because they weren't used to that sort of non-stop movement.

**Martin Johnson:** If you ever need an example of how to play a midweek game on tour against a dangerous opposition in a dodgy place, then that was it. We blew them away early in the game, got into an early 28–0 lead with Rob Wainwright scoring a hat-trick and that was it, they were out of the game. Sitting in the stands you could feel the home supporters thinking, 'We're getting outclassed here.' It was really all over after the first twenty minutes.

The problem you then have is that the opposition can get pissed off that they're being so badly beaten and get desperate to stop a humiliation. You could see more and more digs going in off the ball and you start to think to yourself, 'Christ, let's get out of here now and go.' All I could think was that we didn't want to be losing any players in this game. It's one thing getting injured in a Test match, but it's another getting injured in the sixtieth minute of a provincial game that's already well won.

**Tom Smith:** It was pretty unpleasant. We knew they'd be tough, but we didn't expect them to live up to their reputation in quite the way they did. Poor Doddie Weir was kicked out of the tour in a really brutal fashion and I'll never forget the Mpumalanga manager making a dreadful speech at the reception, saying that 'these things happen in rugby'. Not in my book, they don't. Rugby is about respect, about lines you never cross. The business with Doddie, the speech, the whole day . . . shocking.

**James Robson:** I can replay the actual moment of the injury in slow motion in my mind. There was a ruck on our side of the field and Marius Bosman comes around the side and literally stamps down on Doddie's standing knee.

**Ian McGeechan:** It bent backwards. Horrific. It was a cold-blooded act.

**Gregor Townsend:** The rest of us didn't really notice it at the time because he hadn't been punched and laid out. If it had been a thrown punch it would probably have erupted, but the fact it was a karate kick and Doddie was kind of trying to shake it off, everyone sort of just carried on.

**Ian McGeechan:** The referee saw the stamp and only gave a penalty. It was extraordinary. I wouldn't have blamed our players if it had kicked off then, but hardly any of them saw it.

**Matt Dawson:** I saw it. It was just so bizarre. I'm not saying violence was normal back then but, you know, if you were on the wrong side of the ruck you were going to get a proper kicking. Getting a bit of shoe pie or being kicked at or raked down your shin, that would happen a lot. And when you're playing against Mpumalanga in the middle of nowhere, you know something's probably going to happen.

**Jim Telfer:** The incident was disgraceful. There's a clear line between being hard and being violent.

**Martin Johnson:** It was one of the worst things I've seen on the field.

**Doddie Weir:** I remember his boot coming down and my knee bending – *ooh, ya fucker* – and then hopping away, my leg feeling weird. I didn't want to put my foot down and take any weight on it because I couldn't really feel where I was putting it down. But I didn't know the extent of the damage. I played on for another five minutes, but the knee was wobbling under pressure so I soon had to go off. Icepack on the knee, foot elevated, hoping it would be okay – but with the way the medics were looking, I could tell it wasn't good.

In the changing room afterwards, the camera crew filmed Weir being treated by James Robson. The sting of the tape ripping away hairs on his leg as Robson removes an icepack from his knee seemingly causing more pain than the injury.

'Am I all right, aye?' asks Weir.

'The medial ligaments are gone,' replies Robson softly.

'What does that mean?'

'It means you're finished. It needs fixed.'

'Does it? Will it not just heal in time?' It's a final plea, nails clinging to a last vestige of hope.

Robson shakes his head.

Weir looks around the room. The bottom has just fallen out of his world.

'Ah well, it's been a good old time, hasn't it?' he manages, but as Robson explains what will happen next, it's clear to see how close Weir is to tears.

'Cheers, Robbo,' he says, and cracks a thin smile, but he can't sustain it and has to bite his lip to hold himself together. It's devastating to watch.

**Doddie Weir:** You say it breaks your heart to watch it. It broke mine too. I tried to look cheerful for the boys. It's the way I've always been, to show a positive side. But I was going home and it had been a wonderful trip. The rugby was pretty special, yet the biggest wrench for me was leaving the thirty-five players. Bentos was pretty special. He was my new mate. All of them were. Leaving that was the biggest thing. The video picked that up, our camaraderie.

**James Robson:** I reflect on this a lot – could I have softened the blow a little? I examined him after the game and immediately knew his ACL had gone. And people around me were saying, 'We need to get a scan, we need to get a scan,' but I was confident in my diagnostic ability. If you examine people very quickly after seeing that kind of injury you can assess it before other structures tighten up to protect the joint and you can sometimes get a false sense of security when that happens – and that's when a scan makes a big difference. But immediately post-match, I got him up on the bench and examined him and knew that that was it – tour over. I wish I'd broken the news differently, though.

**Doddie Weir:** Nonsense. Honesty is what you need and that's that. James Robson is an amazing individual. That's the great benefit of playing at the top level – if there is an incident, you get seen straightaway by the best there is and then taken off to hospital. So I was off to hospital that night and unfortunately the next day I had a scan that confirmed Robbo's diagnosis. I was going home.

**Mark Andrews:** Rugby in South Africa is tough . . . but that? There's never been any room for behaviour like that in the game. Sure, I was aggressive when I played and I wouldn't stand any nonsense – but I was never a fighter and I was never dirty. In nearly 300 first-class games I was never sent off for fighting. I know that'll surprise a few people, but it's true. If I wanted to fight I'd have been a boxer. Oh, I'd take care of myself and my teammates. If you were on the wrong side of the ruck I'd hurt you – but I wouldn't ever kick anyone in the head. There's a difference between being tough and being dirty. It's easy to take a cheap shot. What Marius Bosman did to Doddie Weir was dirty, not tough. That wasn't me. I wanted to dominate everyone I played against, but I'd do it within the rules. No one deserves to be injured like Doddie was.

**Ian McGeechan:** Bosman was at it all game. Their coach even tipped off the Sky commentary team beforehand, saying that he could be a decent player if he could learn to discipline himself. We later counted eight separate incidents on the video where he's either been punching, kicking or head butting.

**Ieuan Evans:** He should have been banned for life.

**Martin Johnson:** It's a shame we didn't see the guy again. It's not like he was a Test player that we'd come across later in the tour. He's just some muppet that you move on from.

**Doddie Weir:** You train hard to get to the pinnacle of the game and then something like that happens . . . I dunno, it was tough. Really tough. But I eventually took the attitude that there was no point crying too much about it. It was a massive disappointment but there was nothing I could do. What was also difficult was that my mum and dad were coming out for the Tests on only their second foreign trip in twenty-six years of marriage. So I felt sorry for them.

**Matt Dawson:** There was often rough play in those days but there were boundaries everyone kept to. Eye gouging, for example, or stamping on the head, or doing that type of thing – buckling people's knees deliberately – they were all out of bounds. I mean you could get a good kick in the ribs or a rake down the back or, you know, stamping on your hand, all that sort of stuff just went on and you got on with it. But there were the boundaries and I just remember at the time the shock of seeing Doddie getting kicked . . . it was so blatant, so obvious, so malicious. And you knew straight away. I mean it wasn't like, 'Oh, well, you know, he's taken a bit of a knock there, he'll be alright in a couple of weeks.' From where I saw it, it was like, 'Well your tour's done here, Doddie.'

**Lawrence Dallaglio:** It was devastating for Doddie and for the whole team. When you're a Lion in South Africa, it's you against the whole nation. We came together very, very strongly and it's devastating when someone has to go. I think he inspired us, you know? They were quite violent, the South Africans.

**Ian McGeechan:** The other second row, Elandre van den Berg, wasn't an awful lot better than Bosman.

**Tim Rodber:** Van den Berg's the guy who ripped open Jon Callard's head in '94. Twenty-five stitches.

**Rob Wainwright:** I had my head stamped on. You look back at these things and, to be honest, rugby was like that in those days. You had to look after your head and accept that your body was going to be tattooed a wee bit with some stud marks. But as long as you had your arms, so that you could protect yourself, you were okay. You didn't respect the people that stamped on your head, but then again, you didn't waste too much time chasing them round the pitch afterwards, you just got on with the game. It was part and parcel of being a back row forward that the opposition front five were going to take every opportunity to inflict pain upon you and you were going to take every opportunity to have that pain inflicted by making a nuisance of yourself.

**Scott Gibbs:** The South Africans called it 'tenderising' – when you're in those real small pockets of South Africa where the whole town wants to have a piece of you and if they take one of you out it's part of the national cause. So you know that you're there to be gotten at. If the overall philosophy was about standing up to them and playing them at their game, we'd have got beaten up. Trying to maintain that discipline about sticking to the process, creating quick ball, developing our link play, believing in the talent we had, not putting ourselves under pressure by playing too much football too early and in the wrong positions, but when it was on, we went for it. That was our philosophy. And nine times out of ten it really worked.

**Paul Wallace:** We did really well to keep our discipline. That could have ended up as an all-out brawl. There's no point against teams like that. You can't back down, but what you need to do is up the pace and get around them and punish them that way. You exhaust their energy so they can't get into a fight with you and end up putting yourself at risk of being sent-off or cited.

**Jeremy Davidson:** If we dropped to their level and just got into some dirty shit round the rucks and stuff like that, then we weren't maximising our ability. Our ability was speed of ball, playing fast against these big, heavy South Africans. We knew the provincial teams would try to tenderise us from week to week, give us a good battering – even injure some of us – so it was easier for the Boks by the time it got to the Test matches.

**Neil Jenkins:** In the end, we absolutely gave it to them that day. It was a heavy score, 64–14. I was fucking delighted to get one over on them, especially after what happened to Doddie.

**Keith Wood:** Every single player changed on that day because we felt like we were doing it for one of our own after that.

**Rob Wainwright:** I have bittersweet memories from that game, because in terms of personal form, that's probably as high as I got and it was the type of rugby that Geech had laid down. We wanted to play with a lot of offloading and running into gaps. But it was ultimately all overshadowed by one stupid act.

**Richard Hill:** I was sharing a room with Doddie at the time. He was a lovely, lively character and it was heart-breaking for him. Rob Wainwright appeared with a bottle of whisky and they went off to drown their sorrows.

**Rob Wainwright:** When people had gone, you wept for them briefly and then you got on with things. You had to. But it was probably a turning point for me because Doddie was my best mate on the tour and to lose him was a real blow. When he went home it had a big impact on me. It must have been the day before his birthday. Keith Wood and I took him out for a couple of drinks and gave him a good send off.

**Jeremy Davidson:** I felt so awful for him. Second row competition didn't come into it at all, because Doddie was such a good guy and a good friend. A band of brothers went out for a few beers with him a couple of nights later because his tour was over and we wanted to see him off properly. At that stage of the tour it would probably have been Martin Johnson, Doddie Weir, Simon Shaw and then me after that, so it kind of moved us all up the pecking order a wee bit. I think the Test team would have been Doddie Weir and Martin Johnson, if I'm honest, just because that's the way it was written, and they were complementary, the two second-rows. Doddie was athletic and good in the air, a good jumper; Martin Johnson was your grafter and your leader. So I was probably quite lucky in the fact that Doddie got injured even though it breaks my heart saying that.

**Doddie Weir:** Kathy and I got married later that summer and somebody gave us a boot cleaner in the shape of a hedgehog that we kept outside the front door. We called it Marius and I liked to give it a good kicking every time I went in the house. As boot cleaners go, it had a fairly short lifespan.

Did I ever hear from him? No. He ruined that tour for me but life moves on – and I'm beyond holding grudges these days. Thanks to Mr Richard Branson, I got flown back out again to be with mum and dad for some of the remaining tour games. It was a bit of a haze, though, I have to say. I can't really remember much of what went on and who we spoke to and where we stayed because it was quite a social wee period. How do I look back on it? Happiness. Disappointment as well, but mainly happiness. I loved those guys. It was a special time.

# CHAPTER ELEVEN

# SOMETHING WASN'T RIGHT

IN THE AFTERMATH of Mpumalanga, Marius Bosman and Elandre van den Berg were fined but neither was suspended and the judgement left the tourists incensed. For wrecking Weir's knee, Bosman was docked 10,000 rand, the equivalent of £1,400; Van den Berg got the same sanction for stamping on Wainwright's head. To add insult to injury, sixty per cent of Van den Berg's fine was suspended until December of 1997 pending good conduct.

A replacement was now needed – and Geech surprised everybody when he went for Nigel Redman, the Bath and England warhorse. 'He made his England debut when I was fourteen,' said Johnson. 'He hadn't played for England in two years. I heard he was being called up and I was like, "Really?" And he came out and he was brilliant. Absolutely fantastic.' The thirty-two-year-old was in the last days of his playing career and had achieved fame, of sorts, when somebody worked out that in the course of his thirteen-year Test career he had been dropped more often than any other Englishman in history. 'Jack Rowell, the England manager, took me aside and told me that I was going to South Africa,' Redman recalled. 'I said, "Jack, I don't believe it!" Jack replied, "Neither do I."'

Redman's fairytale elevation wasn't the only curious thing that was going on. The Mpumalanga game had been dominated by the assault on Weir and the horrible stamp on Wainwright, but Jim Telfer was beginning to see stuff that fascinated him. 'In that match we chose a smaller front row for the first time – Tom Smith, Keith Wood and Paul Wallace – and we destroyed the Mpumalanga scrum, which was supposed to be the strongest in South Africa,' he said. 'That got you thinking. Woody was the only one who had been in our minds as a Test contender before the tour, but the way those two boys had played at prop in the scrums and then the way they ran around the field – it was interesting.'

Now they were in Pretoria to face their first Super 12 opposition, the Blue Bulls, or Northern Transvaal as they were termed on the Lions schedule. 'If you take the forthcoming Tests into account, we are about to embark on the toughest month of rugby any of us have ever undertaken,' said Geech.

Northern Transvaal were without five front-line players in André Snyman, Joost van der Westhuizen, Marius Hurter, Krynauw Otto and Ruben Kruger, who were all being rested by the Springbok camp, but they still had a pack of hard cases, some good ol' boys who weren't afraid of the Lions' burgeoning reputation.

**Loose head prop, Lourens Campher:** Wily, no-nonsense, huge.

**Hooker, Henry Tromp:** Our old friend, the killer.

**Tight head prop, Piet Boer:** No frills, just fire and brimstone.

**Lock, Derrick Grobbelaar:** Free Stater, veteran, large.

**Lock, Derrick Badenhorst:** Unsung, hungry, large.

**Blindside, Nicky van der Walt:** Young, fearless tearaway.
**Openside, Schutte Bekker:** Reputation for ruthlessness.
**Number eight and captain, Adriaan Richter:** Ten Test caps, Transvaal legend.

When Henry Tromp played his fourth Test for the Springboks against Wales in Cardiff in December 1996 a protester ran on to the pitch with a banner urging South Africa not to pick murderers. Since then, there'd been very little coverage. The issue had been all played out. Tromp was picked to play against the Lions and there was barely a murmur about it.

**Martin Johnson:** I remember people coming on the pitch in that Wales game to protest about him being there, but I don't remember anything really being made of it on the tour. You barely have time to think. You play a game, you travel, you train and you're straight into the next game. You'll look at the opposition's key players, but you don't really have any time to think of that exterior stuff.

**Fran Cotton:** History books told us that the clash with Northern Transvaal was always regarded as the fifth Test in the days when the Lions traditionally played four. They're a hard breed up on the high veldt. Playing them at Loftus Versfeld is one of the biggest games you will play in your life and I don't know if our lads realised just how much passion these boys would bring on the day.

**Martin Johnson:** Something wasn't right in the dressing room. The anticipation wasn't there, that slight apprehension. You should always have that little bit of fear – fear of what the opposition can do to you if you don't go out there and produce your best form. I felt that that healthy fear of failure wasn't there.

The minute the game began, things started going wrong. We stood off them and let them get the upper hand. Everyone felt sluggish, especially the forwards. We didn't have anything in our legs and no one felt sharp early on. For the first twenty minutes I felt absolutely crap, just struggling to get around the park. I don't know if it was because we had trained too hard in the week, if playing at altitude got to us, or even if it was a combination of both, but we watched them play for the first twenty-five minutes.

**Gregor Townsend:** It was my first game at altitude and it was tough going. It's like a heat or a sharpness in your breathing which means you breathe quicker and you feel less fit. It's tough. I suppose the equivalent would be a frosty morning and you go for a run. And the air is sharp in your lungs. You do feel it when you're playing, especially if it's an open game.

**Martin Johnson:** We tried to put the ball wide straightaway but it didn't open the game the way we wanted it to, not least because Northerns defended better than Western Province. We let them have the ball too easily and made all the mistakes we knew we shouldn't have done. Jerry scored a nice try but to be honest they were running the game.

**Ian McGeechan:** We still wanted to try out different options and Richard Hill had a slight calf injury so we were able to try out Eric Miller at openside. It didn't prove an awful lot because the back row were under so much pressure in the scrums that they spent most of the game on the back foot.

**Eric Miller:** It was a different role for me. It was a bit like when I started playing rugby after always playing Gaelic football, not having that awareness of where exactly I needed to be around the field. I didn't get hands on the ball as much as I wanted and was a little at sea.

**Jim Telfer:** We made so many basic mistakes in the first half that we didn't give ourselves a chance.

**Scott Gibbs:** The boys trained too much in the build-up. The forwards were still flying at it the day before the game and it took a lot out of them. You could see there was no spark there.

**Ian McGeechan:** It was the worst thirty minutes on tour. We thought we could do it without putting in the hard work. We were going through the motions, thinking it would all come right like it had done against Eastern Province and Mpumalanga.

**Jeremy Guscott:** Bentley was giving out a lot of verbals against Northern Transvaal. He was giving their centre [Danie van Schalkwyk] a load of shit, but that backfired against him. It was one of those playground situations where someone's agitating for a fight, but they don't really want to fight, they just want to put them off. Bentos was really running this guy down and the guy ended up scoring two tries and Bentley was taken off. That was the end of Bentos for the first Test – he was out of Test selection on the back of that. He played so badly.

**John Bentley:** I couldn't believe how badly I played. What a difference a week makes. From top of the world to bottom of the heap. I felt so dejected.

**Ian McGeechan:** We were only 18–7 down at half-time – Jerry had fashioned one of his specials, a chip over a flat defence with wonderful timing on the pick-up for the try – and were still very much in the hunt. The last thing that Jim said as we left the field at half-time was that if Northern Transvaal were to score next it would become an impossible task.

They scored next. It was a soft try just fifty seconds after the restart which again came from one of our weak areas on the day: the scrum. We'd done a lot of work that week on it, but there was still more to do. It was a question of getting the collective timing right and of adapting to the way the scrum is refereed there. The South Africans came in from further away, so the hit was that much bigger and they kept pushing on contact. If you didn't meet it right then you lost ground immediately. We were still scrumming too high, which played into their hands. It was a gradual process of refinement.

**Martin Johnson:** Of all the tries we had conceded on tour so far, that was the one which worried us the most, because it came from a scrummage where our back row was successfully kept away from the play, which gave our opponents the room to make the score. We were 25–7 down and looking like we were going to get a whacking, but we pulled it back a little with another try from Jerry and two penalties from Stimmo. At 25–20 down we were back in the game and playing okay when Gregor threw an intercept.

**Ian McGeechan:** Gregor had a free rein to play as he wanted, but we kept impressing on him the importance of collective responsibility – that he couldn't be too loose and he couldn't throw too many slack passes. He threw one against Northern Transvaal that let Van Schalkwyk in for a try. That made the score 32–20, just as we were beginning to work our way back into it.

**Gregor Townsend:** I got a lot of stick for it.

**Ian McGeechan:** He made amends with a try five minutes before the end, but we lost 35-30. I never had any doubts about Gregor's ability. He'd had a difficult season but only because he had so much pressure heaped on him. He was an outstanding talent. It was my job to give that talent the opportunity to come out, to express itself and in doing so, free up other players around him.

**Graham Rowntree:** That game was the final nail in the coffin for my chances of starting the first Test. It was tough going. I've had a lot of Lions experience now through playing and coaching and for these provincial guys it's their World Cup final. There's such a history to the Lions, everyone wants to tell the grandkids about how they destroyed the Lions and this is their one opportunity. So we had to try to deal with that mental and physical pressure.

**Scott Gibbs:** Bentos was having a nightmare and I was sent on to replace him in that game, but I couldn't do enough to change the result. I was really, really revved up and I got cited after the game for supposedly throwing a punch at their centre Grant Esterhuizen. I admit that I caught him in the chops, but I was genuinely trying to go for the ball. Geech and Fran said to me, 'We've seen it on the video. It's nothing, don't worry about it.' That's what I thought too, but the more I watched it the more I thought, 'Hell, it does look bad if you're an impartial viewer; it does look a bit beyond attempting to go for the ball.'

**Neil Jenkins:** Gibbsy got banned for giving one of their guys a clip.

**Scott Gibbs:** Given that I adopted the mentality that I wouldn't be bullied and I wouldn't take a step back, I admit that I probably lost my cool in that Grant Esterhuizen thing. Fran Cotton stuck by me during that episode. He mitigated our legal case which only resulted in a one-match ban. With more camera angles and super slo-mo replays, today I'd have had a red card, for sure. And

I perhaps would have had a few more on the tour, given some of the tackles that were made. There were a lot of borderline hits during that tour.

**Fran Cotton:** It looked like a punch to me, but we went in with the defence that Scott had been trying to dislodge the ball. After we'd presented our case they decided it had been a punch but the game being what it was back then, they felt that if the referee had seen the decision he would have only awarded a penalty. They suspended him for one game and we thought there was no point in appealing; he'd have been rested for the next game anyway, so we just sucked up the media attention and made sure we all moved on.

**Jim Telfer:** It was the wake-up call we needed. Some of the players had been getting a little bit cocky. After that defeat our backs were against the wall.

**Eric Miller:** If we were losing to a Northern Transvaal team missing some key players, what the fuck was it going to be like facing a full-strength Springbok team?

**Ieuan Evans:** The Northern Transvaal game made us realise, 'Okay guys, this isn't as easy as we thought – and it's going to get tougher. But let's turn this around, let's use it.' Psychology is so important, and we're all amateur psychologists on tour because every weakness is exacerbated if you allow it to be. Everything's amplified. And it works in terms of positive aspects as well. You can get carried away with certain things and you can get overly negative. Both aspects can be inflated. It was a dose of reality. We narrowly lost in Pretoria, up on the veldt. Don't worry about it. We still haven't played a Test match yet. The first Test match was still two weeks away, which is an eternity on tour.

Northern Transvaal was the first loss the Lions had suffered at the hands of a South African provincial team since 1968. 'A timely reminder to the tourists of the true worth of South Africa rugby,' reported Clinton van der Berg in the *Cape Argus*. 'Carel du Plessis would do well to look at the video. Again and again. There are crucial lessons to be learned.'

'Hounded and hunted down' read the headline in *The Observer* the next day. 'It was a dramatic afternoon,' wrote Mick Cleary, 'with the Lions so far off the pace in the opening stages it was hard to recall that they had been so imperious over the past couple of weeks.'

'Now the Lions face two extremely difficult assignments over the coming week,' wrote Edmund van Esbeck in *The Irish Times*, 'against Transvaal on Wednesday night and Currie Cup holders Natal next Saturday, before the first Test on Saturday week. What effect this defeat will have on confidence only time will reveal, but it will certainly concentrate the minds and leave not a shadow of doubt about the difficulties that lie ahead. Their character as well as their skill will be tested.'

In the aftermath, Adriaan Richter, the Northern Transvaal captain, brought the analysis back to the scrum. 'We applied a lot of pressure,' said the flanker. 'We closed them down quickly and didn't allow them the platform to use their very quick backs. I was not impressed with their front row on this performance.' The critique was backed up by his head coach, John Williams. 'They have some quality players, but if they want to make a running game effective their scrummaging and their driving must improve to provide the necessary platform.'

**Ian McGeechan:** It was a serious point of the tour. It was the first real test of the attitude in the squad. When you're winning, it's easy to get on well, but when you lose, those relationships can come under strain. When we got back to the hotel in Pretoria, I took the whole squad to the team room for a five-minute chat. I told them that they were still a very special bunch of players and I still truly believed that they had the ability to go all the way in the Test series. I just wanted them to know that I still had faith in them all. If they were what I thought they were, then the experience of defeat would make them stronger. But the way they reacted to the defeat, and the way they trained the next morning, would determine how good a touring party we really were.

# CHAPTER TWELVE

# VICTORY IS A FORMALITY, SAYS OS DU RANDT

HAVING NOT PLAYED a match since December, the Springboks prepared for the Lions with a warm-up match against Tonga at Newlands on Tuesday 10 June, eleven days before they would return to the same ground for the first Test. Despite pulling almost all of his Springboks out of the provincial teams, Carel du Plessis still had only a limited amount of time with his players in the build-up. A large proportion of his squad missed early training camps as they were part of the Sharks side that travelled to Auckland to play in a Super 12 semi-final against the Blues on 24 May (which they lost 55–36).

When they did all finally assemble, Du Plessis had to try and instil a new playing philosophy. In the end, they might have been better off playing an intra-squad game than facing the South Sea islanders. Hardly the most testing of opponents at the best of times, the Tongans were obliterated 74–10. The Boks scored eleven tries and barely broke sweat.

**Gary Teichmann:** We hammered them, which wasn't ideal. It was good to have a run-out, but it was no test. We weren't overly concerned – we were playing the Lions, not the All Blacks. We felt we had more than enough firepower to see them off, even if our prep hadn't been that great.

**James Dalton:** There was going to be nothing gained from the match. It was a glorified contact session in the guise of a Test. Tonga were hopeless and there was no way of making a statement against them.

**Gary Teichmann:** Did Tonga give us a false sense of how good we were? Maybe.

When he took the head coach job, Du Plessis decided that one of his primary objectives was to move away from the Springboks' traditional obsession with physicality. He wanted a more expansive style, more ambition, more pace, more risk. The way the Springboks had been dismantled by the All Blacks in 1996, and the way the Kiwi Super 12 sides had been tearing their opposition to shreds, Du Plessis believed that the game had transitioned from the brutal forward dominance around the set piece and breakdown that had been the Springboks' calling-card for more than a century. But changing such an ingrained cultural style would be no easy matter – and he knew that if he failed, the kickback from the Afrikaner traditionalists would be severe.

**Carel du Plessis:** I spoke to the Sarfu chief executive, Rian Oberholzer, about my philosophy when I first became involved in 1996. I wanted us to attack with the ball, not just grind out games with kicking and using the forwards. That wasn't the game that I'd played and it wasn't how I thought the Boks should play. The All Blacks had shown the way with a fifteen-man game and

I wanted us to follow that style. I looked around the squad and I felt more than confident that we had the players to do it.

**Joost van der Westhuizen:** I was happy with the way we played against Tonga and I understood how Carel wanted us to play, but I think some of the guys were growing tired of always having to adapt to the methods of a new coach. We had had one coach in 1994, another in 1995, another in 1996 and now another in 1997. It made life difficult.

**André Snyman:** And when Carel came in . . . listen, he was a brilliant player, but I didn't rate him as a coach. I think he struggled to transition from being a player to a coach. He was a great *technical* coach, he knew his rugby and everything, but I think he struggled to deliver his messages to the players.

**Gary Teichmann:** In the early training sessions, I could almost see the players standing back and forming opinions on Carel and Gert. Sportsmen at the top level can be ruthless judges. If they sense weakness or hesitation, they can be unforgiving. I'm not suggesting this was the case, but we were still getting to know them and their methods, which stalled some of the momentum from the end of '96.

**Joost van der Westhuizen:** People don't always appreciate the value of stability. They think you should just pull on your Springbok jersey and perform well, but it makes life very difficult when you're constantly having to build a new relationship with a new coach. Some of the players were growing impatient.

**Gary Teichmann:** Some of our training sessions were bizarre. I remember one time being taught how to pass the ball at speed. You could see the guys wincing at the drills. These were international players. If they couldn't pass the ball at speed at that stage of their careers they shouldn't have been in the Springbok squad. Coaching at Test level is not about teaching and practising basic skills, it's about selecting and developing a game plan that the players understand and support and then motivating the squad.

I'm not saying that Carel didn't approach these broader issues, but when he did his inexperience of coaching at that level was pretty obvious. He'd get the whole squad together for long meetings where we'd discuss his vision for how rugby should be played. He'd speak passionately about the importance of skills and movement and versatility, of releasing players from all restrictions, freeing them to play their natural game – but you could see players tuning out.

**Mark Andrews:** That was the time when I felt the most lost with the Boks. Carel was technically very good, particularly when it came to running lines and how to swerve, but everything was very backline-orientated and it just felt like there wasn't any substance to what we were doing. There was no understanding of where we had to be and how the game would flow as there had been under, say, Ian McIntosh. Under Carel, everything was fragmented. We were asked to look at various video clips, but they were never edited to form a holistic picture. It was all theory. We were sitting in video sessions for two hours not knowing what Carel was trying to get across. I remember having to wake up André Venter because he fell asleep.

**André Snyman:** Carel was a very quiet, kind guy. He knew the game, knew what to do, knew how to analyse the game and all that stuff, but I think he lacked the communication skills with the players to properly share his thoughts and share his vision. He had the opinion of, 'Well, you're a Springbok rugby player, you know how to play. I'm not going to tell you how to play rugby. I'm just going to tell you: this is the game plan, go and execute.'

Other coaches, like Kitch and so on, they were proper, proper coaches. They would put us in an on-field situation and ask, 'What are your options? What are you going to do? Okay, now execute that.' You know, with Carel it was more of a free-flowing thing. We'd get to training, do some handling, work on some of our lineout calls, work on some strike moves and then that was it.

**Gary Teichmann:** As the weeks of the tour progressed we were watching the Lions record decent victory followed by decent victory. You could see their confidence was visibly increasing with each win and as the first Test at Newlands approached their performance curve seemed to be moving emphatically upwards. Meanwhile, we didn't have a performance curve – probably because we were still busy in a team meeting.

**Carel du Plessis:** I felt strongly that there was a need to take a fresh look at the Springbok style of play. This is oversimplifying it, but what I was trying to do was to improve the individual skill level of the players and incorporate that into a team environment. I wanted us to have more options and variation in attack and better-equipped players. I wanted to improve the skill level of the players so that they could play the game I thought they were capable of playing.

**André Snyman:** Well, he never explained that to us. Honestly. He never explained to us why we were doing what we were doing. That's why we started doubting him. I mean, we were a team that had just won the World Cup. Yes, there were a couple of players who had retired, but the foundation was there. We were on a high, we had confidence – so why break it down and choose players out of position or bring in players who have never even played Currie Cup rugby? Whether he was clutching at straws or whether he thought we were going to start playing a new brand of rugby . . . I don't know, I honestly don't know.

**Gary Teichmann:** I could sense his frustration that players didn't immediately understand what he was talking about. He was genuinely excited about the prospect of his vision, but his message wasn't really getting through. I didn't fully understand what he wanted either. The vision sounded fine, but it was undeniably fuzzy and difficult to put into practice on the training field. I've always been a Philistine in terms of rugby strategies, believing the game is about winning possession, retaining possession and converting possession into points. I see rugby as a wonderfully simple game and tend to steer clear of analysis paralysis.

Players approached me, asking me to get the meetings cut shorter and for them to be told precisely what was expected of them. I spoke to Carel, but I could see that he was disappointed that I wasn't on board with what he was trying to do.

**Carel du Plessis:** I have never relied on the convenience of hindsight. If I did, I might say now that perhaps I should have looked more closely at how I was going to introduce changes into the team environment. If the members of the team were going to perceive it as a change, then you have to avoid a situation where that change creates uncertainty.

**Gary Teichmann:** I suppose he was maybe just operating on a different level – as he'd done as a player. He was determined to change our underlying approach to the game, but rugby players generally operate on instinct. We just wanted to play. The vision thing was taking up too much of our time and everyone became increasingly frustrated. When were we going to work on set moves? When were we going to go through our defensive patterns?

**Carel du Plessis:** If I had my time over again, I would probably try to continue on the path André Markgraaff had started and phase in the changes subtly and slowly. But at that time, I was convinced that the changes weren't as radical as some people were making them out to be. In my mind they *were* just subtle changes – a change in the way of thinking as much as anything. A lot of people laughed when Mark Andrews was quoted as saying he was being taught how to sidestep, but that wasn't really what I was trying to do. I had no intention of turning Mark into Danie Gerber. All I wanted was a greater awareness of where to run at the tackler; in other words, to run at his arms and not necessarily at his body. It's true that I wasn't a fan of just playing direct rugby all the time. Of course, you have to be direct. But I thought we needed to vary our points of attack and to operate off a split-field attack.

I felt we needed to move away from thinking that we should take the ball up all the time and that we should always take it up through the one and two channels. That works if you have players who are dominating physically, but I felt that to properly manipulate opposing defences, you had to offer more than that. I felt – and I still feel – that we had a massive talent pool in South Africa and the players had the ability to do a lot more than what they were producing on the field.

Despite everything, the Boks had an in-built confidence about themselves. As confusing as things were behind the scenes they were still sure they'd have too much for the Lions. Maybe that was born of arrogance, but they felt that they'd win the series and that it might even be a whitewash. Given that they had growing reservations about their coach and that their preparation had been low-key and lousy, they had an inner steel that trumped all doubt.

**Joost van der Westhuizen:** Looking back on the All Blacks series in '96, with the exception of the last Test when we won comfortably, any of the matches we played against them during the year could honestly have gone either way. They were a strong side, but I think they got lucky at crucial moments and they suffered so few injuries – especially when compared to us. So going into the Lions series there's no doubt that we felt confident. We'd won seven Tests on the bounce, things were going well on the field. The Lions had built up some good momentum of their own, but were we worried about them? No.

**Gary Teichmann:** The speculation around the country was that we'd win the Test series 3–0. To be honest, we expected nothing less. I recall reading articles about the Lions' preparation and the various merits of Fran Cotton and Ian McGeechan, but I was convinced that we would have too much quality in our team. They would be well prepared, well managed and well coached, but they were going to lack the talent to beat us. At that stage, all your focus turns to excitement. We were about to play the Lions for the first time in seventeen years and looking at their squad, despite the success they'd enjoyed on the tour, we felt confident that we were much better than them both individually and collectively.

**Carel du Plessis:** We weren't complacent, but I think the public were. It felt like everyone was expecting us to win the Test series easily.

**Os du Randt:** We probably all saw victory as a formality.

## CHAPTER THIRTEEN

# TOM SMITH, BOSTON STRANGLER

THE LIONS HAD reached a critical point. One defeat was just about tolerable. Two defeats in a row could have been the death knell of the tour – and they knew it. Jim Telfer laid into his players, telling them that they were starting to believe their own press, that four wins against lesser sides proved nothing, that the one time they played against strong South African opposition they'd lost. The entire thing was on a knife edge heading for Johannesburg and a midweek game against the Gauteng Lions.

**Martin Johnson:** I think we'd got a bit cocky and Northern Transvaal gave us a slapping. And suddenly we sort of hit this wall. Jim made the guys who lost on the Saturday stand there for the Monday session and watch him destroy the midweek team who were going to play Gauteng. We had to watch these guys who had nothing to do with the loss on Saturday getting hammered. Properly horrible, a wake-up-in-a-cold-sweat-remembering-it training session.

So he did that to them on the Monday and they played on the

Wednesday. If you asked a player to do that now, they'd go on strike. 'No, no, can't do that – sports science.' But it wasn't about that. I remember Wally carrying Smithy, or Smithy carrying Wally – I can't remember now which it was – and they had to scrum, run, scrum, run and they were having to carry each other through it to get this session done. If you've never scrummed, you have no idea what I'm talking about – but it was horrible. It was a marker from Jim to say, 'Toughen up, we've got more of this to come. If we don't stop the rot now, they'll kill you.'

**Jim Telfer:** It was psychological as much as physical. The players, I take my hat off to them. We must have done about sixty scrums again. And it was brutal. And some people have commented that it was stupid, but it seemed to work. We knew the South Africans would take us on in the scrums. That's always been the case – it's the arrogance that they have to be the best. And they had Os du Randt and Garvey and Drotske and big second rows, and they were going to try to pulverise us in the scrums in the Test matches. So we had to get some kind of parity. We were never going to dominate them, but we had to make sure they didn't dominate us. So we had to improve our scrummaging, that's why we did it.

**Ian McGeechan:** You could sense that lessons were being absorbed and that the players had narrowed their focus. I told them that if they could accept that there was never going to be an easy period in a game, never mind an easy game, then we'd be able to cope with anything.

**Jim Telfer:** We lost two players that week. First Doddie and then Scott Quinnell had to go home with a groin injury. He was replaced by Tony Diprose, who was called over from the England tour in Argentina.

**Scott Quinnell:** I'd been suffering with a double hernia in the build-up to the tour, but I had two cortisone injections and it was decided that these, coupled with strong painkillers, would see me through. But four weeks in, I began to struggle. I knew my hernias weren't going to last out. We had a rest day and Allan Bateman, Barry Williams and I decided to go to the cinema to catch a film. As we crossed a busy road, a car sped around the corner and forced us into a jog to the other pavement. The pain in my groin was so intense. I knew there and then my tour was over.

**Martin Johnson:** I had no idea that Scotty was carrying any kind of an injury so it was a real shock to hear he was going home. All of a sudden, out of the blue, he was gone. It made you start to wonder how many more key players we were going to lose and if it was going to start to affect our chances.

**Ian McGeechan:** On the Monday afternoon we held a clinic in Soweto. It was a very arresting experience. We'd done clinics in different townships down the years but this was different. The very name itself conjured up images of trouble and hardship and violence and poverty. It made you appreciate the reality of the place when the police on our coach strapped on their guns as they got off.

**Rob Howley:** Coming off the bus, there was a line of guards to protect us. You had to watch your back a bit. We were told not to venture down any quiet roads without an escort. We were told to take our watches off and not carry any valuables. There was a wariness.

**Ian McGeechan:** To have a chance to go in and see for yourself – admittedly no more than a snapshot – made a big impact. People are struggling by in this vast, sprawling place, there was rubbish everywhere, yet also real signs of ordinary life.

**Gregor Townsend:** I can still smell and feel that day, like driving through Soweto and there was a rugby pitch there and we did a training session with kids with bare feet. Being there and seeing their reaction. You just felt privileged going into Soweto. It was humbling.

**Ian McGeechan:** I know these clinics were just cosmetic but from our point of view they couldn't be anything else. We had a small window of time and were happy to give it over if we could. On top of that we were directed by Sarfu as to where we should go. I hope the kids we saw got something out of it.

**Gregor Townsend:** I remember thinking at the time that there were a number of kids with great athleticism and they were good with ball in hand. We knew that rugby was still a white sport and it would have been a challenge for those kids to really make it, but you did think, well, there's six or seven million whites playing in South Africa and there's forty, forty-five million blacks that haven't really been allowed to play, or allowed to flourish. If that population got into rugby, South Africa could dominate the game forever.

All these years later, one Lion after another will tell you of the importance of the week they played Gauteng, the crossroads they were at and the heat they were feeling. Even those who weren't in the match-day squad were sweating, knowing only too well that a second defeat could see the entire shooting match spiral out of control.

Gauteng had picked a formidable side with rejected Springboks Hennie le Roux and Kobus Wiese back to have another go at the Lions alongside fellow internationals Chris Rossouw, Roberto Grau, Pieter Hendricks and Johan Roux. They sensed vulnerability and went after Lions' blood.

**John Bentley:** After the defeat to Northern Transvaal I'd gone off tour for a couple of days – I stopped messing around and went away to have a good look at myself. I wasn't just on tour to be a prankster, I wanted to be a Test player. I'd let myself down on the Saturday, so it was a case of showing up and doing what I was there to do.

**Jim Telfer:** It was a make or break game. They had some big names playing for them. Kobus Wiese was back again; they had Roberto Grau, the Argentinian loose head, who'd played the previous weekend when Argentina beat England and André Vos, who would go on to get thirty-odd caps for the Boks, was also playing. Rossouw was a World Cup winner, Le Roux was a formidable player on a mission.

**Ian McGeechan:** We couldn't take two defeats in a row. It would have crippled the momentum of the whole tour. The two replacements, Mike Catt and Nigel Redman, were due their first games. I'd been very impressed with both of them. Mike had been so close to selection in the first place anyway. They were both involved in a heavy contact session we had on the Monday. We all knew we had to find the intensity we lacked against Northern Transvaal. We went with Tom Smith and Paul Wallace as the props. I was keen to see how they would go. They'd done so well against Mpumalanga, but Gauteng was an even bigger test.

Tom Smith's rise had been far from easy. Born in London, his father died when he was only six and after beginning his

176

education at Emanuel School in Wandsworth, he was packed off to boarding school on the banks of Loch Rannoch in his mother's native Scotland when he was thirteen. Rannoch was in the middle of nowhere. The closest rival was Perth Academy, a hundred-mile round trip away, while the schools in Edinburgh and Glasgow were two-hundred-mile round trips.

**Tom Smith:** I wasn't behaving as well as I should have been at school in London; I wasn't working as hard as I needed to,' he says. 'And then I was offered a choice about going to Rannoch and I was glad to go. It was a good place for me; it was a pain in the arse to get to, but it was unique. You used to get the sleeper train up from London and wake up on Rannoch Moor, either freezing cold or with midges everywhere, one or the other. But it was gorgeous.

There was a great rugby ethic there. It was a small school, so we struggled to win many games and half the season was always snowed-off, but it was a great place to play. There was a coach there called Peter Rowan who focused on us being fit and he worked us pretty hard; there were lots of hills around and we'd go running for hours. There were times when it was pretty tough and cold out there but at the end of the day rugby is a hard game and you need to be tough to play it. It was a good foundation for me in so many ways.'

Smith was hard and uncompromising despite his size – at just five foot ten and sixteen stone he was a Mighty Mouse McLauchlan incarnate. That was small for an international player, but then again, the Mouse had done all right during a forty-three-cap career for Scotland and as a cornerstone of two successful Lions tours in 1971 and 1974, playing in all eight Tests. And like McLauchlan, who had learned his trade in the West of Scotland playing against farmers, miners and shipyard workers, Smith had served a testing scrummaging apprenticeship.

**Tom Smith:** When I joined my first senior club in Dundee, there was an old prop called Danny Herrington, a bit of a local legend, who basically shoved my head up my arse in training, twice a week every week for what seemed like years. That's what you call a learning curve. Those training sessions were my classroom. Danny took the view that a young prop should have his share of bad experiences before trying to inflict them on other people.

'From Dundee I moved to Watsonians in Edinburgh and played on the sevens circuit at the end of the year and that was where Jim Telfer apparently first saw me. Back in those days, you'd get a call to come down and do live training against the Scotland team on a Tuesday or Wednesday night before a Five Nations match, so I went down and did a few scrums and what have you, and it all kind of kicked off from there.'

**Martin Johnson:** Tom Smith? I didn't know him from a hole in the head before the tour.

**Ian McGeechan:** Jim rang me up before the 1997 Five Nations when Tom was about to make his debut and said, 'I want you to watch Tom Smith. Don't just look at how he gets on in the scrum, look at how he gets about the field, how he reads the game. He's different – and I think he might be the kind of guy we could use in South Africa.' So I watched him and Jim was absolutely right. He'd only just arrived in international rugby but I could see that he was a special player. He scrummed well, lifted well in the lineout, hit the rucks he needed to hit, was good in defence, but it was the way he handled the ball and the running lines he took and his work rate. That's what really stood out.

**Jim Telfer:** Tom was exceptional. A natural athlete, really strong for his size and he had great skills. You didn't need to roar at him, you knew you would always get 100 per cent. He was unfazed by whoever he was playing against. He was my kind of player, no fuss and no bother.

**Keith Wood:** Tom was small, but he was strong, fast and had the most unbelievable hands – I mean, truly extraordinary. He had this weird low centre of gravity and could catch anything close to the ground and his rucking was superb, like all the Scottish guys at the time who had come through the Telfer system.

He was a constant presence wherever you needed him, he was all over the park. And in the scrum, I loved working with him. It was funny, we toured again in 2001 and as soon as we bound up for our first scrum together in four years, it was like settling down into a familiar armchair. It just felt comfortable and he would do anything to help make your job easier. You would tell him you needed something and he would barely acknowledge it; he would just accept it, no matter what you said, and he would do it. He was properly selfless. I would say, 'I'm going to have to loosen my bind here,' or something, and he wouldn't even acknowledge it, but I'd go and do what I needed to do and he'd let me off with it, you know? His job was to do his job, and part of his job was to make my life a little bit easier and so that's what he did. I thought he was magnificent.

**Tom Smith:** I went on tour with Scotland to New Zealand in 1996, got capped in the Five Nations against England and five months later I was on a Lions tour. I didn't really understand too much about the Lions before the tour. The hype is different these days, every game you play now either puts you in or out of Lions reckoning, even if it's three years out from the tour. So I was gloriously naive at the beginning but the significance of it kicked in pretty quickly. You're at the first get-together of the squad and you're surrounded by these legends of the game. It's pretty intimidating at first, but everyone's just an ordinary person and you're all there for the same reason. That makes you relax into the atmosphere and then the nerves and the energy really get going when the rugby starts. It's difficult to explain, but it seemed a bit lower-key back then than it is now. Nobody expected us to do anything; I think we were going there as lambs to the slaughter. Expectations were quite low and then, obviously, it started to come together.

**Jason Leonard:** Tom Smith is, in my opinion, one of the greatest Lions ever. He went on two tours and played six straight Tests. Hell of a player. People see the Lions in different ways. For me, the jersey was always the focal point. Putting on that jersey, I would think of Mighty Mouse McLauchlan or Graham Price or Fran Cotton – and when you put that jersey on, all you want to do is to live up to those legends. Current players will be thinking the same about Tom Smith.

**Martin Johnson:** No one really knew guys like Tom. He'd only played one year, he didn't play Europe, so we didn't really know him. It was all brand new. And obviously he's very, very quiet as well.

**Lawrence Dallaglio:** I just thought he didn't like me. It made me feel better when I heard everyone else thought he was quiet. He was a man of few words, but he didn't have to say anything; it was his actions – he inspired others through his actions.

**Matt Dawson:** I remember Mark Regan sharing with Tom at one point and he woke up in the middle of the night to find Tom standing over him, stark bollock naked, throttling him. And Ronnie is in an absolute panic, screaming, 'Oi, bab, what yer doin'? Get orff, get orff!' And he threw Tom off, and Tom got back in his bed and knew absolutely nothing about it the next day. He was known as the Boston Strangler after that.

**Mark Regan:** I didn't sleep again while we shared. Fucking shit myself.

**Tom Smith:** Yeah, the sleep-walking was a bit of an issue, apparently.

Sleep-walking wasn't the only concern Smith had, however. When he was eighteen he suffered his first epileptic seizure, a condition he still manages to this day – although not always successfully. 'During one nocturnal seizure I fell out of bed and broke my toe. That was a bit difficult with a high impact game and I missed a few Test matches because of it. Then, around 2005, I started having daytime seizures which caused short-term memory loss and pretty nasty headaches. I played a Calcutta match against England after having a seizure on the day of the game and that was definitely not the best afternoon I've had.

'It wasn't something I really shared with other people, though. I always wanted to be judged by what I did on the field, not by what I did in spite of my epilepsy. There are plenty of people out there playing with epilepsy. They just get on with it. When I went to South Africa, I did wonder if something might happen, if I might have a seizure, but I've been fortunate that, on the whole, my epilepsy hasn't been too serious – on a scale of one to ten of how serious it could be, I'd rate myself just a one. I only had seizures during the night at that stage, while sleeping, and that was a concern before going on tour and sharing a room with another player, but luckily nothing like that happened while we were away. Just the sleep-walking – and apparently trying to murder my roommate.

**Martin Johnson:** Tom was quite hard to get to know at first, but you couldn't help but see that he was a hell of a player. I remember doing lineout drills once and the ball's flying everywhere off the back of the lineout and one of the props was supposed to catch it and run around the corner. And the other prop doing the drill couldn't catch it – I won't name who it was – but he just couldn't catch it. But then Tom stepped up to do it and a terrible ball gets thrown down to him – and he caught it off his bootlaces without even thinking about it. And I remember thinking, 'Okay, this guy's got some skills.' Then you add in his performances – and the Gauteng game was probably the big one. He had to stand up in the tight and scrummage against a big, horrible, nasty team in a full-on Test match environment at Ellis Park, and to do that as well as doing all the other things he could do got him in the Test team. You know, when you hear Jason Leonard talk about the guys in history like Mighty Mouse, Fran Cotton, Graham Price . . . he's right. He absolutely is. Tom is up there with the best ever.

**Graham Rowntree:** Before the tour started, both myself and Jason Leonard were the favourites for the Test spots. We'd had a good Five Nations, our club form had been strong, but it was tough. It was tough. As the games unfolded they got gradually tougher. It was quite clear that some guys will gain some form compared with other guys and it was quite obvious early on that Tom Smith was a special talent. I was aware of Tom, having played against him on his debut in the Five Nations, but he was exceptional. I wasn't involved in the Gauteng game but Tom was and I was astounded by his performance.

There were a few props around that time who changed propping. It wasn't just about set piece dominance anymore – because of them it suddenly became about what you could do defensively, what you could do with a ball in hand, what you could do when you made a break. Nowadays you take that for granted with all prop forwards, but back then it was only Tom doing that and a couple of French props – Christian Califano and Franck Tournaire. And they changed propping. Suddenly this new hybrid mobile, ball-handling prop was everywhere.

*Top*: Where our story begins: President Nelson Mandela presents the 1995 World Cup trophy to François Pienaar at Ellis Park. *David Gibson, Fotosport*

*Below*: The great unravelling: Joost van der Westhuizen tries to escape the clutches of New Zealand's Josh Kronfeld during the second Test of the 1996 series, which the All Blacks clinched to win their first ever series against the Springboks in South Africa. *Mike Rogers, Getty Images*

Assembling the pride: the 1997 Lions pose for their squad photo at the Oatlands Park Hotel. *David Gibson, Getty Ima*

Eric Miller familiarises himself with one of Jim Telfer's nets during a rucking drill. The stick is no doubt in Telfer's hand, ready to remind the players of the body height he wants. *Billy Stickland, InphoPhotography*

Tom Smith shows his dynamism with ball in hand in the opening tour match against Easter Province at the Boet Erasmus Stadium, Port Elizabeth, while Doddie Weir watches on. *David Rogers, Getty Images*

Scott Gibbs hacks the ball ahead in the mud at the Basil Kenyon Stadium in East London as the Lions take on Border. Following behind are Allan Bateman and Paul Grayson. *Billy Stickland, InphoPhotography*

Rob Howley, supported by Graham Rowntree, darts away from Percy Montgomery during the match against Western Province at Newlands in Cape Town. *David Gibson, Fotosport*

Matt Dawson makes a break against Mpumalanga att Witbank, supported by (*from left to right*) Neil Jenkins, Jeremy Davidson, Neil Back and Tim Rodber. *David Gibson, Fotosport*

Martin Johnson wins the ball against Northern Transvaal at Loftus Versfeld in Pretoria. The match would serve as a wake-up call for the Lions. *David Gibson, Fotosport*

ohn Bentley on route to scoring the try of the tour against Gauteng at Ellis Park. *Billy Stickland, InphoPhotography*

The creator: Gregor Townsend bounced back from an error-strewn game against Northern Transvaal to secure his place in the Test team with an outstanding performance against Natal at Kings Park. *Alex Livesey, Getty Images*

Tim Stimpson, in action here against the Emerging Springboks, put in a number of impressive performances to put serious pressure on the selectors to pick him at full back for the Test series. *Alex Livesey, Getty Images*

Carel du Plessis takes a Springbok training session before the first Test with (*from left to right*) Mark Andrews, André Joubert, Joost van der Westhuizen and Gary Teichmann. *Alamy*

teams line up for the South African anthem before the first Test at Newlands in Cape Town. *David Gibson, Fotosport*

The Lions were reeling from the power of Springbok pack in the opening stages of the first Test. The unstoppable force that is Os du Randt trundles over from close range to score to extend the hosts' lead. *David Gibson, Fotosport*

Jeremy Davidson was a hugely important cog in the Lions set-piece. Here he claims another lineout throw from Keith Wood. *David Gibson, Fotosport*

Metronymic: Neil Jenkins bangs over three points with his hugely reliable boot. *David Gibson, Fotosport*

The Rolls-Royce under pressure: André Joubert, normally totally unflappable, was nervy and out of form in the first Test, particularly under the high ball. *David Gibson, Fotosport*

Joost van der Westhuizen spins the ball out to Henry Honiball, harried by Matt Dawson. *David Gibson, Fotosport*

Teichmann and Honiball look on as Jenkins kicks another goal for the Lions. *David Gibson, Fotosport*

Matt Dawson scampers away down the blindside to score the Lions' first try of the series after his overhead dummy fooled half the Springbok defence. *David Gibson, Fotosport*

Alan Tait dots down for the try that nearly blew the roof off the Black Swan pub in Kelso. *David Gibson, Fotosport*

Will Greenwood is attended to by Dr James Robson, Rob Wainwright (also a qualified doctor) and physio Mark 'Carcass' Davies after a sickening head injury suffered against the Free State in Bloemfontein. *David Rogers, Getty Images*

'As I caught it, he was already flying through the air,' remembers Pieter Rossouw of this tackle by John Bentley in the second Test at Kings Park. 'He almost killed me.' *David Rogers, Getty Images*

Percy Montgomery celebrates his try in the second Test after Henry
Honiball fools Alan Tait into passing him the ball. *David Gibson, Fotosport*

Taking no prisoners. Lawrence Dallaglio, supported by Jeremy Davidson and
Scott Gibbs, carries into André Snyman in the second Test. *David Gibson, Fotosport*

The assassin Jeremy Guscott. *David Rogers, Getty Images*

Lion Kings: full time in the second Test. *David Gibson, Fotosport*

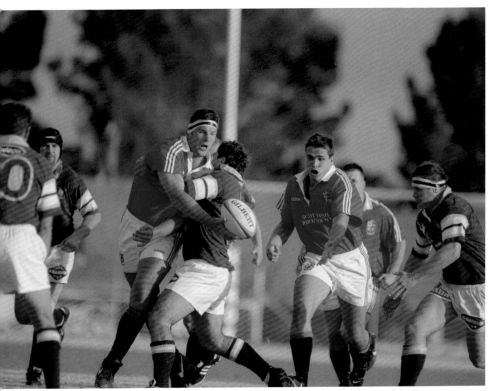

Simon Shaw offloads the ball out of a tackle to Tony Diprose in Welkom during the final midweek match against Northern Free State (also known as 'the Purple People Eaters'). *David Rogers, Getty Images*

The Lions brains trust: Fran Cotton, Jim Telfer and Ian McGeechan during the warm-up for the third Test. *David Gibson, Fotosport*

John Bentley gives a final team talk before the third Test at Ellis Park. *Billy Stickland, InphoPhotography*

Martin Johnson and his team, immortalised by the Test series victory,
celebrate with the specially commissioned trophy. *David Gibson, Fotosport*

And Tom set the standard for that, particularly for northern hemisphere loose head props. Paul Wallace was similar as a tight head. I thought they were exceptional. Exceptional.

While Smith may not have known too much about the Lions before he joined the tour, the same could not be said of his front row ally, Paul Wallace. The red of the Lions runs deep in the Wallace family. His elder brother Richard, a winger, toured in 1993 and his younger brother David, a flanker, toured in both 2001 and 2009.

**Keith Wood:** The genetics of the Wallace family are pretty extraordinary. David was in perfect condition for a flanker, Richie perfect condition for a winger, Paul perfect condition for a tight head. He was like a rhino. He had the best physique of any prop I've ever seen. He wasn't heavy – he was maybe sixteen and a half stone – but that was all muscle and power and speed.

**Paul Wallace:** There was a shortage of props at my school, Crescent College in Limerick, and I was the biggest. I'd never played there before so that was a bit of a jump. But I learned my lessons fairly sharpish. The first few guys I came up against were like Leinster schools props. They were three years older and I got absolutely stuffed. You learn the hard way. I won my first cap at the 1995 World Cup alongside my brother Richard, so it was a huge moment on two fronts – playing for your country and getting to do it alongside one of your brothers. We beat Japan. I was told by one of the coaches, 'Have a good scrummaging game and you'll get picked for the big pool game against Wales.' We scored two pushover tries and dominated them up front all day but, of course, I didn't get a look in. Selection could be like that in those days: very hit and miss. In '98 the two of us were joined by our brother David for Ireland's tour to South Africa.

A few clubs approached me when the game went professional.

When you looked at Saracens and the direction they were going in and the players they were signing with the likes of Michael Lynagh and Philippe Sella, that persuaded me to join. Playing there really took my game up a level. I'm not going to lie, I was disappointed to miss out on the initial Lions squad. I had a bit of a chip on my shoulder about it which, in hindsight, was a good thing. I had a point to prove.

**Keith Wood:** Wally's a great tourist. A *great* tourist. Loves the craic, works hard, is as hard as they come and he brought a dynamic element to the tight head position. And he loves a party.

**Richard Hill:** He *loves* a party. Partied as hard as he played. We were still in a transitional period from amateur to professional and when some guys went out on the town, they still really went out – like they would in the old days. Wally was able to train and drink, train and drink, and just get on with things with a hangover. The only tell-tale sign was that he'd be way more vocal and enthusiastic in training after a heavy session. Back at Saracens, it wasn't unknown for him to visit the Eros nightclub in Enfield on Saturday night, fall asleep in a corner and wake up refreshed just in time for the start again on Sunday. I still don't know how he managed it. He was the same on tour – he would work so hard in training, produce the goods on the field, and then would go out on the smash like he was on holiday. An incredible engine.

**Jeremy Guscott:** The New Zealanders have a saying about walking across the whitewash: 'On the outside of the whitewash, we can do what we want within reason, but show respect; but once you cross the whitewash, it's business time.' In 1993, we had guys who went off tour in a big way and lost interest and it affected the rest of the tour. Now, in '97, we had guys that were fucking loose as fuck when they were outside the whitewash and did some mega socialising, but they all got across that whitewash to train and train well – and, well, you can imagine what it was like with Telfer: he ain't letting anybody get away with anything, especially if you're a forward. Everybody was in shape across the whitewash, and the standards never slipped. It has to be a joint effort for it to be successful. You have to have some people that step up to keep the show going during that midweek phase. And in '93, it just didn't happen, for whatever reason. But in '97 it did.

**Ian McGeechan:** We won that Gauteng game 20–14. It was tight, but South Africa was starting to open its eyes.

**Jim Telfer:** We were 9–3 down at half-time, but Austin Healey scored a superb try to bring us back into the game and then John Bentley scored what most people would say was the try of the tour.

**Neil Jenkins:** The wonder try.

**Jeremy Guscott:** I bet he loved telling you guys about that one.

**John Bentley:** I remember the ball being kicked to Neil Jenkins, who was in our twenty-two and I had loads of time to look up as I tracked back – and the first thing I noticed was that only their hooker and flanker were out wide covering me and I had loads of space to work with. So I knew that something was definitely on.

After that it's a bit of a blur. It's broken-field running. The first bit was planned – going round the first two, although the hooker nearly caught me by the shirt collar – while the second bit was just . . . find the space. I kept going, past defenders down the wing then cutting back in, guys just seemed to fall off me. I remember being aware that there was a blond fly-half, fast, coming across to cut me off, around the ten-metre line. I stepped inside him off the right foot, then went inside another player, then all of a sudden there's another bit of space opened up with some posts in front of me. Someone tried to tap-tackle me, I managed to keep my feet, and then I remember getting tackled over the line by two players, one of which was the same fly-half.

It was all very surreal but wonderful. Nothing was going to stop me. It was probably the best moment of my career but its real importance was that it helped get the tour back on track after a poor performance, not least from me, against Northern Transvaal the previous Saturday.

It changed my life, really. Everyone talks about that try. My wife says: 'You went on one tour, scored one try and you've got one speech. Get over yourself.' I scored seven actually, but that's the only one that people talk about.

**Mike Catt:** Thank God for that try. I missed five kicks out of six and we might have lost if it hadn't been for Bentos – and I'd have got the blame.

**Rob Howley:** Bentos, by his own admission, didn't play well against Northern Transvaal. But then he had his day against the Gauteng Lions, and he was back on tour. You can be a lucky Lion and you can be an unlucky Lion. If you have an opportunity and you take it, you climb further up the ladder towards Test selection. Or your performance can put you at the bottom. Bentos certainly came back and showed some resilience and that was what it was all about.

**Richard Hill:** At that particular point we were a squad that had some results but still needed to build confidence after our loss to Northern Transvaal. It was important not only to get the tour back on track with a performance but also that confidence of winning in a country where we were still not perceived to be as good as them. That performance was a huge boost to us.

**Martin Johnson:** It's things like Gauteng that win tours. Yes, we all remember the tries and the rest of it, but it's times like that when teams come together and things turn. We were in a tough spot after losing to Northern Transvaal and we needed them to dig us out – and they did.

**Jim Telfer:** Afterwards, I remember walking up from the pitch, and the first team, which had been beaten on the Saturday, clapped in the team which, in my opinion, saved the tour. It's moments like that which you never forget.

**Martin Johnson:** When the lads came off the pitch they were sort of, 'We won, but it wasn't great.' They were quiet. But those of us watching it had a better perspective on how massive the win was, how gritty the boys had been. They came back in a bit flat and we basically told them off and reminded them what a pivotal moment it was. We were jumping up and down and going berserk because we were back on the road.

**Will Greenwood:** On a Lions tour, you cannot over-estimate the importance of unity and togetherness. It was onwards and upwards from there.

**Rob Wainwright:** It was a war of attrition: it was a massive defensive effort, and we came through it, and I put that up as one of my favourite games of rugby anywhere, at any stage of my career, because it was such a huge lift to the squad when we came off. The celebrations at the end of that, from everyone, were probably as big as after the Tests. They were absolutely massive.

**Fran Cotton:** Winning that game was a defining moment. All the non-playing members of the squad, including back-up staff, forced their way down through the stands and the crowds to the dressing room to applaud the team in. I knew then that we had real team spirit, and if you've got that then anything's possible.

**Ian McGeechan:** I'd learnt hard lessons from previous tours that the midweek team is essential to morale and momentum. Nigel Redman had only just arrived on tour and he was marking the massive Kobus Wiese, who'd said in the press that he was going to give us all the trouble in the world – but Nigel did a spectacular number on him. That, to me, showed me that we were going to be all right.

**Jeremy Davidson:** The tour took a turn and the coaches' eyes were opening a bit and they were thinking possibly, 'We've got more contenders for positions than we thought.'

**Neil Jenkins:** Before the tour, the coaches would have had in mind a lot of the front-liners, and a lot of them should have been the England boys, and rightly so because they were the best side, there's no doubting that. But sometimes, things happen on Lions tours. Some players get out of their comfort zone, and they're not too happy on the tour, they find they're not front-liners like they usually are and all of a sudden they're thinking, 'Hang on a minute.' Sometimes players don't respond the way you want them to.

**Martin Johnson:** It was tight, like a fourth Test match and I don't think the guys who played realised what they'd done at the time, but when they came off, the ovation they got from the rest of the squad – I'll never forget that. That game was massive. That's one of my favourite moments of being a Lion – and I didn't even play. I was in the stand watching. But it was a very special moment. I think everyone knew – we're back on tour.

# CHAPTER FOURTEEN

# LAWRENCE DALLAGLIO
# AND HIS JUTTY-OUT JAW

EVEN WITHOUT SOME of their stellar Springboks, Natal were favourites to beat the Lions in Durban – in the eyes of the South Africans at least. André Joubert, Henry Honiball, Mark Andrews and Gary Teichmann were locked away in the Springbok camp, but they still had serious firepower. They hadn't won back-to-back Currie Cups without having a squad of players who were up to the mark.

They still managed to pick seven internationals to face the Lions and a number of others who would go on to be capped soon enough. They had Ollie le Roux, a prop driven by his desire to challenge Os du Randt's supremacy with the Boks. Le Roux would win fifty-four caps. Beside Le Roux in the front row was hooker John Allan, who had the rare distinction of playing nine times for Scotland and thirteen times for the Springboks. Granite-hard and hugely experienced, Allan had become a legend of Natal rugby. This was his last dance before heading to Europe and a player-coaching role with London Scottish.

Natal had class and abrasiveness. Captain Wayne Fyvie made his Natal debut on the flank in 1994 and had since clocked up fifty-seven matches for the province while also winning three caps for the Boks. Behind the pack, scrum-half Robert du Preez had seven Springboks caps and had played sixty-one matches for Natal, while Pieter Muller in the centre had made his Test debut for the Springboks back in 1992 and had won seventeen caps by the time the Lions came to town. Muller had enjoyed a varied career – forty games for the Orange Free State, forty-four for Natal as well as two seasons in Australian rugby league and a stint at Toulouse. He would go on to win sixteen caps, becoming a mainstay in the Boks' midfield throughout 1998 and 1999.

Full back Gavin Lawless had been the top scorer in provincial rugby in 1996 while playing for Transvaal and when he moved down to Natal for the 1997 Super 12 season, he scored a world-record 50 points on his debut against Otago. On the bench was John Smit, a nineteen-year-old prop who would go on to captain his country to World Cup glory in 2007 and a series win over the Lions in 2009. This was one dangerous rugby team the Lions were playing.

**Tom Smith:** I remember going to the top of Kings Park after the captain's run. I'd never played in a stadium like that, with these huge steep stands that just towered over the pitch. You could just feel the history leaching from the place. And the buzz around town – I walked through the hotel to get on the bus for the match and the whole lobby was taken over by Lions supporters.

**John Smit:** I think it is almost more of a privilege for us to play against the Lions than it is for someone to get picked for the Lions. If you have that opportunity then you are very fortunate and must embrace it fully. I'd just turned nineteen and I became one of the very few players in history to play against them on two separate tours when they came back again in 2009. We went into that game in '97 and there were basically no other tight head props available in our entire province at the time, so I was put on the bench. I was absolutely shitting myself.

**Gregor Townsend:** I'm not sure how many times a build-up game was dubbed 'the fourth Test', but the media in Durban were at it again with Natal.

It was not a coincidence that Geech had Andy Keast as part of his backroom team. Keast was Keith Wood's and Jason Leonard's coach at Harlequins, but more importantly he had been a former director of coaching at Natal and what he didn't know about South African players, their talent and their mindset, wasn't worth knowing. His inside information was pivotal along the way, nowhere more so than that day in Durban in mid-June.

**Ian McGeechan:** Dick Best was the one who talked to me about Andy. He said, 'You will not have a better source of knowledge of South African rugby and their players than Andy Keast.' Now obviously Andy was a coach, he wasn't an analysis man. So Dick arranged for me to meet him. Well, as soon as we started talking, it was a no-brainer. I did say to him, 'You know you won't be coaching, you'll be analysing, but it'll be the game and how we want to play and how each player's going.' And he said, 'Yeah, I understand that.' He would spend hours and hours on the analysis and the thing was, because it was a coach doing it, he was able to tie his findings in with training programmes and practices. We videoed every training session and we looked at every player in every training session and had a collective conversation about what we were seeing.

**Andy Keast:** That tour was one of those golden passages in your life where the dice always fall in your favour and everything meshes perfectly. It was undoubtedly the highlight of the eighteen years or so I was involved at the sharp end as a coach or analyst. At the time, I just remember working incredibly hard, almost around the clock, with boundless energy and existing in a kind of Lions bubble. Socially, it was exceptional with everybody making friends for life but looking back we had precious little chance to enjoy South Africa. The focus was all on the work we had to do.

**Keith Wood:** Andy Keast never gets mentioned because he's only on the video now and then. He had been an assistant coach at Quins and he had helped me get back from the injury in '95 at the World Cup because I had to kind of rebuild my game entirely and I disagreed with him all the time and we would fight every Monday afternoon at Quins. We'd have a video session and argue and you're on the VHS and you're rewinding, forward and back. Technically, he was very, very good. And like Telfer, he made you a better player. He was brilliant at identifying weaknesses in your game and those of your opponent. He was a really important part of that tour.

**Ian McGeechan:** Natal were the Currie Cup champions and had recently got to the semi-finals of the Super 12. Andy's contacts told him that Natal were out to show that they were the dominant province in South Africa and were hell-bent on using this game as a platform. They had a reputation as the most fluid of the South African teams so we had to make sure we gave them no room. They also had the best goal kicker in South Africa in Gavin Lawless, so our discipline had to be excellent. We made a great start, stringing together good passages of play right from the kick-off.

If at the time you were writing a list of guaranteed Test starters you'd probably have Johnno first and Rob Howley second. Maybe Keith Wood, Gregor Townsend, Neil Jenkins, Scott Gibbs and a few others would have been bankers as well, but Howley was one of the main certainties. With the Lions leading Natal 3–0, a nightmarish scenario began to unfold.

**Rob Howley:** I picked up from a ruck inside their twenty-two on the right-hand side off slow ball. There was nothing on out wide, so instead of passing to Gregor I went myself and ran into Ollie le Roux. It wasn't the best choice I ever made. It was like running into a car. I remember getting a sharp pain in my shoulder. I had a bit of treatment on the pitch and carried on, hoping it would be okay. Within a minute or so, I had the chance to pass off my right hand and it felt fine. But then play moved on to the left-hand side and I needed to pass off my other hand. There was nothing there. I think the ball bobbled along the floor and I knew straight away. Something was seriously wrong.

Howley was escorted from the field by James Robson, who rolled Howley's jersey into a makeshift sling. The footage recorded in the medical room afterwards is sobering. Robson is gentle as Howley's tour collapses around him while the delivery of the Natal doctor's prognosis is jarring in its bluntness.

**Rob Howley:** James looked at my left shoulder and obviously there's a huge bloody point in it, jutting at least two inches higher than it should have been. It was a South African medic who said, 'He's out of the tour.' He showed no empathy. He probably didn't realise what he was saying, but obviously my listening skills were pretty sharp at the time and I was going to hang on to every word either of them said. James never said it. He was keeping his counsel. He was aware that my parents were arriving the following day, along with Ceri and the family. He walked that line where he kept me hoping that I wasn't out. When they injected me on the medical bed, it was pretty obvious from the pain I was in that there was no way this was going to be a week or two weeks. I asked James, tongue in cheek, how long it was going to be. He probably knew that the answer was at least six months.

**James Robson:** As a player and as a tourist, he was such a wonderful man. And it was devastating to bring him off and then to see the extent of his injury. And again, it was one of those 'that's his tour over' moments. He was a shoo-in at that point for the Test matches. It brings tears to your eyes. It doesn't matter how hardened a professional you are. Most of the time I can hold it together, but when you get close to these guys and you're telling them that that's the end of the tour, it's pretty difficult.

It lives with you, you know. You were always the person that told them that their tour was over and although you didn't cause the injury, you kind of develop ownership of it because it happened on your watch. It's hard to not think that you're actually either complicit or guilty in some way of actually causing the injury. I suppose it comes from the respect and admiration I have for them. They're the sons that I never had.

**Martin Johnson:** If you lose someone from a tour who's by far the best player in his position and there's no one who even comes close, then you really feel the loss. There was only one player in the party at that stage who I felt was in that position and that was Rob Howley. When we found out he was going home I can remember the feeling: 'Oh fuck me, please not Rob.'

**Dai Young:** It would have been a hell of a battle to see Rob versus Joost. You work so hard to get on the Lions tour and that happens. It's heartbreaking. At the time it was perceived to be a massive blow for the Lions. Without saying it, everybody realised that Rob was our number one and destined to play in all the Tests. Nobody wants to give that impression because it looks like you're lacking confidence in the other people there, but deep down everyone knew it was a massive blow.

**Neil Jenkins:** I was devastated because he's a very, very good friend of mine. We'd grown up together, played together from under-11s days, and then with each other for Cardiff and Wales. He was an exceptional player and at that time he and Joost were definitely two of the best scrum-halves in the world. For them to go head to head in that series was something that most fans and pundits were all looking forward to.

**Rob Wainwright:** Of all the injuries, his was the rawest. I know watching Doddie's, as was highlighted in the video, was devastating, but Rob . . . his world fell apart when he got injured. I think he'd laid out a path for himself and injury had robbed him of it and it was a very difficult moment for him. I'm sure inside Doddie's head – and all the others that were injured – it was no different, but Rob just wore his emotions on his sleeve far more. It was very hard to see.

Despite the hammer blow of losing Howley, the Lions barely broke stride. Matt Dawson came on and they started dismantling their hosts with the kind of rugby that nobody in Natal saw coming. Jenkins banged over some early penalties, Gregor Townsend slotted a drop goal on twenty-three minutes and followed up shortly afterwards with a try.

**Ian McGeechan:** We were playing really well – even after the shock of losing Rob. There was another nervous period when

Johnno got punched in the face and had to have his cheekbone sewn up. We were worried that he might have broken something, which would have been a real disaster.

**Martin Johnson:** The weird thing was that it was one of those punches that didn't actually hurt at all. It just caught me over the cheekbone and split it. I had to go off and get a few stitches put in. It felt like I was off for ages but it was only eight or nine minutes. I got back on the field just in time to see Natal kick a penalty and for the ref to blow up for half-time, so it actually felt like I had two half-times in the game.

Although the Lions' half-time lead was only 16–9, the run of play had been massively in their favour. Everyone in their changing room expected a major breakthrough on the scoreboard in the second half. And so it transpired.

Townsend orchestrated things magnificently and with Jenkins dead-eye in front of goal, the pressure on Natal just built and built until they could hold out no longer. Townsend jabbed a kick through into the Natal dead-ball area which right winger Shaun Payne was unable to handle and Mike Catt was there to score under the sticks. Six minutes later, on the stroke of full time, Tait and Gibbs battered their way deep into Natal territory before Dawson put Dallaglio in for a third. It finished Natal 12 Lions 42. In terms of sending a message, it was like a bazooka straight into the heart of Springbok country.

**Ian McGeechan:** To me that last try summed up so much of what we were about. Lawrence, like all the players, was very tired at that stage. He could easily have taken a second or two longer to get up from the previous breakdown, but he didn't – he got back to the play, trailed the ball, the Natal defence didn't pick him up and he was through. It proved that we were prepared to play for every second, no matter how badly fatigued we felt.

**Jeremy Guscott:** I have never met anybody with so much self-belief who goes about life with such unerring confidence as Lawrence. He has always had an enormous presence, both on and off the field.

**Keith Wood:** Before I met him, I thought he was a big, arrogant Englishman – and he is. Big jutty-out jaw, puffed up chest, incredible confidence, he's all of those things. But you also realise that he's half-Irish, half-Italian, with a fairly wicked sense of humour, a class guy. But the thing that really hit you was his work ethic. I'm not joking, the work ethic was just incredible. And the charisma of the guy. Unbelievable.

**John Smit:** I came on with about fifteen minutes to go and John Allan, our hooker, came over to me. John was a bit of a legend. I'm not sure if he felt I had what it took to be out there. I remember being terrified of playing the Lions. John came over and headbutted me three times, we chest-bumped five times and by the time we scrummed down I was more afraid of my own hooker than I was of Dai Young, who I was scrummaging against. John had learned a thing or two about dealing with young players from his days being coached by Jim Telfer in Scotland.

After the game, Dai came to find me to swap jerseys, but I couldn't give my Sharks jersey away because it was the first jersey I was allowed to keep. It was a one-off version done specifically for that game. So Dai came in and said, 'Do you want to swap jerseys?' and I said, 'Man, I'd love to, but I've been dreaming about playing for the Sharks since I was eleven years old and if I give this jersey away, I'm not sure if I'll get another one.' So

Dai nodded and said, 'No problem,' and he went back to his changing room.

**Jason Leonard:** Dai came back in and was a bit miffed. I asked him what the problem was and he said, 'The young kid didn't want to swap shirts.' I said, 'You do know he's a baby? This is literally his first start in his representative career, of course he isn't going to swap. What do you care, Dai? You've got Lions kit coming out of your ears – you should be handing it out.' I love Dai to bits but it was obviously in his head that you had to swap.

**John Smit:** A few minutes later, Jason came in to our changing room and asked for this youngster John Smit.

**Jason Leonard:** I tapped on the door and Ian MacIntosh opened the door. He's a lovely guy, but his eyes were going in different directions. He asked what the matter was. I asked to speak to the young kid and I remember him barking, 'Smitty! Smitty! Come here!'

He came to the door and saw me with the kit and he was very polite. He said, 'Sorry, Mr Leonard, but I can't swap shirts because it is my first season playing.'

**John Smit:** And Jason said, 'No, you have it wrong. I've not come here to swap. I'd like you to have my jersey. I heard your story and I want to wish you all the best for your future – I'm sure you'll have a long career with the Sharks and the Springboks.' And he handed me his shirt, which was just magnificent of him. That for me summed up what rugby was and is and what the Lions are all about. I wouldn't have thought it possible at the time, but three years later I started my first Test as a hooker against England at Twickenham and I didn't think Jason would have even remembered this young ginger prop that he'd handed his Lions jersey to, but after the game I folded up my number two jersey and went and found him, reminded him of the story and gave him my shirt. We had a few beers together and have been friends ever since. That, to me, is what epitomises rugby.

**Jason Leonard:** I've still got it and have a lot of pride in that shirt. It's a nice story; it's what our game is all about.

**Tom Smith:** Our scrum had struggled against Western Province and that was followed by defeat against Northern Transvaal the following weekend. I didn't play in either game. Instead, I was picked for Mpumalanga in midweek, where we won by sixty points, and then again for the Natal game, where we did well. Sometimes, your star rises when you're not involved. I had a bit of luck because those fixtures in Cape Town and Pretoria were good ones to miss and after Telfer had beasted us in training, we were starting to scrummage much better together.

**Gregor Townsend:** People would have thought Tom might struggle in the scrum because the weight he was conceding would have been huge – and because of that they would have written him off for the Tests because everyone knew what was coming with the Springbok props. But he held his own in the scrum and what he did in the loose was unbelievable. He was so talented. I played with Tom at schoolboy level – he was a year older but I played in fifth year and he was in sixth year – and they put him at number eight for a couple of games. He was so good in the loose. He could pass off both hands, he was quick and he read the game so well. I remember he once put Chris Paterson in for a try against Wales when he grubbered the ball down the five-metre channel. What kind of prop can do that?

Tom Smith had been among the stand-out performers against Natal along with Keith Wood, Eric Miller, Lawrence Dallaglio, Richard Hill and Martin Johnson. Dallaglio had done well to shrug off a cynical knee drop into his back from lock Wikus van Heerden. The Wasps captain held back from retaliating at the time, but made Natal pay by putting in a world-class performance. Beyond the nightmare of Howley's injury there was the dampener around Allan Bateman, who was forced off with a hamstring injury.

**Jeremy Guscott:** Bates was a fantastic all-round player. He was fit, he was quick, his defence was better than mine. He didn't have a great kicking game, but his work rate was phenomenal and I knew he was my main challenger for the Test team. He was one of the fittest guys on that tour, but he kept on getting niggles and that played in my favour. Had Bates been fully fit, he'd have been a huge challenge. He could also have played inside centre. He was tough enough to take those hard running lines that Gibbsy could do. He also had good hands. He was a very accomplished player, Allan Bateman. He just couldn't get fit enough or stay fit for long enough.

Against the best provincial side in South Africa, the Lions had just triumphed 42–12. 'Lions prey on Sharks' read the *Mail & Guardian* headline. There was no doubt that it was a huge win for the tourists, although much of the post-match analysis concentrated on the loss of Howley just seven days before the first Test. Howley says the long journey home was one of the most difficult trips of his life. He was empty. 'It was heartbreaking, but you always learn something from adversity, you always try to draw on the positives.' He could have become demoralised and disillusioned by his fate or he could use it as fuel. He chose the latter. Four year later, in Australia, Howley became a Test Lion at last.

In South Africa, he left behind a squad with an increasingly interesting dynamic. Players were moving up the pecking order and others were moving down. Tom Smith and Paul Wallace were continuing their charge. Jeremy Davidson was now looking like a Test player from top to toe.

**Neil Jenkins:** Without doubt, that Natal game was when my Test ambitions solidified. You're thinking, 'I've got a chance here, a massive chance.' And it's a case of batten down the hatches, get yourself physically right, mentally right and do whatever you can to perform well. Natal were a quality outfit. I never ever thought I'd be picked for the Test, I'm not going to lie, but after that game . . .

**Scott Gibbs:** Up until the Natal match the talk was that the coaches hadn't made their minds up who they wanted in the Test side – even with Johnno. A lot of guys put their hands up that day and it was a game that rescued my Test ambitions. I'd been injured and I missed nearly two and a half weeks of football. I went over heavily on my left or right ankle; I can't remember which. And it was a question of – it's not broken, but it's severe. It's a three-week injury. Can we accelerate the healing to around ten days so we can make a decision as to whether I have to go home or if I'm still on the tour? Thanks to a great medical team, and my own self-discipline in following all the right procedures and giving myself the best opportunity to get back on the field, I was off the practice field for around eight days before starting to gently get back into it. So I missed a lot of the early games when people started to stake their claims and there was some amazing football played.

There was speed across the field, but also footballing ability in abundance. Guys like Neil Back and Lawrence Dallaglio – they all revelled in that environment. The key axis was the link between the backs and the forwards. Continuity. If we could create quick ball, we had the experience and the ability to beat them on the outside, and on the inside. But we needed to have that continuous level of support through the mid-line of the field. A lot of rugby is won or lost in that middle thirty.

**Mark Andrews:** Maybe we should have released more Springboks to play the Lions earlier in the tour. We allowed them to build momentum and they went from an ordinary team at the start of the tour to a good one. If we could have disrupted them early on, we might have split them.

**Ieuan Evans:** That's the thing about Lions tours – we're not supposed to peak until the first Test, possibly the second Test. It takes a while, and home sides tend to pay too much attention to the initial games and think, 'There's nothing much here.' Well, we're not supposed to be perfect against Province or Border or Mpumalanga. You're supposed to be perfect by the time you hit Newlands and Kings Park for the Tests. We're not trying to paint a false picture, but that false picture can be painted because you're trying things out, people are getting to know each other, you're not quite on the same wavelength, you're not quite hitting your straps, you're tweaking things, so it does catch out the home teams. They'd have looked at the Border game, they'd have looked at the Province game, they'd have looked at the game against Northern Transvaal and they'd have thought, 'We don't need to be worried here.' All of a sudden, they're hammering the Sharks and the South Africans are thinking, 'It ain't gonna be quite as easy as we thought. They ain't quite as mediocre as we believed.'

The circus moved on, heading south to Cape Town for a game against the Emerging Springboks at the Boland Stadium in Wellington, a farming community an hour or so from the big city. Nick Mallett, the man who many thought should have been South Africa coach ahead of Carel du Plessis, was in charge of the Emerging Boks. None of the team had yet been capped, but plenty would be – Deon Kayser, Percy Montgomery, McNeil Hendricks, Warren Brosnihan, Braam Els, Niel du Toit, Dale Santon and Robbie Kempson.

Geech and Telfer had their minds made up on most positions for the first Test but the centre partnership was still causing them some thought and they wanted another look at Jeremy Davidson in the second-row, just to reassure themselves that he was the man to partner Martin Johnson.

The Lions beat the young Boks out the gate, Nick Beal scoring three tries with Graham Rowntree, Tim Stimpson and Mike Catt contributing to the annihilation. 'We underestimated them and we got a hiding,' said Dale Santon, the beleaguered Emerging Springbok captain. 'We were a talented team and expected to turn them over. I can't remember the final score. I've blocked it out of my memory.' It was 51–22.

The midfield combination of Will Greenwood and Allan Bateman had worked a dream. Now that he was fit again, Bateman was occupying Geech's thoughts as he contemplated selection. 'I thought I had as good a shot as any,' he said. 'I suppose that shows just how good the management were – no one, except maybe Dai Young, felt left out of their thoughts. I never understood why Dai only started two matches before the Tests, why Telfer was so dismissive of him. But fair play to Dai, he remained upbeat and was a great tourist.'

John Bentley had put in a storming performance on the wing. He was another one who thought he might make it. 'We were finding out who was in the team for the first Test the next day and I felt good, felt like I had a great shot of being named. The waiting part was horrible. You're just on edge the whole time, counting down the minutes.'

Neil Back was continuing to play on Jim Telfer's mind. Against the Emerging Boks he'd been outstanding again, perpetual motion in the back row, a whirling dervish of energy and action. On account of his diminutive size, Back hadn't been selected for England in two years, a rejection that weighed heavily on him. He admitted that when he got the letter telling him that Geech and Telfer wanted him as part of the Lions squad he sat in his kitchen and stared at the invitation for minutes before breaking down in tears. 'It was like a dam had burst,' he said.

Now Back was forcing the management into a lengthy conversation about who should play on the flanks in the first Test. 'I thought I was playing as well as, if not better, than Hilly [Richard Hill], but I had a feeling they would go with him. You never knew, though. In those situations you just have to keep plugging away and play the best you can. It's the way I'd always been. There's nothing more that you can do.'

**Martin Johnson:** Of all the guys selected for the tour at the outset, I was most pleased for Backy. He was such a class player and had worked so hard for years, but he'd been overlooked for a couple of seasons for England because of his size. He's one of the all-time great players.

Across town, Carel du Plessis was naming his team for the first Test. He kept faith in most of the men who did a number on Tonga, the only change being Mark Andrews' return in place of Fritz van Heerden. The campaign behind Kobus Wiese had failed. The Springbok coach was satisfied that he had the forward firepower and the backline nous to put the Lions to sleep, regardless of how good they looked.

As well as Os du Randt, Mark Andrews, André Venter and Gary Teichmann, the Springboks had another fierce competitor in their pack – Ruben Kruger, a horse of a man who had scored the game-defining try when the Boks beat the French in the World Cup semi-final in 1995. That game was played in a deluge on a surface at Kings Park that was more akin to a swamp than a rugby pitch. In the most horrible conditions imaginable, the ogre revelled. Kruger was outrageously good that day. At the end of 1995, it was Kruger, not captain François Pienaar nor drop-goal hero Joel Stransky, who was named as South African player of the year.

Quiet, unsmiling and full of dog, his combination with Teichmann and Venter was one of the best in the world. The three of them working together was a back row that, if allowed to function unchecked, could well determine the fate of the series. As Chris Hewett predicted ominously in *The Independent* that morning: 'Teichmann's men are not looking for mere victory over the Lions, they are looking to humiliate them.'

Publicly, the Boks had confidence bordering on arrogance but privately, there were doubts. Most of their misgivings were left unsaid, but they ate away at some members of the team none the less, the captain Teichmann among them.

'We trained incredibly hard that week,' he said. 'Gert Smal was another disciple of setting scrum after scrum as a way to build up fitness. André Markgraaff had done the same when he took over in 1996, but he changed later in the year and it made a huge difference. Now Gert was in charge it felt as if we'd taken two steps forward, three back. It was so frustrating. I went to speak to Carel and Gert about over-training the guys and leaving them fatigued for the match, but they didn't listen. It was old-school and it was how they wanted to do it. That close to a Test match, can you really build your fitness up? Yeah, probably – but it will leave you knackered for the game. And looking at how the Lions played – that fast, offloading game – I was getting increasingly concerned about the threat they were going to pose while realising, at the same time, that our preparation wasn't going well.'

# CHAPTER FIFTEEN

## DO A JOB ON JOOST

THE TIME HAD come for Geech and Telfer to name their Test side. The players would be told in the very early morning by way of a letter slid under their hotel room door. There were three groups of players at this point – those who were pretty certain they were in the team, those who were pretty certain they weren't and those who felt they were on the cusp, possibly in the team, possibly on the bench, possibly nowhere. The stakes were too high for slumber.

**Tim Rodber:** Geech hated confrontation, so he put the letters under the door at six in the morning – and no one went to bed. Everyone stayed up. There's that great video of John Bentley, knackered. Hasn't been to sleep.

**John Bentley:** I decided to film my reaction to receiving the envelope that would tell me whether I was in the team for the first Test or not. I'd scored four tries in five games and thought I must be in with a chance. I couldn't sleep, so I waited outside the lift for Samantha Peters [Lions administrator] to deliver the letters.

**Gregor Townsend:** I was sharing a room with him and you see it in the video, him in the corridor, which I didn't know he was doing at the time. I remember the light switch going on several times through the night, him looking at the door and then the light going off again. This was before everyone had mobile phones or anything. A bygone era. So you had to wait for the letter to be pushed under your door. I think it arrived at something like five or six in the morning, and he came back into the room and went to the bathroom and filmed himself opening it.

**Jeremy Guscott:** I had a good feeling about being selected. I hadn't played for about eight days, but I was flogged pretty hard at the beginning of the tour. There were some injuries. And then to give everybody a game, I was set aside for a little bit. I just had a good feeling I'd be there or thereabouts. We played against Transvaal. We lost, but I knew I'd played well. I was part of the side against Gauteng when Bentley scored. I put myself in a decent position. Bateman needed to play out of his skin, I thought, to edge me out. It wasn't a sure thing, but . . .

Fifteen players got positive news under the door shortly before dawn in Cape Town.

**Full back, Neil Jenkins:** I was rooming with Tony Underwood. He was a great guy. I think I roomed with him for about twenty days on tour in total. I'll always remember the different experience we went through when we had our letters. I was lucky enough to be selected, and Tony wasn't. Tony left me to go for a walk and gather his thoughts. It's hard, you know? He's your roommate, he's a good man and I felt for him. I wanted him to play and vice versa. You're both thinking the same. For one to be picked, and one not to, it was tough. But the feeling for me was incredible.

**Right wing, Ieuan Evans:** I was the oldest player on tour and got a fair amount of stick for it, as you might imagine. I very nearly didn't make myself available because I'd just had a new baby, but my wife supported me to go and I'm so thankful that she did. But being the elder statesman, I got some amount of grief. Keith Wood liked to call me 'Dad' and I remember at one dinner, Dai Young chirping up, 'So Ieuan, what was it really like in the Boer War?' Comedy geniuses, both of them.

**Outside centre, Scott Gibbs:** If you love the game, you know exactly where you were when you watched your first Lions series – it stays with you forever.

**Inside centre, Jeremy Guscott:** We had a very decent team that was capable of beating anybody in the world. There was no such thing as a fear of their players.

**Left wing, Alan Tait:** Competition was pretty intense in the centre. I was more than happy to fit in on the wing. Geech was grilled by the press about my selection when the team was announced. What it came down to was defensive qualities. Bentos's defence was capable, but he'd made some bad decisions at unfortunate times going into the Test series and I think that's what swung it in my favour.

**Fly-half, Gregor Townsend:** You're so nervous when the letter comes through, but I'd played in every Saturday game, so I was probably thinking it would be a surprise if I didn't make it. If they wanted Tim Stimpson to play, they might have picked Jenks at ten and Mike Catt had come out and played well, but in the back of my mind I was thinking, 'If they wanted either of them at ten, they would have played them in the Natal game.' The Natal game was billed as the fourth Test and that was probably my best game. But when your roommate gets disappointing news, you have to temper your excitement. The emotions are probably greater when you miss out than they are when you get selected – when you're named in the team, your focus immediately shifts to preparing for the game.

**Scrum-half, Matt Dawson:** I'm sure at the time Austin and I both thought we were the best scrum-halfs out there, but the reality was perfectly clear. Howlers was quite rightly the number one choice. So in the previous weeks, the focus for me and Austin was that whenever you got an opportunity, you had to try and make the most of that opportunity so that you were the guy who was going to be backing up Howlers. And Austin certainly did that against Gauteng, while I managed to put in a good performance against Natal. I mean, no one would have finished the Natal game and thought, 'Oh my God, Matt played well,' but I think what I did was fit into the way that the team wanted to play. And I think it was probably important to Geech and Jim that I was a relatively low-risk replacement for Howlers because they knew what they were going to get out of me.

**Loose head prop, Tom Smith:** I think rugby is a sport where you're only as good as the person next to you and I feel fortunate and honoured to have been surrounded by so many players that led the way. You're just part of a jigsaw. In '97, I was as green and as young and stupid as it was possible to be. And you were running around with players of the calibre of Jason Leonard, who shared his wisdom and his experience with you – and that is essentially the Lions. The team is more important than any individual ambition and I was fortunate enough to play with these great guys and these great players.

**Hooker, Keith Wood:** We were in our own little bubble. This is really important to have as part of the narrative. We weren't getting access to newspapers at all. No internet, no Twitter, no camera phones. We weren't getting any of it. A different age.

**Tight head prop, Paul Wallace:** I was sharing with Tommy Smith and I don't think we even checked our letters, we were just rushing down to breakfast before we even looked at them to find out if we were in the starting line-up. I hadn't had that many opportunities because of the experience of the other lads. Even though I'd been playing well I didn't think that getting selected would actually transpire – and I think Tommy had felt the same.

**Second row, Martin Johnson:** I can't ever remember being as nervous as I was on the day of the first Test.

**Second row, Jeremy Davidson:** I got a lot of games at the start of the tour because they were trying to see what level of player I was. I was a young international and I didn't have a big brand name like a Rodber, a Dallaglio or a Guscott. Two or three games and you know Guscott is ready for the big match against the Springboks, you know you can throw him in there. Before the first Test I played a midweek against the Emerging Springboks and I think that was another big test for me and I came through it reasonably well. My roommate Graham Rowntree woke me up. Handed me the letter. He told me he hadn't been picked and he asked me to open my letter to see if I'd been picked, which was quite strange considering I didn't know him that well. He was shaking me in bed saying, 'Out – open your letter.'

**Blindside flanker, Lawrence Dallaglio:** No Lions team had won a tour in South Africa since 1974 and even the All Blacks had taken until 1996 to win a tour in South Africa. So I think we all knew we were up against it. And shitting ourselves, if I'm honest with you. When you look at most rugby teams nowadays, they're all pretty much the same size, but in those days, I'm not sure what the South Africans were up to, but they were the biggest race of human beings I'd ever seen in my life. They were enormous and terrifying to play against. I think we knew we had to come together very quickly and for all of us, it wasn't just about you as a rugby player, it's as a human being, getting to know the other guys in the team, start to share that intellectual property that you have and put it all out there on the table because the only way you can be successful is if you give everything on a Lions tour.

**Openside flanker, Richard Hill:** It was an incredible feeling. I remember looking around the other players and thinking, 'This isn't a bad room to be in.'

**Number eight, Eric Miller:** I remember getting the letter under the door telling me I was starting. Incredible.

**Tim Rodber:** It was a strange few days. I'd spent my whole life dreaming of playing for the Lions in a Test series and when the squad was announced, I wasn't even in the twenty-one, let alone the starting side. I'm reading the letter and I'm thinking to myself, 'What? What's gone wrong? Now, we've all agreed that if you didn't get picked, you want to be a good team-player and support the guys who've made it – but of course I was absolutely livid and I ran around the field on the training day smashing into people, got bollocked by Jim Telfer for going too hard and all this sort of stuff. I was so angry when I got the letter.

**Eric Miller:** I started to feel unwell. There was a bout of flu going through the camp and it hit me. I got taken down to one of the gyms and they put me on the treadmill and the energy just wasn't there. So I knew in my head I would never have been able to take the field. A couple of the lads got sick in different stages during the tour and I was just unlucky to get it then. I got it at the wrong time and it was a pretty bad dose.

So the same day that I was told I was starting, I was then told I wasn't in the squad because of the flu. And then I was lying in bed that night and I got a call from home with the news that Liam Grant, a good friend of mine from primary school, had taken his own life. It was horrendous. It was one of those days when everything is just heaped on you. My dad was so distraught for me he went down to the pharmacy and got me some flu medication which we didn't realise had all these banned substances in it. I didn't think twice about it and took the pills, but when I told James Robson he was horrified.

**James Robson:** If he'd recovered enough to have played the game and then got tested afterwards, he'd have faced a massive ban. His reputation would have been in tatters. It was an innocent mistake but there would always have been a question mark about whether he'd taken those pills for another reason. I had a talk to the whole squad about not taking any over-the-counter medicines without us checking them first. It was probably just as well we did because a lot of the boys came down with flu over the next few weeks and if we hadn't flagged it then we might have had all sorts of problems.

**Number eight, Tim Rodber:** I was put in – and so I suppose it's a lesson in life that you never know what's going to happen. Mentally, I was probably more focused by the fact that I was dropped than I would have been if I was playing, so it kind of worked out well in the end.

**John Bentley:** I filmed the build-up, but, when I found out I hadn't made it, I was crushed. The letter started 'Congratulations', so I thought I was in, but then I read the rest of it – which told me I was a substitute. The video doesn't show how I reacted because I didn't turn the camera on again for two days. It was hard.

**Ian McGeechan:** Allan Bateman was the unluckiest player of all to miss out on a Test spot because he played some fabulous rugby, but so had all the other centres. It was the hardest combination for us to pick.

**Allan Bateman:** Jerry was a much more attack-minded player and I was much more of a defensive player. We could both do the other bit, of course, but it seemed to me that Geech wanted to play a more expansive sort of game – so that's how I comforted myself: they wanted to play an attacking style, so they went with Jerry. If the game plan had been to deliberately just go out and defend, he might have opted for me. That's the way I saw it. I was never upset that I wasn't in the starting line-up for the Tests because I was just happy to be there. I suppose I could be one of these people that thinks I should be selected every time, but I was never like that because I always thought, 'The coach knows what he's doing and he's picking the team he thinks is going to win,' and that was all fair and good to me.

**Jim Telfer:** The Springbok way is to dominate you physically. Humiliate you. You looked at their pack and it was fucking enormous. So how do you deal with that? One of our key aims was to withstand the pressure in the scrums from the start and during the last few games before the Test match it was fairly obvious that the lower the props could get the better it would be. So we picked Tom Smith and Paul Wallace as the props, both technically good and able to get lower than their Springbok opponents Os du Randt and Adrian Garvey, who were both well over six feet. Keith Wood was the outstanding hooker, so he was picked. I went out with an open mind about the Test team, but Tom Smith had only played three Test matches for Scotland and was seen as a surprise choice. We still had Jason Leonard, Graham Rowntree and Dai Young, who were scrummaging forwards, but as time went on it became apparent that they couldn't play the fast-moving type of game we wanted to play. So, I suppose we were quite brave in going with Tom Smith and Paul Wallace in the front row and for Jeremy Davidson ahead of Simon Shaw, who was several inches taller and a couple of stone heavier, in the second row. But Jeremy was the in-form second row, so he had to go in alongside Martin Johnson.

**Jason Leonard:** I didn't have a great tour, so it was right that Paul and Tom were the Test props, which didn't mean that I didn't support them every inch of the way and do all I could to help them in training. I'm as competitive as the next person but Lions tours are different. I knew I wasn't going to make the Test side so I decided to try and help the other front row players as much as possible. I did everything I could, whether it be scrummaging sessions, lineouts or rucking and mauling sessions.

**Jim Telfer:** Jason Leonard is a superb guy. He came with sixty odd caps and was on his second Lions tour and he could play tight head or loose head. He captained the team in the first game when Martin was being rested. I think a lot of people would have expected him to play in the Tests, but by the time we played Natal we were playing superb off-your-shoulder rugby, carving the opposition into ribbons with our angles. After that we decided on our Test team and Jason Leonard took it like a man. He came in and helped both Tom and Paul. He must have been disappointed, but he never let it show – and that culture we had developed of everyone working for the cause shone through.

**Dai Young:** I don't hold any grudges. I thought Tom and Wally played really well. If I remember correctly, it was all geared up for the England front five to be playing in the Tests, and if you look at the games prior to that, it pretty much suggested it. The majority of the England front five had been playing and getting it wrong. I think the plan with the England front five didn't work and they had to kick on and look at other options. Both Tom and Wally deserved it. I hadn't had many opportunities but selection didn't go my way. Wally, in fairness to him, was a very destructive scrummager. He got himself in a position that was very difficult to move. And Tom Smith's work rate around the field was phenomenal. I don't think that was the plan, but when things didn't go as expected, they took their chance.

**Jim Telfer:** There was some debate about the back row.

**Ian McGeechan:** Rob Wainwright had shown what he could do in the right environment – he scored a hat-trick against Mpumalanga and had been very influential against Gauteng too, but Lawrence had been an outstanding figure, mature beyond his years. His input and attitude were first-rate. We then had a difficult choice between Eric Miller and Tim Rodber at number eight. Whoever we picked there would have a bearing on who we picked at openside. If we chose Eric, then it was to the cost of Neil Back because we'd be too light in the back row with the pair of them. We went with Eric in the end.

**Jim Telfer:** Which meant we went with Richard Hill at seven, mainly because he was such a hard, intelligent player with a high work rate. But I still felt I wanted to have Backy in at some point. Then Eric got ill and Tim came in. That just hammered home the depth of squad we had.

**Jeremy Guscott:** Van der Westhuizen was being talked about as one of the best in the world, but you looked at our scrum-half, you looked at our back row. Our back row was bloody good, so he was containable. Everything was containable. It wasn't like Jonah Lomu was on the other side. Okay, Van der Westhuizen was a threat, but he was containable. He wasn't going to win that Test series on his own.

**Neil Jenkins:** Joost van der Westhuizen was an absolute freak of a player. He was a one-off. An athlete and nasty. He had everything. People talk about Gareth Edwards – he was just as good, Joost. He was right up there. A born winner. The message for us was 'Contain him. Do a job on Joost, and the rest looks after itself.' He could conjure something out of nothing.

**Lawrence Dallaglio:** He was a warrior, Joost. I first played against him for English Students when Pretoria University were on tour in the early 1990s and he was man of the match – just as he was many times afterwards for the Bulls and the Springboks. He was an unbelievable player. We knew how important getting to him was to us stopping the Springboks.

**Matt Dawson:** We did a lot of homework on Joost and felt that we knew how to handle him and that we could read him quite well. You were never going to be able to completely put a blanket over him the whole time, but it was a matter of the half a dozen breaks that he would make in the game week to week, could you squeeze that down to one or two? That was our plan: to close the door on him.

**Jim Telfer:** One benefit of having Andy Keast with us was that he had been an assistant coach at Natal for two years. He put together videos of key players who he felt were vital to how South Africa played and that shaped how we approached games. Andy knew how Henry Honiball, the stand-off, in particular would play, and he was a vital cog for South Africa. Honiball liked to take the ball to the line a lot and use players all around him, inside him and outside him, so with Scott Gibbs, Gregor Townsend – who was quite a good defender as well – and the flankers coming out at him, we might be able to shut down their attack.

**Andy Keast:** Looking at the Springboks, their continuity was at times breathtaking. The forwards were hitting rucks and mauls in threes and fours – and the ball was gone.

**Ian McGeechan:** A video was put together by a lecturer from Cardiff University who from afar had been analysing and studying playing statistics from the tour. He compiled a twelve-minute video set to music, the first half of which highlighted every player contributing without the ball. The second six minutes was about our attack. The night before the first Test I showed it to the players. The silence was deafening. That night it must have been replayed thirty times. Every time I went past the team room, it was on.

**Gregor Townsend:** The night before the first Test, Daws and I didn't go to bed for ages. We were playing darts and pool and table tennis, just trying not to think about the next day. Eventually it gets to about one in the morning and we say, 'Look, we need to go to bed.' But we both knew we were going to be lying there, staring at the ceiling, just hoping to eventually get some sleep. But the adrenaline, all the thoughts in your head . . . it's hard going. Really hard. It's about to be the biggest day of your life. How do you switch off?

# CHAPTER SIXTEEN

# EVEREST

TABLE MOUNTAIN WAS invisible above the Lions' hotel on the day of the first Test, shrouded in mist that had crept in from the sea overnight. The already gloomy morning darkened around midday as storm clouds gathered and the wind gusted through the city. The air of tension around Newlands was tangible as the crowds began to gather.

Telfer called a forwards meeting. When the players entered they saw a circle of chairs in one corner next to a flip chart and, beside these, another circle of chairs covered by the net that Telfer liked to use during his rucking drills. He told them to sit. Eight starting forwards, three subs. And Telfer.

**Lawrence Dallaglio:** I'm never going to forget his speech. It's seared on my memory forever. You could have heard a pin drop.

**Jim Telfer:** I was setting out the room in the hotel, putting the chairs in a circle and draping a net over other chairs to remind them of the height they had to be in all the forward exchanges.

It was a psychological thing: I wanted them to be lower in the scrums, lower in the driving, lower in the tackle and the only way for us to succeed was to be lower than that net.

**Keith Wood:** Jim Telfer's speech before the first Test . . . it was a slightly out-of-body experience. He was a bit mad. He was. But he got it. Jesus, did he get it.

'The easy bit has passed,' began Telfer. 'Selection for the Test team is the easy bit. You have an awesome responsibility on these eight individual forwards' shoulders. An awesome responsibility. This is your fucking Everest, boys. Very few ever get the chance in rugby terms to get to Everest, the top of Everest. You have the chance. Being picked is the easy bit. To win for the Lions in a Test match is the ultimate. But you'll not do it unless you put your bodies on the line. Every one Jack of you for eighty minutes.

'Defeat doesn't worry me; I've had it often and so have you. It's performance that matters. If you put in the performance, you'll get what you deserve, no luck attached to it. If you don't put it in, if you're not honest, they'll second-rate us. They don't rate us, they don't respect us; they don't respect you, they don't rate you. The only way to be rated is to stick one on them, to get right up in their faces, to turn them back, knock them back, out-do what they can do, out-jump them, out-scrum them, out-ruck them, out-drive them, out-tackle them – until they're fucking sick of it.

'Remember the pledges you made. Remember how you depend on each other. You depend on each other at every phase. Teams within teams. Scrums, lineouts, ruck balls, tackles. They are better than you've played against before. They are better individually or they wouldn't be there. So it's an awesome task you have and it will only be done if, as I say, everybody commits themselves now.

'That was written yesterday about us.' He pointed to the chart where he'd written extracts from the previous day's newspapers. 'Read it silently, take note of it, and then make a pledge. You are privileged. You are the chosen few. Many are considered but few are chosen.

'They don't think fuck-all of us. Nothing. We're here just to make up the fucking numbers. *Their weak point is the scrum . . . The Boks must exploit this weakness . . . The Boks must concentrate on the eight-man shove every scrum . . . Scrummaging will be the key . . . Their weakness is the scrum.*

'Nobody's going to do it for you. You have to find your own solace, your own drive, your own ambition, your own inner strength, because the moment's arriving for the greatest game of your fucking lives.'

**Duncan Humphries:** You would hear Jim rehearsing, all grumbling and mumbling. And then he would deliver it perfectly, and you would think, 'Where did that come from?' I was a table away when I filmed it, but I don't think the players even knew we were there. They were so, so focused.

**Paul Wallace:** I was sitting next to him. It was absolutely phenomenal. Immense.

**Rob Wainwright:** Jim was one of the most incredible speakers I've ever heard when his dander was up. You would leave the room and would be climbing the walls wanting to play right then and there.

**Jim Telfer:** There was no great thought process in it. When you think of it, Everest is the ultimate and the Everest of rugby is winning a Test series with the Lions. I hadn't done it as a player and I hadn't done it as a coach. I was in a Lions team that lost a series in South Africa, so I had personal experience of not doing it, of failing at base camp. It just seemed at the time the right thing to say. It didn't look like I had written things down but being a teacher I was very conscious of preparation and so all my speeches were written and rehearsed to an extent, but I put the notes away and I remembered the buzz words. I had a flip chart in the room and I had those buzz words on it. 'They don't respect us.'

You can use your voice in certain ways. You can go quiet then come out with a volley. Silences were powerful. Often in team talks I would say, 'Sit and think about what you are going to do here today.' I'd even say that with the Melrose under-18s. Oh aye. They deserved good speeches as well as everybody else. I would say the same things to them, maybe not swear so much, mind you.

**Lawrence Dallaglio:** There's not a huge amount a coach or a player can do or say which will change much technically in the build-up to a game, but where you can make a difference is finding the right emotional connection between the group. Jim was able to do that, find a theme and really play to the emotions of each of us. If you are able to do that it becomes very powerful. It doesn't matter who is in the changing room next door. You're ready to win.

**Matt Dawson:** I wish I'd heard that Everest speech in person. There was a forwards meeting and a backs meeting. The backs probably played a bit of pool and darts. I can remember walking past the meeting room and we could see Jim setting it all up, wandering and pacing around the room, rehearsing his lines and knowing what he needed to do. Even then I don't think we fully understood the power of that speech until we watched the video. Certainly both Geech and Jim, one of their great strengths was being able to make you realise where you could put your mind and how influential your mind was in performance. The time, the effort, the energy and analysis that went into it was beyond where we'd been before.

**Fred Rees:** It's one of the magic things that we managed to capture. Jim and Ian making these amazing speeches. They have no ego, those two. It wasn't about them. It was all about the players.

**Ian McGeechan:** It's the happiest I've ever seen Jim. That was his true personality coming out.

**Martin Johnson:** I can't ever remember being more nervous than before those first two Tests in the series. Suddenly everything has gone up a gear with the media, the fans, your own expectations and fears. It's Test match time. It's suddenly so intense. Frightening. You go down and have a meal and you sit round and there's not a lot of talking. You're all getting ready: you know what's coming. Well, you think you know what's coming. They're nervous, nervous, long days. Then you're going to the game and everyone's jumping up and down as they see the bus, and you're just thinking, 'Jesus Christ, why am I putting myself through this?'

**Tom Smith:** I remember sitting on the bus and they had flags hanging on all the lampposts on the way to the stadium with a springbok stamping on a lion. And I was like, 'What the hell am I doing here? Why am I doing this to myself?' The pressure was just so intense. It's funny how you look back and remember things – half the emotion going to the game was fear. You know, 'If this goes wrong, it's going to really go wrong – these guys are enormous and such good players.' But, fortunately, we had that togetherness, that thing that's difficult to quantify in many ways in rugby, but can give you an edge. If you had a formula to build the togetherness we had on that trip you'd do very well.

One of the things I look back on with my rugby career is that I regret that I didn't always live in the moment. Often I was quite stressed, quite nervous, and there was an element of fear – fear of failure, which I think drives so many players. It certainly drove me. Later on, you reflect and you enjoy these moments retrospectively. But at the time? No, it was tough and I went through those games consumed by fear, worrying about what could go wrong. That was the negative part of my character.

**Jeremy Guscott:** People cope with pressure in different ways. Jenks would always be throwing up. Sometimes he had nothing left and would just be dry-retching. I just tried not to think about what else was going on. I was always in the moment. 'I can only control what I can control. I can't put the ball into the scrum, I can't push against the loose head. I can't jump up in the lineout. I can't do everything and you can't be all things to all people. Just get on with what you've got to do.' I understood what the collective was and the best way to be part of the collective was to do what you could do and do it as well as you could and don't piss off the other guys who were trying to do what they could do as well as possible.

**Neil Jenkins:** I saw my mum and dad the day before the first Test and my mum said she thought I looked ill. In the dressing room before the game I was literally sick with nerves. I was always spewing, on the toilet, heaving, dragging up stuff. It was a constant, never just once or twice. The boys at Ponty and Cardiff will tell you the same. It didn't matter who I was playing; it could have been a cup game at Felinfoel, and I'd still be heaving. I do it still now as a coach if we've got big games for Wales. I still get nervous and drag up a little bit. Not as bad as when I was a player. I used to say to Warren Gatland, 'Christ Gats, I always thought this would get easier as I got older, but it's worse sometimes.' Gats would laugh and say, 'I'm the same, I'm the same.' I just accept it now. It's part of my make-up.

But no wonder I was nervous. That Test at Newlands was supposed to be the first step towards the Springboks underlining their status as world champions. Everyone in South Africa expected them to win the series 3–0. Despite how well we'd done in the build-up, I still think most people had written us off.

**Jeremy Guscott:** I looked at our pack of forwards – our pack of forwards were fucking brilliant. I didn't think the Boks could bully us, I didn't think they could run us off the park. I didn't think there was anything they could do that we couldn't match or surpass. We had good reason to believe we could win.

**Ieuan Evans:** Newlands is one of my favourite stadiums in the world. It's a fabulous place to play rugby. I loved the crowd being on top of you. You interact, you feed off each other and those big pockets of Lions support, in the corners, where the Lions supporters tend to be put. The stands are really quite severe in terms of their angle – you feel the history, you feel the energy of the crowd. Playing in front of vast, empty, soulless stadiums where the crowds are a hundred metres away from you, you don't quite get that buzz. The potency of that is intoxicating, it's special, and you feed off it. In Newlands, they're not the biggest of changing rooms and when you come through the tunnel, it's quite compact, it's quite squeezed, but that adds to it. It reminds me of the old stadiums and you get that feeling . . . the legacy of previous players, or previous games, of previous moments that have happened when you run out in stadiums like that. You're certainly conscious of that when you go to Newlands. It probably helped us that we'd already played there on the tour, we beat Western Province there, so it held positive memories for us.

**Gary Teichmann:** The first Test of a three-match series is always pivotal. I don't know how many sides in history have lost the first and recovered to win the next two, but I don't think it can be very many. Winning the first Test changes the pressure completely. After that you only have to win one of the two remaining games, but the losers are loaded with pressure because they can't afford another error.

Carel knew this, I knew this – all the players knew it. On the morning of the first Test at the Cape Sun Hotel you could sense the tension among the guys. I think, if we were all honest, it was because none of us felt well enough prepared for the challenge. But then I looked around our changing room before kick-off and I saw world-class players everywhere. We were struggling with our coach but I knew there was more than enough talent in our team to beat the Lions – and probably beat them comfortably. But our confidence wasn't bulletproof and it meant that going into the first Test, instead of believing we would win, we were just desperate not to lose. That's a significant difference. That's what I said before we went out – but you can sense when the guys are taking in what you say and when they're not. And they weren't.

The atmosphere. They all mention it. The riotous commotion, the ground-shaking thunder of the home crowd, the fire and the fury, the almost maniacal din that greeted the teams as they emerged into the 50,000 crowd at Newlands. 'Where does that noise come from?' Teichmann mused later on. 'The roar that seems to come from the depths of the earth when a Springbok team runs on the field in South Africa? It's different to anything else I've ever heard. Even if the team scores a great try or wins a tight match, the crowd's reaction isn't the same as when the team runs onto the field. It is soulful, emotional and timeless. Leading the team out into that will stay in my memory so long as I draw breath.'

**Paul Wallace:** Fuck me, the noise from the crowd was unbelievable.

**Keith Wood:** Jesus Christ. The whole place was shaking as they ran out.

**Paul Wallace:** Os du Randt was down on the programme as twenty stone but he was at least twenty-two stone. Over the years I propped against a lot of guys who were twenty stone and he wasn't twenty stone. He was a huge man. And he also had a massive back-five behind him. André Venter on the flank was probably the biggest man on the pitch.

**Tom Smith:** I was five foot ten, around sixteen stone, and Os du Randt, playing in the same position, was six foot three and twenty-one-and-a-half stone. I was up against Adrian Garvey and he was much the same. They were all big boys.

**Keith Wood:** Wally was sixteen stone at the time. I was about seventeen-and-a-half, nearly eighteen stone. Tom Smith was about sixteen stone. Opposite us, Os du Randt was twenty-one-and-a-half stone, Naka Drotske was nineteen-and-a-half stone and Adrian Garvey was nineteen-and-a-half stone. They were *huge*. Tom was a couple of inches shorter than me; Wally and I are about the same six-foot height. Those guys were towering over us.

Neil Jenkins kicked off, the ball climbing into the sky and over the left-hand touchline. Out on the full. A horror show. Scrum South Africa. The packs converged on the halfway line; the first test of the first Test had arrived. All the blood and sweat that Telfer had spoken about, all those sessions on that bastard scrummaging machine, all those hours on training grounds in

Port Elizabeth and East London, Cape Town and Witbank, Pretoria, Johannesburg and Durban had all been for this. *They don't respect you. They don't rate you. They don't think fuck all of you.* That's what Telfer had told them only a few hours before. The opening scrum. *This is your Everest, boys. This is your Everest.* The front-rows fired into one another. The Lions shuddered and then went skidding backwards. Four, five, six steps. It was stunning. Du Randt, Drotske and Garvey left their opposite numbers in a heap as Newlands all but climaxed as one at the sight of the Springboks reducing the Lions to baby cubs. Joost van der Westhuizen didn't hang around. He moved the ball to his right to Honiball standing on the ten-metre line. Honiball sent a missile into the left-hand corner. It bounced twice and spun into touch, just five metres from the Lions' line.

**Fran Cotton:** And the thought hit you, 'Oh God, this could be a difficult eighty minutes.'

**Paul Wallace:** The scrum was my fault.

**Keith Wood:** Actually, it wasn't.

**Paul Wallace:** I decided to take on Os straight away and do battle with him through power alone. I left a big gap between the two of us before we engaged. The result was the biggest hit in a scrum I'd ever experienced in my life and our pack was catapulted backwards. I'd completely underestimated his power.

**Keith Wood:** I set the height of the scrum and I wanted to hit them as hard as I possibly could and I let that get in the way. So I set it, Wally was too high, without a shadow of a doubt. I'm glad he's taken the blame, but it was my fault. He was too high but it was because I set it too high and I called the hit in the scrum.

So, I put him under pressure by setting it at this height because there was no way he was good enough at that height. And they knocked us back. Now, again, this is memory, but I felt it went back about five yards – and I nearly shat myself. I said, 'Oh, my God, is this what we have now?'

**Os du Randt:** It was an interesting choice that they picked Wallace over Leonard. Before they left Britain, I'd fully expected to pack down against Leonard in the Test series. I didn't know much about Wallace, other than he'd been a late replacement for Peter Clohessy. He was small – they were all small in the front-row – and we wanted to dominate them early and show they were going to be in for a long night.

**Martin Johnson:** They detected a weakness in our scrummaging and destroying you up front is in the DNA of the South African forwards. They want to physically destroy you, to scrummage and attack you in that area of the game. And for us to pick a relatively small front row, they were licking their lips.

**Jeremy Davidson:** You felt the hit from the scrum and then it felt as if you were falling into the Grand Canyon – you're just going backwards and you're on your arse and everybody's on top of you.

**Keith Wood:** So you've just been monstered in the first scrum and now you've got to throw the ball in on your own line. What a lovely start to the match. I throw it to Johnno, but he doesn't win it cleanly and they get awarded a scrum. Fucking hell.

**Paul Wallace:** I went in too high on the first one and I went in too high again on the second one. In those first two scrums I hadn't appreciated the simple physics of Os being four or five stone heavier than me and also having a huge back-five behind him. I got fucked both times. We were shell-shocked. Johnno just gave me a look and I said, 'I'll sort it.' Johnno only ever needed to give a look. The Springbok pack might be fearsome, but it was nothing compared to one of those looks from Martin Johnson.

**Keith Wood:** We got the height much better in the second scrum, but they knocked us back, I'd say, two metres and I was so relieved to be only knocked back two metres. We were under colossal pressure in every scrum. Everything was pressure, pressure, pressure.

**Martin Johnson:** It was the worst start possible. We kicked the ball straight out and they drilled us back at the first scrum. They kicked it to the corner, won the lineout, drove us, smashed us at the next scrum. I mean, it was a terrible start.

Teichmann sped off the back of that second scrum but was met by Richard Hill and Tim Rodber and stopped in his tracks. The ball came back for Joost, who fed big Naka Drotske. The hooker was enveloped by Johnson, who clung on on the ground to slow the ball up. The presentation of the Lions captain lying prone on the ground was a gift for the Bok forwards and Garvey and Andrews gleefully climbed all over Johnson's back and ribs, raking him away from the ball. 'Hey, hey, hey, don't start that,' said referee Colin Hawke, holding out his arm South Africa's way for another scrum. 'Give him a chance to roll off.'

**Martin Johnson:** Nah, that was fair enough, I was deliberately lying all over the ball.

**Mark Andrews:** Rugby is about intimidation and I wanted to make sure Johnson knew who I was throughout that game. We had a few little moments. He was the captain of the side and if he lost his concentration it might detract from the way he led them. If he started losing his cool and the rest of their players started losing their cool, it would only be a good thing for us. I was just checking the guy out.

Scrum number three. Already. The Boks piled in again. The Lions juddered. Hawke called for a reset. They engaged again. Hawke blew again. Reset. They engaged for a third time and Wallace was forced inside by Du Randt. Hawke had seen enough. Penalty to South Africa. Teichmann pointed to the posts.

**Os du Randt:** As a rugby nation, scrums will always be an area where we try to dominate. In those days we worked really hard to manipulate the scrum to get a better angle for the backs to attack from. I don't remember any meetings where we said we were going to scrum for penalties but as a South African front row you are always going to try for push-over tries when you're near the line. We'll always go for that. We pride ourselves on that mentality.

**Tom Smith:** Penalty to them. Not the best of starts. It felt like the game had been going on for about an hour already. How long was it? Three minutes?

**Paul Wallace:** We were reeling.

Edrich Lubbe, winning his second and last cap, stepped up to take the kick. Fifteen yards to the left of the posts, just inside the twenty-two. He hit a beauty. 'It's a brilliant start for South Africa,' observed Hugh Bladen in the commentary box for the South African broadcast. 'And it all came, basically, from a mistake from Neil Jenkins at the kick-off.'

Jenkins had a second chance now. This time he judged it perfectly, hanging the ball high above Mark Andrews, who took it at full stretch just as the Lions stampeded into him. Andrews' control was good. André Joubert then smashed a long spiral that bounced out on the Lions' ten-metre line. It was a text-book exit.

Having failed on his first throw to Johnson, Wood now hit Jeremy Davidson in the middle of the line – the first clean piece of possession that the Lions had had so far.

**Keith Wood:** For me, Jeremy Davidson was extraordinary. Not only was he a beast in the scrum, he was outstanding at the lineout. I was having huge trouble with my lineouts at that stage. I had a bad shoulder, couldn't practise as much as I'd have liked and my throw was not a natural throw – it was staccato, it just wasn't good. But he could pick any ball I threw to him. I could have thrown a dead duck at him and he'd have caught it. He was phenomenal. In that match he caught three balls one-handed – and I don't mean palming it down, I mean catching the ball in a claw at the top of his reach.

**Jeremy Davidson:** If you go out there for the Lions against the Springboks you've got to have a bit of confidence in yourself, you've got to be able to back yourself in the lineouts and I knew I was capable of winning whatever ball was called to me and, luckily enough, Johnno called to me a lot. It's not often a captain does that, but it shows you what a good captain Martin Johnson was. Getting so much ball helped me play a bit better. People remember me for that Lions tour because of the quality of the lineout, but you know what, Paul Wallace lifted me from the front: he was probably one of the best lifters in world rugby, and Rodber behind me, so you had to be good yourself and then thankfully the players around you made you look even better.

Neil Jenkins' boot levelled it at 3–3 as the Lions started to show intent in attack. Short pop passes, tip-ons, runners offering themselves all over the place, but the defence was ferocious and Townsend, dancing into a gap, was walloped in a double tackle from Teichmann and Du Randt. Despite the shuddering impact of the hit, Townsend still managed an offload to Matt Dawson, who was in turn smashed by Hannes Strydom, but he too managed to slip a pass to Davidson – only for it to drift marginally forward.

**Alan Tait:** That link game, that offloading game, was key if we were going to get the better of the Boks. If they don't win that contact and you get the ball away, it definitely upsets their rhythm in defence and you're stopping them getting their big men in the tackle and slowing the ball down. And it would also knacker their big boys out, while we had lighter, quicker forwards who were all fitter.

Scrum time again. They Lions creaked and Du Randt got an angle on Wallace, but it was a much more even contest than before.

**Paul Wallace:** We had to forget the idea of power-scrummaging and go back to the northern hemisphere tactic of more technical scrummaging, trying to manoeuvre them into uncomfortable positions. And if you can do that, you can negate their power. And after those first two scrums we managed to control things better in terms of angles.

**Os du Randt:** They were a narrow front row compared to us, so they were tricky to scrummage against. Once they sorted their height out, it was much harder to dominate them. They adjusted well.

**Lawrence Dallaglio:** What those guys did in the front row was phenomenal. I've never seen a bigger front row in my life than Adrian Garvey, Naka Drotske and Os du Randt. Monsters.

**Martin Johnson:** You can't use words any more without them sounding clichéd, unfortunately, because they've all been used so often, but you're going into those games and you know if you get it wrong, the Springboks will kill you. They will destroy you. Not just points on the board: they will destroy you in every way possible. I haven't really got the eloquence to say it, but in a situation like that you've just got to back each other up for the whole game; whatever happens, keep on going at them. And you only really have each other out there. We had a few thousand fans, but it's an away game and you're surrounded by a rabid South African crowd, you're playing the world champions, they've got some great players, they're the Boks, they're a side full of monsters. And you've got to bring out something special, you've got to find something special for yourself and as a team. Even more so as a team. You can all be trying hard yourselves, but it's got to be a cohesive effort. And you've got to have a bit of skill, as well. You've got to have the skill to do it. You've got to produce not just the guts, but you've got to produce the moments where you take your opportunities and score points.

With thirteen minutes gone on the clock, Small popped up at scrum-half on the Boks' ten-metre line and boomed a huge box-kick downfield. Both Jenkins and Tait were caught out of position; Jenkins scrambled back and gathered it inside his twenty-two but under pressure from a charging Venter, he sliced his clearance into touch.

**Alan Tait:** Jenks wasn't a renowned full back and I wasn't a renowned wing so I thought South Africa might pick on us there, and they did a couple of times. There was that early box kick and then about a minute later, Van der Westhuizen picked from a scrum and came round, put it through his boot and I was beat out the traps. Dead and buried. But Jenks had read it perfectly and dealt with it – but they'd obviously practised it. I remember thinking, 'We're getting tested here. You're going to have to be on the money to get through this.'

Jenkins didn't deal with it quite as perfectly as Tait remembers – the full back did indeed gather the ball but, under pressure from Joubert, he was forced to run it out five metres from his own line.

Mark Andrews was unable to take Drotske's throw cleanly, but Hawke judged that this was because he had been pushed by Rodber – although the replay cast some doubt on that – and South Africa were awarded a penalty. Lubbe set the ball on the tee – and hooked it horribly to the left of the uprights as great jeers rang out from the Lions support in the stands.

'I think he was just trying to give it a little bit extra because he was kicking it into the wind,' said Bladen in commentary. 'But the pressure is on.'

**Matt Dawson:** It was probably the most mentally taxing game that I'd ever played. With the noise of the crowd, the intensity that the South Africans brought, you felt that if they got anywhere near our line, they were probably going to score.

But the South African lineout was malfunctioning badly. For the third time in a row, Drotske failed to find his man and Kruger conceded a knock-on. The resulting scrum was solid as a rock and Dawson cleared superbly downfield, finding touch just shy of the halfway line.

Drotske threw to Andrews – and Davidson got a huge paw to the ball and tapped it down. The loose ball was gathered by Van der Westhuizen and quick hands down the touchline released Strydom into space. A pop to the supporting Drotske took the Boks to the twenty-two and they began to build the phases, Honiball bringing his backs in on sharp lines and Van der Westhuizen releasing the heavy hitters around the fringes. But the red line held firm and eventually Dallaglio got his hands through to jackal the ball and Kruger was penalised for holding on. The stands shook as the Lions supporters roared in delight and the Springbok supporters booed Hawke's decision. The intensity of the collisions throughout that whole passage of play had been out of this world.

**Jeremy Davidson:** André Venter and Ruben Kruger were tremendous athletes. Just big beasts, incredibly aggressive in everything they did, whether they carried the ball or they tackled you or they hit a ruck, you felt it for days afterwards. A different level of intensity, of physicality, and, you know, it's almost going as far as you can take rugby in gladiatorial terms, where it was a 'hurt or be hurt' kind of thing. The Boks had an incredible back row; but so did we.

**Richard Hill:** Their back row were totally uncompromising, particularly Venter and Kruger. Unbelievably physical – but in a largely legitimate way. There were some cheap shots flying around, but those guys weren't really the type to throw too many cheap shots. Great players, big ball-carriers, tough in the tackle. I think they were probably some of the biggest learnings for me in that part of my career: how physical the tackle was, how brutal a defence could be. I'd only played in four Five Nations matches by that stage and the physicality of the tackle wasn't anywhere close. Yes, you'd have the isolated ones, from Scott Gibbs and people like that, but this was consistent throughout the whole team. I'd never imagined anything like it before.

**Lawrence Dallaglio:** Any back row forward will tell you that their effectiveness depends on the five forwards in front of them. A back-row's talents can be completely erased if they don't have a front five platform because rather than being a launch pad for your own side's attack you become involved in a holding operation, spending all your time trying to dump the opposition runners.

It was our game plan to throttle the Springbok half-backs. Our strategy was to hound them mercilessly and deny them space. That meant Hilly arrowing in on Honiball while Rodders and I closed down the inside space. The pincer was completed by having a heavy hitter like Scott Gibbs in midfield, forcing them inwards.

**Neil Jenkins:** Whenever you play South Africa you have to stand toe-to-toe with them, and let them know that you're there. The side we picked in that first Test was one of those sides. It was a side that was going to stand up to them. You had Johnno, Lawrence and Gibbsy. Three of the most physical players to have ever played the game and that's including the South Africans. You had three men there who were going to say, 'Yep, we're more than happy. Bring it on.' The rest of us just followed them.

**André Snyman:** Scott Gibbs tackled me and tipped me over and drove me into the turf. That was a moment when you go, 'Hang on a second, this is a new level.' There's an action photo of me with my legs right up in the air. Nowadays the rules would have given him a red card, but back then it was all just part and parcel of a big defence. When that happened, for me, it set the tone. 'Hang on, we need to pull up our socks here. We're in a real game now.'

**Lawrence Dallaglio:** Gibbsy absolutely emptied him. The whole stadium went ballistic.

**Jeremy Guscott:** He was always shouting at the opposition, Gibbsy. I remember him shouting at Teichmann a lot, giving him some verbals. It's not something I ever did. I didn't want to encourage people to run at me. Gibbsy was doing it to make them run at him, put them off whatever their game plan might have been – and it worked. You've got to be slightly dull to want to run at him, thinking you're going to run over him.

**Scott Gibbs:** Jerry was a guy you needed to create space for. And I was the guy, either by being a decoy or by doing some of the early hard stuff where I'd get across the gain line and he could benefit in the second phase. We are very different in many respects, but a centre partnership has to have counterparts, it has to have an axis. All good selections in the midfield have traits that either one of them can't replicate. When you look at the way Carling and Guscott performed in the midfield, it was pretty much seamless and the same with Tim Horan and Jason Little. I think I made his life a little bit easier, doing the trash talking and some of the heavy lifting. He worked very hard, but you couldn't expect Jerry to do the stuff that I could do. And I could never envisage doing what he was able to do.

**Jeremy Guscott:** I was able to read Gibbsy. I had an ability to read a game pretty well, understand where players were going to go and work off it. I just got him; it was almost telepathic. We did it without thinking. It's not unique. I had it with Simon Halliday at Bath, more so with Halliday. I didn't quite have it with Carling; I linked better with Gibbs than I did with Carling. I loved playing with Gibbsy.

Two minutes later, the Boks had a scrum on the right-hand touchline, ten metres from the Lions' line. Wallace was penalised for his angle and Hawke had a word with him. The Boks elected to kick to the corner. Drotske hit his man. Andrews took the ball down and shifted it to big Os, who peeled around the openside with Venter and Teichmann driving him on. He thundered towards the line, Dallaglio and Hill hanging off him, Dawson and Tait trampled before him. It was like trying to stop a tank. Impossible. The first try of the series.

**Lawrence Dallaglio:** I challenge anyone in the world to try and stop him from two yards out like that.

Edrich Lubbe lined up the conversion but sent the kick to the right of the posts. 8–3 to the Boks.

Having claimed the restart, Joubert hit a punt down the middle of the field, but Jenkins had positioned himself well and returned the kick with interest, spiralling an absolute beauty that bounced into touch a yard from the Springbok try line.

Honiball cleared from the lineout, but Davidson was then taken in the air just outside the twenty-two and Jenkins had a chance to reduce the deficit to two points – and it was a shock to see him slide it to the right of the posts.

**Neil Jenkins:** Ah, mun, you can't get them all, can you?

**Jeremy Guscott:** I bet it still annoys him.

**Neil Jenkins:** Of course it does.

He had a chance to atone for this a few minutes later – after Davidson once again claimed the lineout and the Lions pack got a maul rolling, which the Boks pulled down – and this time he made no mistake.

The Lions felt momentum swinging their way again and they upped the pace. Evans kicked a huge up and under and chased hard and Joubert was found wanting under the high ball. He spilled it forwards just outside his twenty-two and the loose ball was pounced on by Dallaglio, who rolled and then popped to Johnson. Mark Andrews dived off his feet to kill the ball at the ruck and Hawke's whistle pierced the air again. There were just minutes left to go in the half. Up stepped Jenkins and a moment later, for the first time in the match, the Lions were in the lead, 9–8.

**Martin Johnson:** South Africa are a team, like France, that can come out and blitz you for twenty minutes on emotion. They can come out and hit a level for twenty minutes that can blow you away, but it's so incredibly high that it's unsustainable. So you know that if you can live with that and stay in the game, they can't keep that up forever. It's impossible to play like that for eighty minutes. Them coming out all pumped up was no surprise. So we just had to hang on; we just had to stay in the game. You're going to bleed a little bit, but don't let them kill you. If they score two tries in twenty minutes, it's probably game over. So you just have to stay in the game, stay in the game; get a foothold, get a foothold. And we did.

Henry Honiball, flustered, banged his kick-off far too long and Townsend touched it down in the in-goal area. The Lions scrummed solidly as 'Flower of Scotland' echoed around Newlands and then the fly-half arrowed a kick into the Springbok corner.

The camera cut to the sidelines where Carel du Plessis stood, rubbing his chin. 'A worried man at the moment,' observed

Bladen. 'What a pressured job he has.'

The Boks defended the lineout well and Honiball cleared to halfway, where play largely remained until Hawke blew for the break.

'Gary Teichmann will be a little bit worried that South Africa haven't turned their superior possession into points,' said Bladen as the players jogged for the tunnel. 'But full marks to the British Lions for their defence – and Martin Johnson, I'm sure, will be a happy man.'

**Gary Teichmann:** We were trailing at half-time but I told the guys I was pleased with the overall performance. We'd dominated them physically and Os had scored a great try. We just had to press on and the points would come.

**Ieuan Evans:** You know what still gets me is their tactical naivety. Jenks had only played a handful of games at full back and I was astonished that they didn't bombard him with high kicks, especially in that first half. Tactically you have to look at that and wonder what the hell were they thinking.

**Scott Gibbs:** I wasn't surprised because when you look at Henry Honiball as a number ten, his first reaction was always to run. It was in his DNA, and that's what made him so dangerous. That didn't make him predictable by any stretch of the imagination. I kind of knew that the kicking threat was going to come from Joost. He liked the little kick, the little 'worm' ball, the little ball over the top. And I think they thought that turning the wingers would prove far more effective for chasing down and creating pressure than it would be to put Jenks under pressure.

**Ieuan Evans:** They were cocky. That's part of their strength. I don't think the Springboks really looked at their game management –

they just wanted to run over us. I don't think they'd worked out the technical aspects and that goes back to a bit of inexperience on the coaching side. They should have taken advantage of Jenks being a fly-half playing full back. Carel du Plessis didn't have the experience of Geech and Telfer. We brought a strong kicking game and we put them under pressure. In that first Test, I'd never run so much in my life. We tackled and tackled and tackled. The important thing was to stay in the game and then strike when the opportunities arise. And they always arise.

**Ian McGeechan:** We talked at half-time primarily about keeping hold of the ball. We had to be patient because they weren't threatening us and we had showed that we could create. We knew that they would put in a big fifteen minutes again after the interval and we just had to ride that out. Unfortunately, we gave a stupid try away just four minutes after the restart.

Russell Bennett had entered the battle as a half-time replacement for Edrich Lubbe. When Kruger rescued possession on the Lions twenty-two, the Boks struck out, Teichmann thundering past Gibbs and then finding Bennett with a round-the-corner pass that put the Border man away in the corner. Newlands erupted. Soon, Honiball banged over a penalty to extend the Boks' lead. Jenkins put over a fifth penalty to narrow the gap to one, but the respite was brief. Venter lined with Bennett and the substitute went over once again. At 21–15 and a conversion to come and all the momentum in South Africa's favour, the Lions looked in mortal danger with just twenty minutes to go.

Touch judge Didier Mené got involved in that moment, telling Hawke that Venter's pass to Bennett had gone forward. Hawke cancelled the try; 21–15 became 16–15 again.

**Os du Randt:** It was a huge moment. The pass didn't look

forward to us.

**André Venter:** It wasn't forward. Watch it on the video. Watch it.

**Martin Johnson:** We were hanging on by a thread. They were enjoying all the territory, had just scored a try and a penalty and then came the disallowed try from Bennett. If that had stood they would probably have been out of reach. That's how close the margins are in these games. Was the pass forward? Possibly. Did we get away with it? Possibly. Tiny margins.

**Gary Teichmann:** There was a period after half-time when we could have ended the contest but we let a couple of chances slip – a couple of passes didn't go to hand, we gave away some silly penalties – typical of a team lacking a bit of confidence, I suppose. A few months earlier we wouldn't have made those mistakes.

Darkness fell over Cape Town and with it came the rain. If Bennett's second try had been awarded, the Springboks would have had clear breathing space, but they were still in a dog fight, the Lions refusing to lie down.

**Martin Johnson:** The game was on a knife edge. A penalty, a drop goal, a referee's decision. We knew it might all depend on all those little bits.

**Jim Telfer:** Ian always said, 'If we're within touching distance with ten minutes to go, we have the players who can win it for us.'

**Ieuan Evans:** Keep them worried, keep them on edge. Just because they went ahead, it didn't really faze us. We had enough experience, enough people who'd been around the block to realise that the game can ebb and flow. There are periods when each side has good and bad moments, the key is to make sure you capitalise on your good moments.

**Keith Wood:** In the last five minutes of the first half we got a scrum and I felt as if they were tiring. And then, when we went into the second half, I would say with twenty minutes to go, I felt they weren't tiring, they were tired. I felt we'd the upper hand. And we had the upper hand because of Wally. Now, we all did our part, absolutely. Wally got penalised a lot for going in and going down and should he have been penalised for it? Yes, he should have been. But the times he didn't get penalised were the ones that made the difference. There's a psychological impact on a team who know they're bigger and stronger and heavier and more powerful but despite that they can't get in control of the scrum. They weren't destroying the opposition scrum and it became demoralising for them. What we were doing seemed to take away some of the mystique of their pack. Wally holding his feet, scrummaging with his nose on the floor without collapsing, was central to that. I still think he was amazing, for the size he was. I did think of him as a big guy before the tour, but he was tiny compared to who he was playing against. We had to fight for every single second of every single scrum, but we ground them down. They were bigger, but we were fitter and willing to work – and we knew that every time we went down for a scrum if we didn't get it exactly right we'd be belittled and that's a great driving force.

**Tom Smith:** I think sometimes when you play against a team that's expecting to dominate so much and they can't, then even if you're just playing at parity it puts you in a stronger position in some ways. They came into the game with expectations that they couldn't necessarily fulfil. I wouldn't say we were dominant in the Test matches, but we weren't dominated, and that was, in some ways, as good as being dominant because they'd expected to dominate us completely, and Christ, they were big guys.

**Os du Randt:** The ref should have taken stronger action. Wallace scrummed illegally against me most of the time.

**Keith Wood:** Was Wally's scrummaging illegal? Of course it was illegal. But that's what scrummaging is about. The amount of carping that went on afterwards was absolutely fantastic. Look, it was a confrontational battle – and Wally was magnificent.

**Paul Wallace:** Du Randt's scrummaging was only a small part of his game and because of his weight and long back it could actually be his Achilles heel if the scrum was brought low enough. He tended to tire quicker than most because he was carrying such a heavy frame around the pitch and I felt that he could be put under pressure later in the game if he was pinned down into an uncomfortable position.

**Os du Randt:** Wallace was street-smart.

**Keith Wood:** Playing against Os du Randt, nobody expected anything of him, but because he scrummaged low he ate Du Randt alive. Not from the start, but by the end of the game Wally had him inside out, a guy four or five stone heavier. He was showing that form in the last week or ten days before the first Test, but it was still a surprise he was picked. You see, you can never make presumptions about yourself or about anybody else on a Lions tour.

**Paul Wallace:** Os was quite a clean player, to be honest. There were no digs or anything flying in, just a good clean scrummaging battle. But I put my hand down on the ground at one point and André Venter stamped on it and broke it.

**Gary Teichmann:** We were still in the lead. It was 16–15 with eight minutes left. And then Matt Dawson had his moment of magic.

**Gregor Townsend:** Matt was a controversial selection because he hadn't played much for England at that stage, but he turned out to be an inspired choice. Geech knew his players.

**Matt Dawson:** Up until that point, Tim Rodber had been picking the ball up at the back of the scrum and he'd been getting smashed by Venter and Kruger and Teichmann. He was just getting battered. We were awarded a scrum on the right-hand side and he gave me a look that said, 'I've had enough of having my head kicked in, we need to mix this up.' So he called 'solo', which meant that he would put the ball wide on his right foot so that I could scoop it up and try and arc around the blindside flanker and then look to link with my winger. So that's what we did.

As Dawson burst into the gap between Kruger and André Snyman, he was pursued by Teichmann, Venter and Van der Westhuizen, while Joubert glided across to cover in the backfield. The scrum-half looked for Ieuan Evans on his outside, but the winger had instead cut back inside looking for the switch. The movement from Evans forced the scrambling defence to check slightly. They prepared themselves for the pass inside from Dawson to Evans, but it never came.

**Matt Dawson:** You look back now and you realise that was a moment when we benefitted from me being such a surprise selection – no one had a fucking clue who I was. I'd only played five Tests for England and had only played a little bit on tour. If Rob Howley had been playing, he would never have got away with that break because they would have known that he was a world-class threat and they would have shut him down. There was obviously a split second where you can see them thinking, 'We don't need to worry about him, he's going to give it to Ieuan Evans, the legend,' and they check their running.

André Joubert, who was one of my favourite players ever, was charging across, but seeing him check was my cue to hold onto the ball. I shaped to pass inside to Ieuan, but I held on and Teichmann, Venter and Joost all bought the dummy because they didn't think that this nobody playing at nine would have the balls not to pass it inside to Ieuan Evans.

**Ieuan Evans:** I came in off the wing on the scissors and every defender came with me. When Daws went to lob the ball back inside, I expected to receive it as well – but if he'd thrown the pass, I doubt whether I'd be alive to speak to you now. There were four of them waiting for me and I'd have had to reach up to catch the ball, opening up my ribs to them. They'd have smashed me to pieces.

**Matt Dawson:** Because Joubert had slowed up, when he realised I was still going he couldn't catch up and I was in.

**Jeremy Guscott:** To beat Ruben Kruger for pace off the back of an attacking scrum and then sucker Gary Teichmann, André Venter and Joost van der Westhuizen with a dummy is no mean feat. It was an incredible try. An iconic moment.

**Gary Teichmann:** It was a simple lack of communication. We should have buried him.

**André Snyman:** Ja, I should have tackled him. I was playing out of position on the wing. If we'd had a genuine wing there instead, would he have stayed out and made the tackle? Maybe. Maybe. Dawson was away into space and he crossed the line in the corner without a finger being laid on him. Dotting the ball down casually, he bounced over the foam advertising hoarding at the edge of the pitch and made pistols of his hands as he celebrated with the Lions support in the stand.

**Ian McGeechan:** To see Matt having the confidence to do that was fantastic. We'd chosen him because we knew what he was capable of when others thought he was our third choice.

**André Snyman:** It was a brilliant try. He went around the corner, threw the big old dummy over the head. He was a skilful player, made the right decision at the right time and fooled all the defenders around him. And you could see that try meant a lot to him with the celebration. I mean, it's an absolutely brilliant individual try. It came at the right time and he did the right thing.

**Paul Wallace:** It was all down to the scrummaging, by the way. I managed to get my right shoulder up on Os and that created the angle.

**Martin Johnson:** He's making light of it, but it's true. I remember saying to Wally at the time that it was his try because he got the right-hand side up a little bit against big Os du Randt. I hadn't seen the detail of what Dawson had done at that point because I was still in the scrum. I didn't know anything about the try in terms of how it had happened, but I remember saying to Wally that he had been the one who had created it. Os was a big, big man; an enormous guy in a world of big people. There are very few people on the planet who are built like an ox – not fat, but a huge, muscular man. And Wally moved him just enough to give Daws the space he needed.

**Gregor Townsend:** There was just no space that day. It was the hardest match I ever played. The South Africans were just so quick and so hard you could hardly draw breath. So we couldn't play the kind of attacking rugby we'd done against the provincial sides – but the challenge was tremendous. And, near the end, the emotion was so high, especially when Matt went over for his try. I can still see us now, jumping up and down as he went in – and that's why you play rugby, for those intense pleasures.

**Rob Howley:** I watched the game in Bupa in Cardiff because I'd had my shoulder op the previous day and I was on the toilet when Matt scored. In my rush to get up, I nearly fell over trying to balance myself with my left arm in a sling and I nearly did my shoulder in again. So I didn't see it live, but I got back into the room in time to see the replay. It was a fantastic dummy. I don't think Teichmann had taken many dummies like that before. Daws was outstanding, especially when you consider he wasn't number one for England at the time. Geech put his faith in him, and he didn't disappoint, did he?

**Joost van der Westhuizen:** We were all a bit stunned by that try, but Gary pulled us together as they took the conversion and just said, 'Keep going, guys, keep trying.'

The Springboks surged forward after the kick-off, but Honiball made the mistake of carrying the ball flat down Scott Gibbs' channel. Having missed the tackle on Teichmann for Bennett's score, Gibbs wasn't going to let the same thing happen again. He crashed into the Springbok ten and forced him backwards. Van der Westhuizen tried to make a break, but was hauled down by Rodber.

**Jeremy Guscott:** Some of the hits were so brutal. I remember wondering how some of them got back up.

**Ieuan Evans:** All of a sudden, they were under the pump. Seeing a team feel that uncomfortable doesn't half give you a little helping hand, doesn't half give you a vote of confidence and a spring in your step when you see a side scratching their heads and thinking, 'This isn't supposed to happen.'

**Gary Teichmann:** We were starting to panic by that stage and you could see us trying things out of desperation. We became individuals, which is the last thing you want happening.

Back in Springbok territory, the Lions were awarded a scrum five metres out and, almost unbelievably, they shunted the Springboks back over their line.

**Tom Smith:** It's one of the dynamics of scrummaging that in the first couple of scrums, everybody's fresh and then you get a bit of running into your legs and the balance between size and strength and the fitness side of it comes into play a bit more. We'd had eight weeks of rugby by then and if you stay healthy and play games, you get very, very match-fit. One of the benefits of such a long tour, as it was back then, is that by the time you hit the Test matches, you're flying. We overcame the tough part, got parity, and then got stronger – and we definitely finished the match stronger. Even so, pushing them back over the line surprised us all.

Under a mass of bodies collapsed around the try line, referee Hawke couldn't see whether Rodber had grounded the ball so awarded another scrum to the Lions. This time the Springboks countered and the ball was whipped from the base by Dawson. Townsend ran a short scissors with Gibbs, who sped into the Springbok midfield. A quick recycle and the Lions were away again, Rodber floating a deft little pass out to Jenkins. Honiball, the last defender, had to make a decision – to commit to the tackle on Jenkins or drift wide onto Tait who was now running free down the left-hand touchline. He went to make the hit on Jenkins, but the full back slipped it to the Scot who roared over unopposed, touched down, and, like Dawson before him, made pistols towards the crowd in celebration. The extraordinary had happened. It was 25–16. Time was almost up. The Lions were ahead in the series.

**Alan Tait:** My gran was passing the Black Swan pub in Kelso and heard an enormous roar at the precise moment I touched the ball down. She said she thought the roof was going to blow away.

It was started by a great run by Gibbsy that got us yardage, and then Tim Rodber, of all players, threw the pass out to Jenks – I'd never seen him offload before. He got that ball away because he knew what we'd practised for six weeks, keeping the ball alive, and I was lucky enough to be on the end. Jenks's ear will still be hurting now the way I was shouting for the pass.

I put it down and just thought, 'We've won it!' You knew that was it, we'd won the Test. I have no idea where the pistol celebration came from. It was a moment of pure elation, knowing it was game, set and match to us and it was a kind of victory salute to all the fans who had travelled to watch us. It's not a bad thing to be remembered for, scoring a Test-clinching try. I turned around, I could see all the players celebrating, I looked towards the Lions fans and you could see all the colours and the roar they were making and it was just a sight to behold.

**Jim Telfer:** The last ten minutes of that match encapsulated everything we'd been planning to do. Hold them, hold them, hold them, stay within touching distance, tire them out, let Neil Jenkins kick his goals and then punch them at the end and draw away. Matt got his try and then a few minutes later we had some great hands across the backline, with forwards and backs interchanging, to put Alan Tait in at the corner.

**Gary Teichmann:** Those final eight minutes . . . They were like a blur. Suddenly, we'd lost by nine points. The result absolutely shocked me, maybe because I'd never even considered it as a possibility. It felt far worse than defeats against the All Blacks or Wallabies. I could see our guys were genuinely stunned, left almost speechless.

**Mark Andrews:** The Lions were smart, they stopped contesting the lineouts in the last six minutes and they just built a wall to keep us out. There was nothing we could do to get back in it before we ran out of time.

**Joost van der Westhuizen:** The changing room afterwards? Devastation.

**Carel du Plessis:** We played poorly, but even then we still had a reasonable chance of winning the Test. Dawson should never have scored his try near the end. Japie Mulder had injured his shoulder and was playing nowhere near his potential. He didn't want to come off the field, but we should have forced him off. That was the turning point.

**Ian McGeechan:** Sport, like anything, like the arts, like music, can touch your soul. Rugby, when it's right, touches somewhere really deep. When you slow down some action and out of all the physicality comes a piece of sublime skill and balance within a physical context, there is a beauty about it.

Rugby is emotional and instinctive as well as scientific and a coach can either encourage that side of the game or discourage it and play to rigid patterns. You have to have a structure and a self-discipline that allows you the freedom to express yourself. I don't think you can have one without the other. If Shakespeare hadn't got the grammatical skills at his fingertips, he'd never have got anywhere near the brilliance of his language.

Those two tries we scored to win that Test match – they were sublime. They're among the happiest moments the game has given me in my life.

# CHAPTER SEVENTEEN

# I TROD IN A DOG SHIT

SOUTH AFRICA WOKE bleary eyed, the Sunday newspapers reflecting the shock the whole nation seemed to be feeling at the loss of the first Test. 'Bokke, O Bokke!' cried *Rapport*, the major Afrikaans newspaper, while the English-speaking *Sunday Times* lamented 'Boks, What Went Wrong?' and the *Sunday Argus* headline simply read: 'Boks Blow It'.

The reaction in the UK and Ireland was equally stunned. 'Lions come roaring back to rock Boks' said *The Observer*. 'The date and the happening will be an indelible entry in the chronicle of rugby achievement,' went the lead report in *The Irish Times*. 'June 21st, the shortest day of the year in the southern hemisphere, will go down as one of the sweetest and certainly one of immense significance in the history of Lions rugby.'

'The two props, Tom Smith and Paul Wallace, together with lock Jeremy Davidson, appeared improbably fresh-faced to face the Springbok fury,' wrote Stephen Jones in *The Sunday Times*. 'They held out and confounded us all.'

One-nil up in the series, the Lions enjoyed their Saturday

night, but the job was only half done. The second Test loomed at the end of the week and they knew that the level of ferocity from the Springboks was only going to rise now that they were fighting for their lives. Rob Louw, the former Springbok back row and a hero of the 1980 series against the Lions, was stung by what happened in Cape Town but could not see it being repeated in the second Test in Durban. 'You could pick the worst Springbok team and send them out to Kings Park and they'd win,' he said, bullishly. 'That's what the Springbok jersey does for players. The Boks will win convincingly.'

Before the countdown to the second Test started, the dirt-trackers had to head to Bloemfontein to face the Orange Free State, the last of South Africa's Super 12 teams.

**Jim Telfer:** After we won the first Test, the midweek players had a training session while the Test team rested. Johnno said to Ian, 'We're still on tour – everyone will come out and work on Sunday morning.' And even though they didn't do very much, the team that won the Test match helped the other players in the squad prepare for their next game. That was an unbelievable act. It defined that squad – and Johnno's leadership – in my mind.

**Martin Johnson:** It was Gibbsy's idea, actually. One of the big things on that tour, like the Transvaal game, was that we all got on the coach after the Test, the whole tour party, and there was this sense of 'Phew, we've kicked them in the balls, what a great feeling.' But we've also got to play Free State a few days later and the announcement went out on the bus, 'Guys, there's a training session tomorrow morning at 8.30 for the midweek team. So anyone who's not played today, anyone who's not played in the subs, meet at eight o'clock.' And it's a bit of a soberer, because the boys are going to have to cut a little bit of the celebration.

Gibbsy turned to me and said, 'Johnno, we all should go and train tomorrow.' And when he said it, I went, 'Mate, that's totally right.' So I got on the mic and said, 'Boys, we're all there tomorrow. Everyone down there tomorrow, we'll meet at eight and we'll go and do this training session.'

**Neil Jenkins:** That's what characterised us – one for all and all for one. It was the most harmonious group I'd ever had the pleasure of being a part of. Before we'd even left, Geech had instilled in us that we weren't English, Irish, Scottish or Welsh, but one team representing one of the greatest rugby brands in the world. We were all Lions together.

**Ieuan Evans:** You've already played a long, hard season domestically and internationally so it's really important you take the opportunity to enjoy yourself and switch off, because it's uber-intense. So the challenge, if you had a couple of drinks, was that you had to be there in training the following day. It's part of the mystique and part of the reality of being a successful touring side. Some guys are fortunate enough to play Test rugby, but there are guys who won't have played Tests that are just as instrumental in winning that Test series. So you have to repay them and make sure that whenever their next game is, you help them. You're there to hold the tackle bags, you're there to make sure that they're at their best, you're there to put the hits in, you're there to push things and you're there to encourage them. It has to be that way, otherwise it doesn't work.

**Martin Johnson:** The next morning we got on the bus and we went to somewhere, God knows where, in Cape Town. The night before we'd won under the lights at Newlands in one of the greatest Test matches of our lives and then the next morning we get off the bus at an open playing field, like a recreation area, and the wind was coming in and the rain was coming down and I got off the bus and I trod straight in a dog shit.

**Ian McGeechan:** The pitch was on a patch of ground that was part of a steel works. It was pretty grim. I don't know whether it was John Bentley or Scott Gibbs, but one of them said, 'Can you imagine where they'd have sent us if we'd lost the Test?'

**Martin Johnson:** So we did the session, all back on the bus, all back to the hotel and all our gear has been packed up to send on to the next hotel and I've got this dog shit all over my bloody trainers. I thought, 'I can't get on a plane with that, because it stinks, it's horrible.' I hate dog shit, it's one of the worst things in the world. So I thought, 'I've got to clean these shoes somehow.' So I'm in my room and I had a mate over and he's knocked on the door, the door's open, I say, 'Come in,' and he's walked in, still full of the celebrations and the joys of the day before, to see me with my toothbrush, cleaning dog shit out of the trainers. And he's just like, 'This is not the glamour I expected.'

We went over to Durban, and the lads then headed up to play the Free State. What's amazing, when you look back now, is that because we only had a squad of thirty-five and twenty-one had played in the first Test, someone from Saturday's starting team was going to have to double up and sit on the bench on the Tuesday. It was Jenks who got the short straw. Can you imagine that happening now? Your main goal kicker sitting on the bench for a midweek match between Tests. And the way it panned out, he ended up playing more than half the game.

Geech had a problem. On the Monday evening before the Tuesday clash with the Free State he came down with a bug. He was still keen to fly to Bloemfontein with the team, but James Robson was concerned that in the tight confines of the plane, he might infect the players. It was decided that he would remain in Durban and Telfer would take charge of the team on his own.

**Fred Rees:** Dunc flew with the team to the Orange Free State game and he said he'd never seen Jim as nervous, as freaked out as he was on that plane and during the build-up to that game. Suddenly, he was on his own.

**Duncan Humphreys:** I thought he was going to have a heart attack. I mean, I genuinely thought he was having a heart attack. But when they got up there and got settled into the pre-match routine, he relaxed a little. And I think the best speech he delivered was the one he did before that match. That was an amazing speech.

'Right,' said Telfer, 'from now on, all we think about is the game. We're professionals – and professional has nothing to do with mortgages or making money. It's about performance. Mental and physical performance. And from now until quarter past seven you mentally get prepared for the biggest performance of your life. The next challenge is always the biggest one. The next challenge is the one against the Free State tonight.

'We're not underestimating them. They're a *good* side. But from now on, we only think of *our* performance. Any sort of standard to set ourselves – the fifteen guys who went out to represent us on Saturday set the stall really high. But instead of saying, "Well that's it, we can't reach it," that to you fellas should be the challenge. They've set the stall out, those fifteen guys, but it could have been the fifteen in here.

'Most of you played last Tuesday. The standard was high; on Saturday it was higher. We can go higher and higher still. Let's think of it, gentlemen. For six weeks we've worked like beasts together. Blood, sweat and tears on the practice ground. We've eaten together, we've drunk together, we've sung together . . . If I were you, I'd be relishing going out tonight. All that work together – to be afraid of this crowd? No, no. The greater the challenge, the greater the response from us. We go out there to put all these things together, all the things we've built up over the five weeks, to come out with a fucking crescendo. We don't fear them. We respect them. But that's it. We're up for the challenge, aren't we? We're up for the challenge. The bigger the challenge, the bigger the response.

'Think of it: we've beaten Eastern Transvaal, we've beaten Western Province, we've beaten Natal, we've beaten Transvaal, we've beaten the Springboks. We can beat anybody if we put our minds to it. If we don't perform tonight it's nothing to do with them – it's to do with us.

'The bigger the challenge, the bigger the response. We want the challenge. I think Geech said last week, "Go out and enjoy it." I wish I was you, boys. All that ability in here. All that individual skill. All that preparation. This is the scene you wanted, this is the stage where you perform. Don't let yourselves down, don't come off the pitch and say, "I left it in the dressing room," or "The fight was too long." Don't make excuses. The real professional never makes excuses – because he's no excuses to make because he's given his all. We're going to do it against the toughest team below the Springboks. When we get it right, we're absolutely fucking breathtaking. When we get it right, we are superb.'

**Will Greenwood:** By the time he had finished I felt like I could run through a brick wall and then beat up the whole of South Africa when I got to the other side. The Boks were relying on the Free State boys to dent our physicality and psychology. 'Ollie' Redman was captain that night; I couldn't believe how hairy he was – everywhere except on his head. Strange memories.

**Allan Bateman:** We were expecting to get booted in that game. We were told how physical they were in Free State, but we just got stuck into them.

**Neil Back:** The Test team stayed behind and it was the first time on tour that the squad had been divided like that. It had a bit of an effect on some of us because it felt like we were going to struggle to get a Test spot. But we embraced the challenge and probably played the best game of the tour. Fran later described it as the best ever performance by a midweek Lions side between two Tests. It was probably the best game of rugby I ever played in.

**Eric Miller:** The ground was hard and fast and because the chemistry of the group was so good, there was always someone off your shoulder. It's just the moment in time and it's the blend of the people and the motivation and the meaning behind it. We blew them apart.

It was a little edgy at first as Tim Stimpson and Free State fly-half Jannie de Beer swapped early penalties but then the Lions began to roar. In front of a huge and boisterous crowd, they ran from everywhere, cutting angles off one another, offloading, always keeping the ball moving. From a tap penalty, Mike Catt sent an exquisitely placed cross-field kick into the arms of Stimpson to score before Bentley tore the defence to shreds on his way to a quick double. Left-winger Stephen Brink crossed for Free State but the Lions responded almost immediately when Greenwood carved through the midfield to set up his centre partner Bateman for an easy run-in.

**Fred Rees:** They played this most amazing rugby and I loved how we were able to capture the pleasure on Jim's face. When he cries, 'Peach of a try!' when Bateman goes over, it's just so lovely. His love of it, for them and for what they're feeling, it's so great.

**Will Greenwood:** We absolutely destroyed them in that opening half. The game was over by half-time – but so was my tour.

**Mike Catt:** Will took a switch ball from me and was caught by the top of his jersey by Jaco Coetzee, the Free State number eight, and swung round.

**Will Greenwood:** There was nothing illegal about it. He swung me round and threw me to the floor, my arm pinned to my side. The rest, I am afraid, I have had to put together down the years by watching the incident on tape and talking to old pals. The next thing I really remember is being in Durban for the second Test four days later. By all accounts, things had gone very wrong very quickly on the pitch.

**Mike Catt:** His head landed at right-angles to his neck and he just lay there, sparko. Austin Healey reacted quickly, getting him on his side and removing his gum shield.

**James Robson:** Rob Wainwright was playing in that game and immediately attended to him because Rob was an army doctor. In those days you just had the team doctor on either side and it was then variable about who else was there. And coming off the pitch to find somebody wasn't stepping up to kind of help me made you realise that all of a sudden it was all on you. And that's a scary thing. It was relatively easy for family to get down to pitch-side. Unbeknownst to me as we're bringing Will off, his mum had got down and her cry of horror still moves me to tears and literally makes the hair stand up on the back of my neck. She said, 'Oh Will! What have they done to my son?'

**Will Greenwood:** My mum was sprinting down the steps and was about to charge on to the field when Jason Leonard pulled off one of the great last-ditch tackles. 'Come here Mrs Greenwood, there's nothing you can do, he's in good hands, let's just get him off the field first.' He saved me from total humiliation – a mother on the pitch in the middle of a Lions series – imagine.

**Simon Shaw:** When someone's knocked out, it's always a worry and then seeing Will taken off on a stretcher was upsetting. It was the tour's darkest hour. But as players, you've got no option but to concentrate on the game and we just had to get back into it.

**Tim Stimpson:** You're used to players getting injured and going off. Your job is your next job and you remain focused on the game. It's just part of your conditioning that people go off on stretchers. You hope they're fine, but by the time you've had a swig of water you're thinking about your next challenge. I only found out the extent of what happened with Will when I watched *Living with Lions*. When people say he nearly died, you're like 'Oh, shit . . . what?' James Robson – the legend that he is – was fishing his tongue out of his throat and saving his life.

**James Robson:** He was unconscious and when that happens everything becomes loose and his tongue had fallen back in his throat and was blocking his airways. So we had to get him in the recovery position to try and clear that. Fortunately, we didn't have to take any more drastic measures than that, but every time I watch that piece of footage, it makes me go cold. He was out for two or three minutes – that's a long time. We got oxygen on and you're just trying to maintain the airway as we took him off to make sure he was breathing because you're always worried that any moment you may lose that airway. There was real anxiety that we were going to lose him.

**Allan Bateman:** I saw he got carried off and saw his mother and tried to calm her nerves a bit, but I don't think I realised how serious it was until I saw the footage later. You've got to put that kind of thing behind you. People break legs, and worse. If you start letting that affect you, you'll never play another game.

**Will Greenwood:** As we passed my mum, she cried: 'William, William, what have you done?' It's not a video I want to see again, but if you watch it, the footage in the medical room shows you all you need to know. Robbo was white and shaking, my mum was distraught in the background. I'd swallowed my tongue, my pupils were not reacting to light, my throat was about to be cut open to free up the airways. Robbo said later that he thought I was going to die.

**James Robson:** Fortunately, he came round and we were able to get him off in an ambulance to the neurosurgery unit. I stayed overnight with him because of the severity of the injury and I remember taking him out of hospital and getting on a plane the next day.

**Doddie Weir:** He's an amazing guy, Robbo. He understands the player, he understands the medical industry, he saved Will Greenwood's life, he knows exactly what's going on. And he's so easy to get on with. He understands the body so well and we all had total and utmost respect for him. When you've been on six Lions tours, it gives you an indication of how good he is.

**James Robson:** It took a couple of days for the exhaustion from the whole thing to kick in because you're so intensely focused still on everything that's going on. The whole scenario, you know. I still relive Will's injury and you can't help but think if something else had happened, I might have lost him. It was difficult to watch the video of it all again when it came out.

**Will Greenwood:** There was no out-of-body experience, no going towards the light. I just wasn't going to wake up. Then it happened. With Robbo's help I came to. What was the first thing I did? I told my mum to go away because she was embarrassing me. I was taken to hospital where they gave me brain scans and a bed. I rang my wife. She tells me we chatted for an hour. I don't remember a word. I have one hazy memory of that time. I woke again at 4.30 a.m. and all I could hear was Afrikaans, I had no idea where I was. I lifted my sheets and was still in full Lions kit and I thought I was dreaming.

**Graham Rowntree:** He didn't get over that for a long time, you ask him about it. He had a fear in his game for a long time. He could have died. Terrible. Jesus.

**Mike Catt:** It took him a good year-and-a-half to get over it.

**Will Greenwood:** It was the fact that my shoulder got mangled at the same time – that was the thing that took a long time to come back from, not the head knock. When I came back the following season, the shoulder was still giving me problems and made me fall off my game slightly and when that happens it eats away at your confidence. The head knock? I couldn't remember it; it didn't bother me afterwards.

**Simon Shaw:** We got a great win and then it was a case of getting into the dressing room as quickly as possible to find out how Will was. The minute we discovered he was making a good recovery and that any element of danger had passed, someone inevitably made a joke about it and we moved on. It's just the nature of rugby teams, I suppose – gallows humour, don't show too much emotion. But it had been a scary moment.

**Neil Back:** We won 52–30 and I felt that our performance, and more importantly our attitude, meant that they might look again at one or two of us for the second Test.

**Rob Wainwright:** It was one of the greatest displays of free-flowing rugby that I was ever involved in, without a shadow of a doubt.

**Jim Telfer:** That win showed everyone the strength of our squad and built up our own confidence even more. Guys like Tony Underwood, Mike Catt and Tim Stimpson couldn't get into the team for the second Test, which is amazing to think. If Will Greenwood hadn't been injured, I'd have put him in the mix as well – he'd been outstanding.

**Martin Johnson:** We sat there in the team room, watching it, and apart from Will Greenwood getting injured, it was an unbelievable game. I remember Gibbsy saying, 'I wish I was playing.' So they turned it from a game of 'No one wants to be playing against the Free State,' to 'God, I wish I was playing in this.' It was just inspiring.

**Os du Randt:** André Venter and I didn't play in that game, but we still had outstanding players like Helgard Muller, Brendan Venter, Jannie de Beer, Rassie Erasmus, Charl van Rensburg, Braam Els, Ryno Opperman, Charl Marais and Willie Meyer in our line-up. The way the Lions beat us showed they were a side to be reckoned with. When a squad's second-string put in a performance like that it makes you think.

# CHAPTER EIGHTEEN

# GARY TEICHMANN'S PAIN

GARY TEICHMANN STRUGGLED to sleep in the week of the second Test. He lay awake in bed wondering how the hell the Boks had got themselves into this mess after such a promising end to '96. He'd believed that the wins over France had sparked a renewal but the Lions had just put paid to that. 'Where had we gone wrong?' he asked himself. 'What had I done wrong?'

Three days after the defeat at Newlands, Carel du Plessis turned thirty-seven. There were no celebrations. The head coach was visibly on edge as he sat on a chair at the Beverly Hills Intercontinental hotel in Umhlanga Rocks and announced his team for the make-or-break second Test. The pressure on him and his players was increasing by the minute and injuries in his squad weren't helping. James Small, Japie Mulder and Edrich Lubbe were out. In their place came Pieter Rossouw, Percy Montgomery and Danie van Schalkwyk. They had a total of four caps between them – all belonging to Danie van Schalkwyk. On the bench, Krynauw Otto and Dawie Theron were gone, replaced by Fritz van Heerden and James Dalton.

**Pieter Rossouw:** I was sitting at home watching the first Test and was pretty surprised at how the Lions played. They were much better than I thought they were going to be. The next day I got the call from Carel telling me that I'd made the side for the second Test – and at that stage I was laughing because I thought it was a friend playing a prank. In December of '96 they'd picked a wider training squad of seventy-two players and I wasn't part of it. So for me to be picked six months later in a Springboks side for a pivotal Test against the Lions – it was totally unrealistic. I'd also missed the Western Province game against the Lions because of injury so I was sure it was a prank . . . but eventually I realised that it was Carel. It felt unreal. I had to go to Sarfu head office to get my kit and the next day I flew to Durban to join up with the squad.

Dawie Theron [Springbok tight head] picked me up at the airport and I told him, 'Listen, I've brought two balls with me that I want the Springboks to sign. I'm not sure how long I'm going to stay here.' Now obviously I hadn't been a part of everything running up to the Test series and I had to try and learn so much that week, but fortunately I fitted in quite nicely and there were a few other new guys in that team – Percy, Russell Bennett, Danie van Schalkwyk – so that helped me a lot because I wasn't alone as a newbie.

Of all the changes Du Plessis made, Montgomery's selection was the most contentious. He had played against the Lions at fly-half for Western Province and in the centre for the Emerging Springboks. Du Plessis selected him in the midfield to replace the injured Mulder. There were many in the South African press who felt that he wasn't physical enough and that his defence would be found out.

**Pieter Rossouw:** Percy hadn't played all that much in the centre and the big thing for him was getting used to defending in that thirteen channel, which is a very difficult position to defend. He could defend at ten and defend at fifteen, but at thirteen there's a lot of space for you to manage, so you've got to be pretty sure of what you're doing. And I think he was still struggling with that. He wasn't that confident about who he had to mark. Later on, he got better and better, but at that stage defence was his weak point.

**Carel du Plessis:** When I picked Percy, I backed his attacking qualities ahead of any possible defensive vulnerability he might have. I was always willing to invest in an outside centre whose strength was to attack from first phase and create try-scoring opportunities because of his out-and-out pace. There was no other outside centre in the country who could match him for explosiveness. I made a call to go for a player who gave me more in attack than defence. That was a risk I was willing to take and I was prepared to live with the criticism of him missing some tackles because of the attacking dimension he gave our backline.

Percy was a player I had identified as having the potential to break the mould of South African outside centres because he was not physically imposing and didn't weigh 110kg, but he had an understanding of space and movement, and a natural feel of when to run and when to pass. I also rated the quality of his field kicking and, to me, we had something rare in an explosive left-footed outside centre who was as quick as anything I had seen over the first twenty metres. I had to play him against the best in the world to confirm my gut feeling that he was good enough and I never doubted he would make an impact in Test rugby.

**Percy Montgomery:** I remember walking into the Springbok team room for the first time. There were no welcomes, no smiles, nothing. In all the years I played for the Springboks afterwards, I never experienced anxiety like that again. I've known tough times and there were difficult years but that week was something else. There was a lot of emotion in the squad and I sensed that there wasn't a lot of confidence in Carel and Gert Smal, with the media writing them off and the senior players not convinced they were good enough to be there. But I thought they were brilliant because they were the guys who were about to make me a Springbok. I tried to distance myself from the negativity – I was just desperate to do well and I wanted Carel to succeed.

When I got to Durban I was excited, confident, I felt I could do anything against anyone. There was nothing to be scared of because by being selected, I already felt like I'd won. I was young, ignorant about the history and tradition of the Lions and, as far as I was concerned, I was bulletproof. I saw it as my first Test and not as a Test to save the series against the Lions. It would take another ten years of playing Test rugby for me to understand that some Tests are bigger than others and that a series against the Lions is the biggest thing outside of the World Cup.

**André Snyman:** Some of the senior players started doubting – and I keep on saying the word doubting, but that's what happened. We doubted. We were asking questions and the questions were never answered. Why did he select me on the wing? I'm a specialised centre. I've been a centre my whole life. Why does he pick me on the wing if we have wingers already? Why do you take my best position away from me and put Percy Montgomery at 13 if he's actually a full back? It was just really confusing. So we'd be like, 'Hang on a second, does this coach know what he's doing?'

**Gary Teichmann:** You can't fault Carel as a person, but he didn't have much coaching experience and at that level it counts for a lot. When you are an international player and you are being taught how to pass the ball, you know there is something wrong. There was no definite plan; everything was wishy-washy. And that wasn't a strong Lions team. We should have beaten them. We were at sixes and sevens on and off the field and that was down to a lack of experience. For example, just before the game, we'd go through a whole lot of scrums and shit with Gert, as if we were doing pre-match cramming, when we should just have been preparing ourselves mentally for what was to come.

After that first loss in Cape Town, and by the time we got to Durban for the second Test, we had gone into panic mode. There was intense pressure on us to win the next Test, or we'd lose the series. When the pressure mounts to that extent, it does funny things to people.

**James Dalton:** Carel du Plessis is an amazing man and the best wing to ever play for the Springboks. He was a remarkable rugby player but he had no clue about coaching an international team. As a person, he was softly spoken and very gentle in his communication. You couldn't help but like him. I had so much respect for Du Plessis the rugby player but as a coach he was a joke.

Carel did things as a player very few others would have been able to. He did them naturally and with such ease, but he found it difficult to articulate the most basic aspects of the game to the players. Gert was similar. He made such an impact as a player, but as a coach I found him one-dimensional and he had an archaic and outdated approach to training. He was very uninspiring as a coach.

Look, there are so many permutations and options and opinions, particularly when it comes to selection, that coaches are never going to get it completely right. It is not possible to select a Springbok team where everyone is happy with all the names. But Carel got it more horribly wrong than most other Bok coaches.

We should have annihilated that Lions tour side and we didn't because of bad team selection. I am not shifting the blame; that was just the nuts and bolts of it.

**Os du Randt:** The pressure that week was huge. If we're to stay in the series, everything now rests on the second Test. We were highly motivated. We were hurt. And all of South Africa was on our backs. To lose a Test like that . . . everything was on the line. You'd literally be willing to die to keep the series alive. So we relied on our hurt and our pride to get us ready. The message was: 'Make sure everyone goes out there and does their part. And with the goal-kicking of Jenkins, make sure you don't give away easily kickable penalties.'

**Mark Andrews:** The first Test had been a game that we'd lost rather than the Lions had won, so I wasn't all that concerned about the outcome of the series. The simple fact, in my mind, was that we'd made too many mistakes. You can't lose five lineout balls, kick three balls directly into touch and expect to win. Yes, the Lions played well, but you can't make that many mistakes at Test level and expect to win. At the same time, had Russell Bennett's try been allowed, which it should have been, I really felt that we would have beaten them easily.

**André Joubert:** I knew myself that I hadn't had a good game in the first Test, but my attitude was that there was always the next game to focus on. There was no point reading the papers that week because you knew what they were going to be saying. They even had Desmond Tutu coming out and saying that we were playing poorly, and that our selection and tactics were wrong. But I was convinced that we were all going to play better – and I was going to play a hundred per cent better.

**Percy Montgomery:** I don't remember having any big one-on-ones with Carel that week. I think he pretty much confined his talking to me at training. I remember him telling me to do a bit of goal kicking because I might get used in the Test. I didn't seriously think I'd be kicking because Henry Honiball and André Joubert were starting and they were the top two in the pecking order. Teich never mentioned to me in the week that I'd be used as a kicker during the match and my preparation was about playing centre and doing it as well as I had for Western Province in the 1997 Nite Series, which we'd won.

**Os du Randt:** We trained very hard for the second Test in Durban, as we'd done before the first Test. Gary Teichmann had to complain to Carel and Gert Smal before the first Test that they were driving us too hard. He was worried we'd be too weary come Saturday. We may have been, I don't know. But we trained the same way before the second Test, too. I suppose we wanted to train hard – as I say, we were hurting badly, the pressure was on and we were angry. We were going to throw everything at that second Test.

**Percy Montgomery:** The weirdest thing was being in the changing room with guys like André Joubert, Henry Honiball, Os du Randt, André Venter, Ruben Kruger, Mark Andrews, Joost van der Westhuizen and Gary Teichmann. They were Durban, Bloemfontein and Pretoria-based players, but more importantly, some of them were World Cup winners in 1995 and all of them were Springbok icons. I was shy by nature and in that kind of environment, I kept to myself. It wasn't the era in which young okes would hang out with the Bok captain, invite him for a cup of coffee or join his table. It just didn't happen in the Bok set-up then.

As a youngster, you also didn't have an opinion and if you did you didn't share it with guys who'd won the World Cup. I shut up and spoke when spoken to, which wasn't very often that week.

What made it a bit easier was that Danie van Schalkwyk, who made his Bok debut in 1996, had also been recalled to play inside centre. Danie played for the Bulls and was in his early twenties and we got on well. I enjoyed his vibe. He was a funny guy, outgoing and didn't take himself too seriously. We had so many people doubting our ability and questioning how we were going to stand up to Gibbs and Guscott. They were world-class performers who'd played everyone and we were two kids who'd only just met and would be playing together for the first time. But Danie seemed very relaxed and I was calm because I backed myself to do well.

**Danie van Schalkwyk:** I came in with the unique experience of being the only guy in the squad to have played the Lions on the tour and beaten them [with Northern Transvaal]. But you could see that the Lions were a different team at that stage to the one I'd played before. I was feeling good. Confident that I could do a job. I wasn't overly intimidated by the prospect of facing them.

**Percy Montgomery:** It surprised the older guys that Danie and I seemed so comfortable with the occasion, even though they never said anything to us. I can't recall much being said by the senior players and with so many of them being under pressure after losing the first Test, each guy seemed to be looking after himself. It wasn't a 'them and us' situation but because of all the uncertainty about individual places in the team and pressure on winning the Test, each guy, whether it was his first or fiftieth Test, had to fend for himself.

I found Danie easy to get on with and we seemed to enjoy the same things. He didn't think there were many combinations better in the game than Gibbs and Guscott. He respected what they had achieved but, like me, he wasn't overawed by their reputations. Carel believed we were good enough to handle them and that was good enough for me.

**Gary Teichmann:** I spent a lot of time during the week sitting down with players one-to-one to make sure they all understood exactly what was expected of them on Saturday. We couldn't afford any misunderstanding or uncertainty and I told every one of them that while the Lions were clearly a strong side, in terms of talent they weren't in our class.

**Percy Montgomery:** There was no fear of the Lions. The fear I felt in the squad was about the Springboks failing again. The players couldn't believe they'd lost in Cape Town and were convinced they were too good to lose again in Durban, even though they knew they would have to play well to win.

**Gary Teichmann:** I was in the hotel early in the week and Carel, Gert and I went up in the lift together to the top floor – and no one spoke. And I remember thinking, 'Jeez, is it me?' But I think it was just a case that we were all quiet, reserved guys and there was no dominant leader in the group. That was a dangerous mix because you need a central figure to take control at the heart of a team, especially in South Africa. You can see that in all the most successful teams we've ever had: Kitch Christie, Jake White, Nick Mallett, Rassie Erasmus.

Throughout the week I got Mark Andrews and Joost van der Westhuizen to help with motivating the squad. It may have been a funny word or two over a meal or just an aside to a player, but things needed to be said to certain people. We needed to restore confidence, self-belief, even a bit of arrogance to the team. I wasn't a great orator like François had been, but I was absolutely determined that we wouldn't lose to the Lions. We all knew that we had to throw absolutely everything we had at them. It was going to be brutal. We were going to war.

# CHAPTER NINETEEN

# THE ASSASSIN JERRY GUSCOTT

HE DIDN'T KNOW it at the time but Newlands was to be the last we saw of Ieuan Evans in a Lions jersey. The little twinge he'd felt in his groin just before half-time in the first Test turned out to be something more problematic. He thought three days' rest might fix it, but when the Lions went training on the back pitch at Kings Park, Durban, the groin went entirely and took a segment of bone with it for good measure. A horrible tear followed by excruciating pain. Another Lion down. To add to the upset, Evans' mum and dad and his wife and daughter had just landed in South Africa, full of the joys and counting the minutes before he ran out to face the Boks in the second Test.

**John Bentley:** After the team was announced, I went to see Ieuan on my own. There wasn't much I could say. We both knew the situation. I told him I was sorry his tour had come to an end. I was pleased to be in the team, but it wasn't the way I would have preferred. I understood how he felt and would try to fill his boots. He said, 'You deserve your chance, so take the opportunity.'

**Ian McGeechan:** Bentos coming in for Ieuan was the only change we made to the starting line-up. The main focus we had in selection was over the bench. We wanted to have more flexibility there so that we could make tactical switches rather than just replace someone through injury – which was still quite a revolutionary way of thinking at the time. We went for four forwards and two backs instead of the three-three split that was generally used back then. Having been selected to start the first Test only to miss out through illness, Eric Miller made it onto the bench as did Neil Back. They had both played superbly in Bloemfontein, so deserved to be there – and they could change how we wanted to play.

**Eric Miller:** I was just in pieces after I didn't play in the first Test, but it wasn't meant to be. I thought, 'I'm going to go out next week and get back in the team,' and that was probably the right way to go about it, but I was naive. It's very hard to break up a winning side, but I had a belief that I was going to play. If I got picked for the first Test why wouldn't I get picked for the second? I didn't get selected to start, but I made it onto the bench. It wasn't quite what I hoped, but I was determined to give it my all if I came on.

**Richard Hill:** They selected Backy as a replacement, which put some added pressure on my performance. As an out-and-out number seven, he could only really come on in place of me. Telfer felt Backy could provide a different threat out wide if it was needed, while also knowing that by having him on the bench I had to play out of my skin if I wanted to stay on the pitch. It was a sort of blackmail.

**Ian McGeechan:** The two backs subs we picked were Mike Catt and Austin Healey. Between them they could cover every position from nine to fifteen and play each one to a world class standard. As it was, Aus came on and played on the wing.

**Martin Johnson:** In the team meeting on the Thursday night Geech spent forty-five minutes discussing how the Boks would play now that Lubbe and Mulder were out injured. With Montgomery and Van Schalkwyk coming in they were going to have to change their tactics to kick more and drive at us through the forwards, which meant we needed to hold onto the ball more.

**Richard Hill:** We'd put an end to South African claims that we were pussycats. We had celebrated the Test win, but it hadn't been crazy and the next day we got straight back into our routine. As Bentos told a team meeting that week: 'You've won fuck all yet!' And he was right.

**Martin Johnson:** He was spot on. And we knew what was coming our way. Nothing pumps you like a loss, especially a loss at home, and all week they'd been getting it from their fans. The feeling of frustration and all those things: we've all been there, we've all produced performances in those situations. So a storm was coming. And we had to try and back up our performance from the first Test. Again, the nerves are brutal. You know you're going to have to put your body through a battering and, mentally, you have to be on it for every second of the game, which is even more exhausting.

**Ian McGeechan:** I always used to go for a walk in the mornings of games to get my head right and a lot of what I said to the players later came from those walks. Before the second Test I started thinking about the 1974 tour. I remember I had to go to the Leek and Westbourne Building Society and ask the manager if they could hold the mortgage for four months while I went to

South Africa. Those were the days when the local manager could make those calls. I bet you a lot of the other boys on that tour would have similar stories. We were in Port Elizabeth and we were 2–0 up in a four-Test series. The Springboks were coming for us. They'd never lost a series on home soil before so we knew what was going to happen. That was the hardest rugby I ever played. We couldn't get out of our own half. They kept coming at us and we kept putting them down. Tackle after tackle after tackle. You made one, you got up and made another. No words were necessary. We were just operating on instinct and we survived. We won the match and took the series and none of the Lions who were on the field that day will ever forget what it was like.

At 3.30 p.m. the Lions were gathered in the team room at their hotel. All forty-seven members of the tour were there. Fran Cotton spoke to them all about the collective effort that had got them to that moment and emphasised that they had a chance to seal the series that night with a game to spare. Cotton then took his leave of the room along with all those who weren't playing. Twenty-one players with the destiny of the tour in their hands. There was dead silence as Geech moved to the front of the room.

'There are days like this that many rugby players never have,' he began. 'They never experience it. It is special.

'I can tell you that I've given a lot of things up. I love my rugby. I love my family. And when you come to a day like this, you know why you do it all. You know why you've been involved in this. It's been a privilege; it *is* a privilege, because we're something special. Because you'll meet each other in the street in thirty years' time and there'll just be a look and you'll know just how special some days in your life are.

'We've proved that the Lion has claws and has teeth. We've wounded a Springbok. When an animal is wounded, it returns in frenzy. It doesn't think. It fights for its very existence. The Lion waits and, at the right point, it goes for the jugular, and the life disappears.

'Today, every second of that game – we've talked about what they're going to do, or everybody else has – we go for the jugular. Every tackle, every pass, every kick is saying to a fucking Springbok, "You're dying. Your hopes of living in this Test series are going." And on that field sometimes today, all it will be between you is a look. No words, just a look. It'll say everything. And the biggest thing it will say is, "You are special."

'You are very, very special. It has been, and is, a privilege. Go out, enjoy it, remember how you've got here and why. But finish it off, and be special for the rest of your lives. Good luck, go for it.'

**Martin Johnson:** It was awe-inspiring. Exceptional. It caused me real emotion – not something that many pre-match speeches did during my career.

**Gregor Townsend:** I remember it word for word. I remember sitting in that room and him talking about the sacrifices that are made and that stuck with me. And having 'the look' probably didn't register as much at the time, but you realise later the guy's a genius. Because that's what's happened. Twenty years later, you've not seen a guy for years and you can see him and remember exactly where you were on the field that day or during that tour. And from a coaching perspective, what did Geech put into it? He told us what it meant to him personally and how he had sacrificed things for his family, but that it was worth it because he was there with us in that moment. And that meant a lot.

**Ian McGeechan:** I thought about both my parents when

writing that speech. I go back to both my parents, really, but my father, I suppose because he died so young, was particularly in my mind. I thought about how he would walk to work the last two days of the week to give me a fiver in my pocket so I could stand rounds at the bar after the games when I was playing in Headingley's first team. That was a quarter of his wage and I didn't know that until after he died, when my mum said, 'You know, your dad used to get up an hour earlier on Thursdays and Fridays and walk to work.' When I found that out, it motivated me so much. I would never do anything half-cock, I would never half-prepare, I would never take anything for granted, I would never not do anything a hundred per cent because I know what other people had given up to allow me to have the opportunities. I was a kid from a council house and I went on to play for and coach the Lions.

**Matt Dawson:** You think about the first Test and Jim's Everest speech and Geech's speech and it was probably easier to tap into the players' emotions before that match because everyone had written us off and we were coming in as the underdogs. It's a very, very different skill to be able to come up with a motivational speech in week two and week three that still resonates with the players. To be able to hit the same emotional notes and drive the motivation of what was a pretty cynical bunch of individuals was incredible.

**Gregor Townsend:** I think the analogy that really stood out for me was of the springbok and the lion. That really stuck with me. A springbok's wounded; what does a springbok do? It comes out fighting for its life.

**Matt Dawson:** When he started to talk about the springbok being injured, you weren't just thinking about an animal, you were visualising Joost and Venter and Teichmann and Joubert, you were visualising those players hurting and being angry and being bloodied and embarrassed in front of their nation. It was an amazing metaphor. You could have walked out of that meeting and played the game there and then. The real battle was to try and maintain that emotional intensity for the next two and a half hours until kick-off.

**John Bentley:** Some of the lads would talk on the bus to the ground, but most of us were silent. We had a police escort and as you got closer to the ground it was harder to remain focused and not notice what was going on outside. There were Lions fans everywhere, cheering and waving and obviously tons of Springbok supporters. I was impressed that they never stuck two fingers up at us, but they were all jeering and saying, 'You're going to get your arse kicked.'

It was quite intimidating entering Kings Park because when you get off the bus you have to enter the stadium and walk up the touchline to get to the changing rooms. There was another game going on as a curtain-raiser and although a lot of the crowd were having barbecues in the car park there were already 20,000 people in their seats and we got a great reception.

Everyone gets themselves ready in different ways. Then we get in a huddle, just a minute or two before we go out. Some will shout and scream, others dead silent – Jenks is throwing up – and then Johnno has the final say.

The atmosphere at Kings Park was electric. Two hundred Zulu dancers took to the field before kick-off to entertain the crowd and whip the Springbok supporters into a frenzy. Approximately 10,000 travelling Lions fans roared their team onto the pitch, but their cries were nothing compared to the commotion when Gary Teichmann's men sped out of the tunnel.

**Neil Jenkins:** When we ran out, the sound was unbelievable. It gives me goose pimples thinking about it. We'd run out and then they came out and I remember thinking, 'Jesus Christ' – they'd come out that fast and that hard, I thought they were going to run through the stand at the other end of the pitch. You're thinking, 'Here we go. This is proper. This is what it's all about.'

**Jeremy Guscott:** The atmosphere was a different level. We came out of the tunnel and were hit with this wall of noise. It was electric – there were huge blocks of fans in red all around the stadium shouting, 'Lions! Lions! Lions!' Johnno pulled us into a huddle on the halfway line while we waited for the Springboks to come out and Gibbsy started jabbing the air shouting, 'We have to raise our intensity. They're going to come at us with everything they have but we have to smash them back. We have to be better than last week, we have to play harder than we've ever played before.' Then he stared us all in the eye. 'This is ours.'

**John Bentley:** When they ran out . . . I'd never heard anything like it. The noise that came from that stadium was absolutely frightening. We were all gathered in a tight circle and I was shouting, 'Listen to that, let's shut this lot up, we don't want this lot on our back all afternoon.' Nobody could hear me.

**Pieter Rossouw:** The build-up to the Test match . . . ooft. I was quite nervous. It was a big experience. And then when we got out there . . . it was unreal.

**Lawrence Dallaglio:** We're lining up for the South African anthem, I'm between Johnno and Tom and I just remember trying to control the tears in my eyes; the emotion of the moment was so intense. When they finished singing, we turned around and said, 'We're going to do this.' For those of us who were lucky enough to be at Newlands and then in Durban, we experienced something that has bound us together to this day. It was the greatest rugby tour I ever went on and probably the greatest rugby experience of all of our lives. To share that as a group was incredible.

**Martin Johnson:** After we beat them in the first Test, they were doubly determined to try and destroy us in the second Test. At the start of the game, when they get so fired up and they're so passionate you have to try and hold them. The first Test was tough. The second Test we kicked off and I think they drove us back thirty yards. They steamrollered us. I remember I was on the floor, penalised, and I looked up and caught Lawrence's eye, and we knew we just had to hang on for the next fifteen, twenty minutes and try and weather the storm, weather that intention they had to just completely destroy us. 'Christ, we're getting a shock here.' They were so up for beating us. They hate losing to the English and the British particularly for historical reasons.

'We knew that the Springboks would come out steaming,' wrote Stephen Jones in his match report for *The Sunday Times*, 'but the intensity, even the brutality, of their response to the media and public savaging they took last week still took the breath away.'

**Tom Smith:** The South African public doesn't accept defeat easily. The second Test was one of the most intense matches I think I've ever played in. I haven't watched it for a very long time, but I just remember the pace and intensity of the game was extraordinary.

**Richard Hill:** We kicked off and it was immediately clear that Geech was spot on about the frenzy we were going to face. They were way more physical and when they hit contact, there were boots flying everywhere. You could feel the genuine rage in them that we'd beaten them in the first Test.

**Lawrence Dallaglio:** The second Test was the most physical game I played during my entire career – and the first five minutes was complete mayhem. The Springboks came out of the traps and just wanted to blow us apart. They smashed into every contact and looked to dominate us completely. It was a psychological as well as physical confrontation and if we had crumbled then the whole game was gone. We just had to do our best to repel them – but they just kept coming in wave after wave of attack. When we had the ball it was all we could do to try and hold onto it as they smashed us with tackles. But if you can hold out against that kind of physicality and in that kind of environment then you have a chance. Rugby is a game of confrontation, not a game of containment, and it's virtually impossible to win if all you do is contain. Virtually impossible – not impossible.

When the Springboks won an early, and kickable, penalty, Henry Honiball stood up – and missed. When they won another penalty soon after it was Henry Honiball who stood up – and missed again. Six minutes had been played and the Boks had already spurned six precious points.

The Lions had hardly touched the ball. They had one chance to get on the board – and they took it. In a rare lifting of the siege they got into Bok territory, Ruben Kruger dived off his feet to regain a loose ball and referee Didier Mené whistled for a penalty. Where Honiball missed, Jenkins scored. He banged it over with ease. Given the balance of play it was laughable, but the Lions led 3–0.

The Boks were almost feverish in their aggression now. They tore after Honiball's restart and regained possession, then set into a pattern of pounding at the Lions' defence through their massive forwards. Du Randt took a short ball from Van der Westhuizen and made ten yards despite the entire Lions front-row battling in unison to bring him down. Pick and go, pick and go, pick and go – with liberal use of the boot on any red shirts lying on the ground.

**Lawrence Dallaglio:** The South African game plan has pretty much always been the same throughout history. They have some wonderfully talented ball-players, but they've learned that they can win matches in a very simple way. They will run hard and fast at you. If that doesn't work, they will run hard and fast at you. If that doesn't work, they will run hard and fast at you. Over and over again until the opposition breaks. And, to be fair to them, most of the time, the opposition breaks.

**Matt Dawson:** You were just tackling. You knew you were going to be doing a lot of defence and a lot of tackling, a lot of organisation, sticking to the game plan. My role was just to do the things that I practised. Get the ball away, organise. I remember doing so much organisation, talking and organising around the fringes, man-marking Joost.

Having tested and probed the back three with little chips and high balls, the Boks pinned the Lions into the left-hand corner of the field. A scrum penalty against Paul Wallace allowed André Joubert to dink the ball into the corner. The Lions knew what was coming. Du Randt had trundled over with ease from the same position a week earlier.

Andrews won the ball and his forwards piled around him. Big Os quickly took possession and the Boks heaved. The Lions stood firm and the maul collapsed – legally, according to Mené – and play continued. Van der Westhuizen screamed and cajoled and beat his players with his fists to get them into position to go again. They drove forward. Again, the Lions just held out. The Boks were just a foot or two away from the line now.

**Os du Randt:** I was at the forefront of a lot of our driving moves but the Lions' defence held amazingly well. We dominated them, we were just unable to score. Tim Rodber and Scott Gibbs, especially, tackled their hearts out.

**Alan Tait:** Lawrence and Tim were pivotal in stopping the likes of Teichmann supporting Honiball in open play. The way we planned it, Honiball had to be checked because he was one of the best ball-players I'd ever seen – he could offload a pass at any time and in any situation. But, if the support runners were covered, he'd have no one to offload to. So Lawrence and Tim worked hard on taking out Teichmann and Venter and Kruger and also working hard to smash the other Springbok forwards when they came round the side of rucks.

**Ian McGeechan:** They couldn't work out what we were doing with Honiball. All they could see was that he wasn't playing like he usually did, they didn't see it was because we were putting players in certain positions to manipulate him.

**Martin Johnson:** Honiball was a huge focus for us. We knew that their biggest attacking threat in the backs was Honiball coming up fast to the line with wingers either side of him and he'd either carry or dummy. What was his nickname, the Blade? Killing people. We just had a very simple defence against him – go up to the line, put forwards in places giving him no space to run while ensuring that his runners were all covered. And by doing that we negated Honiball as an attacking force. They scored tries, but they didn't score them through him particularly. We took him out of the series.

**Gary Teichmann:** I think it's fair to say that their defence surprised us. They were pretty much a scratch team, but they defended so well for large chunks of the series, as if they'd been working together for years. We got on top of them as a pack, but they managed to hold out on a number of occasions when it looked like we were about to score. We were dominating but they defended their line very, very well.

**Os du Randt:** They had a huge amount of passion for each other and that helped them play beyond themselves, to withstand us. It was a do-or-die game. And it was an epic occasion of two sides going hard at it – one to seal the series, one to stay alive in the series. Take Martin Johnson – you could see the passion in him. It was so big you almost hated him for it. He was in your face and shouting and rallying everyone around him. That's the picture I remember. As a leader he pulled the others players up and they wanted to follow him.

The Springboks had another penalty. Gary Teichmann contemplated his options for a few seconds but eventually settled for the pragmatic choice and pointed to the posts. This time, however, it was Percy Montgomery who lined up the shot. It was from a straightforward position – on the twenty-two and fifteen metres in from the left-hand touchline. His contact was horrible. The ball torpedoed wide past the left-hand upright. Three attempts, three misses, nine points wasted.

The psychological game within a game carried on when Jenkins rifled over his second penalty, cool as a breeze. The Lions had no ball, no momentum, had spent much of the game hanging on and yet led 6–0.

**Neil Jenkins:** If as a goal kicker, your mentality is, 'why has all this responsibility fallen on me?', more often than not, you're going to miss. You have to want to do it. You want that kick to win a Test match, you want to be in a position where you think, 'Crikey Moses, this is all about me. I'd better put this over.' Not once do the demons come inside your head. There's none of that. You think, 'This is what I've built for, this is what I do, this is an opportunity for me to win the game for the boys and for my country.' That's what it comes down to. That's why you practise so hard and put the hours in.

**Jim Telfer:** A lot of our players froze in the second Test and we didn't play well at all. But we hung on in there and that was the key. Neil just kept slotting over the kicks and kept us in it – but to be fair, we were getting ourselves into pretty good positions and then they'd give away a penalty to stop us. Neil wasn't the longest kicker, but he was so accurate.

Back came the Springboks. They had a lineout close to the Lions' try-line. Drotske to Andrews to Du Randt and the maul began to trundle. One again it was repelled. Van der Westhuizen fed Kruger down the blindside, but he was barrelled into touch right on the corner flag by Davidson and Tait. Mené brought them back for a penalty, Van der Westhuizen didn't hang about. He tapped and fed Kruger again, who was stopped inches short. The pack began to pick and go, waiting for a crack or a fault in the defensive wall. 'I can't believe what I'm seeing,' said Stuart Barnes in commentary. 'The power that South Africa are exerting is unbelievable.' Teichmann picked and darted blind. He was brought down by Dallaglio and in the chaotic few seconds that followed, Van der Westhuizen spotted a gap and went over.

**Carel du Plessis:** There were obvious weaknesses in Joost's game. He sometimes lost control of his skills, notably in kicking, but he was such a unique opportunist. He was daring and impulsive. My overall approach was to give players the space and freedom to play their natural game. I hoped Joost would learn to conceal his weak points if he could be liberated from instructions. I wanted to create an environment in which he felt confident in himself. Then we'd benefit from his hard, elusive presence on the field. That was my general philosophy.

**Matt Dawson:** It was so frustrating because we'd done so much homework on him. Our fringe defence had been pretty good until then, marshalling the fringes verbally, shouting, 'Here comes Joost, no dummies, no dummies, don't fall for it.' You'd be eyeballing him, watching him thinking about making those breaks, but you just couldn't take your eyes off him for a second.

The conversion fell to Montgomery – and he missed again. Four shots at goal, four failures, eleven points that they might have had but didn't. Instead of being halfway towards victory, the Boks trailed 6–5.

But they could still sense blood. Honiball laced another superb kick deep into the Lions' twenty-two and his forwards roared at one another to keep the pressure up. The Lions needed an act of inspiration to regain a foothold in the game. On thirty-seven minutes, they found one. From the lineout, Dawson sent up a towering box kick to clear. Underneath the catch was the debutant Pieter Rossouw, who had barely been involved so far in the game. His only act had been to collect a high ball from a Dawson box kick after which he had been clattered by his opposite man, John Bentley. History was about to repeat itself.

**Pieter Rossouw:** I'd watched him on tour and knew he was a big ball-carrier and that if he got any possession, I had to tackle him as soon as he got the ball to try and stop him. Well, neither of us had done much in the game up to that point, but then they kicked a big up-and-under and I realised that the ball and him were going to be coming to me at the same time. As I caught it, he was already flying through the air. He almost killed me.

'What a tackle!' cried Miles Harrison in commentary for Sky. 'And it's won the penalty.'

**John Bentley:** I didn't play particularly well in that match, but I did get a couple of good hits in on Rossouw.

It was a moment that released the pressure. Dawson tapped and darted and then fed Dallaglio, who broke into midfield and passed to Guscott. Play broke down there, but Dawson had caught South Africa offside with his tap and go and the resulting penalty allowed Jenkins to kick the Lions down the far twenty-two. In the space of the a few seconds they had worked their way from one end to the other. Momentum felt like it was shifting.

**Lawrence Dallaglio:** I remember getting into the changing room at half-time and everyone was so exhausted that it was pretty much silent for the first two or three minutes – you were just sucking in oxygen. It's funny, when you're watching a game you don't realise just how fatigued the players actually are. What you don't want in these half-time moments is a long essay of what needs changing. Ordinarily the mindset is to get two or three bullet points that you can remember to take into the second half. Geech spoke to the backs, Jim to the forwards, then Johnno spoke to everyone. I think Woody and myself probably then piped up something, but I also remember Jerry speaking.

**Jeremy Guscott:** I thought we'd gone into our shells. You're lucky to have these moments at half-time to speak to everyone in a relatively calm environment, and you don't want to waste them. We were close to making history and to freeze, which was pretty much what we were doing, would have been absolutely tragic. We weren't playing our best rugby, and we were more nervous than we should have been – but that's the occasion. They weren't letting us play and they were preferring to give penalties away to stop our attack. If they hadn't given so many penalties away, maybe we'd have scored tries.

'If we work as hard in attack as we are in defence, we'd fucking wipe them off the field,' said Guscott at the break. 'There's no ambition in attack at the moment. We're just happy to go from one set piece to another; we're not working any phases of play. We have to work *twice* as hard in attack. Defence is what we've worked on all tour – it's in our heads, it's natural. Now we've got to work some attack. Just pop the ball up. There's one person running, there's another person outside him – let's fucking use him. They're lining us up. Now let's play some fucking rugby.'

**Jeremy Guscott:** There are moments when you feel you've just got to say something. If you don't say it . . . I didn't want to have any regrets. There was so much at stake. The first Test was relaxing in comparison. If South Africa lost that second Test, they had no chance. It was over. If they won it, all the momentum was going to be with them going into the third Test. We were at an absolutely critical point in the series and the pressure was unbelievably intense. There are some players that are better at coping with it than others. You think about Keith Wood, Martin Johnson and all these great players. They're able to deal with it. For a forward, it's a different proposition, because the intensity is always there. You're always in the game, you're always in the mix, you're scrummaging, you're working at lineouts, at the breakdown. It must be brilliant to be a forward because you're just *in it*, all the time. When you're an outside back, sometimes you think, 'Bloody hell, I hope I don't fuck this up.' You might not have touched the ball for ten minutes. *I* never thought like that. *I* never had any doubt about what I could do and what I couldn't do. I wanted the ball – give it, let me have it. Your subconscious will take you to different places. It's about dealing with the pressure and trying not to let it affect you.

Neither side had made any changes at half-time and while Guscott had been extolling the need for more creativity in attack, the Boks had obviously been making some tactical decisions of their own. With Honiball having caught Jenkins out positionally a few times with his raking touch-finders, he now wanted to challenge the converted full back's ability under the high ball. The second half was just thirty seconds old when he slammed a huge high ball into the heavens. Jenkins came forward to gather it just outside his twenty-two, but bobbled it and lost control. Tait was able to gather the loose ball and he stepped off his left foot to try and get away from the smothering defence that was suddenly all around him. Under huge pressure he tried to keep the ball alive, slipping an offload out the back of his left hand. But there was only one player standing there – Honiball. The stand-off skipped into space, drew in the covering Gibbs and put the ball on a plate for Van Schalkwyk. Guscott tried to shut him down, but the centre drifted a lovely little pass over Guscott's head to Montgomery who flew in for a try on his debut.

**Alan Tait:** We were inside our own twenty-two and as I was scrag tackled I heard a call of 'yep' next to me, so I passed inside – only to realise it was Honiball who'd called for it. Try-time to the Springboks. For a moment all I could think of was how horrific it would be that if we lost that Test and then the series it might all be traced back to that single moment. And to me.

**Jeremy Guscott:** We're standing under the posts and I'm thinking, 'Well, my speech didn't do much good.'

**Gregor Townsend:** It did, though. Jerry was absolutely right, we needed to play more. Yeah, Taity shouldn't have been trying to offload when we were under pressure like that in our twenty-two, but at the same time we had to try and be a bit more ambitious. It was a massive setback to lose that try so early in the second half but from there we continued to try and play and it forced them into giving away penalties to stop us.

Montgomery lined up the kick to convert his try. This time, instead of hooking it, he sliced it past the left-hand post. Five kicks, five misses, thirteen points left behind them. The Lions trailed two tries to nil but were just four points behind on the board.

**Keith Wood:** People say they didn't go in with recognised kickers. They did. They had really good kickers but they crumbled under the pressure of the series. Whatever it is about the Lions, there is a crazy intensity. Crazy. And mad things happen in that sort of pressure.

The Lions were in trouble, but they weren't dead. They needed something to happen, some reason to believe. When it came it was Scott Gibbs at the centre of it. In the grand scheme it was just a big carry, but it meant so much more than that in the moment. The Welshman went blasting at Os du Randt and put the big man on his arse. It led to a penalty which Jenkins put over. Even all these years later people still talk about the collision between Gibbs and Du Randt and how Gibbs left him behind like roadkill.

**Fran Cotton:** Scotty gave us hope with that run. To this day I can see him glancing casually down on poor Os as he struggled to get his senses together.

**Dai Young:** It's gone down in history. That was a big deal for the South Africans, they were showing that on every TV screen in the country. That would have shaken them up and it went a big way to proving we were more than capable of mixing with them physically.

**Jeremy Guscott:** Gibbsy wanted to take on the Springboks all by himself. He was so pumped up that he just wanted to smash anything in a green jersey. He wanted to smash them to the ground. He's not the biggest bloke in the world, but he would have taken on anyone that day. That moment with Os du Randt . . . it was one of the most inspiring moments I've ever experienced on a rugby field.

**Richard Hill:** It was one of those moments you're never going to forget. I can still hear the collision.

**Scott Gibbs:** I hit Os good. He was definitely winded. It doesn't happen often, but when people get really walloped, and they get winded, they start to sound like a cow, you know, 'Mooooo'. And that's what happened to him. It tickled Jerry more than it tickled me.

**Os du Randt:** Ja, it was a big hit. Still makes me pretty angry that he got through.

**Dai Young:** Gibbsy could do anything. He could run over people, he could run round people. He was a real driver of standards as well. We all saw what he did to Os du Randt and you just can't help but look up to him, can you? Jesus Christ, let's follow him.

**Jim Telfer:** When I first met Scott Gibbs, he was so intimidating. He used to shout at the centre opposite him in games: 'I'm gonna get you! I'm gonna get you!' And then he would. By Christ, he would. And that kind of thing would lift the spirits of the other fellas around him.

**Jeremy Guscott:** We won a penalty from the ruck when Gibbsy was eventually brought to ground and as he jogged back I heard him say to Du Randt, 'Get up, you fat ox.'

**Scott Gibbs:** I've always liked to do a bit of trash talking. I got really into it. In the first Test, Japie Mulder was tearing his hair out because he just wanted to throttle me. He was trying to get close and trying to get a good hit. I know he was getting frustrated because I remember Joost telling me a story later on about it. He was saying, 'I'm going to rip his head off, but I can't get to him!' With the midfield, you never really defend your opposite number. That's not the guy giving you any trouble. It's the guys coming on the inside. The sevens and sixes of the world. They're the biggest nemeses for a number twelve. They're the people you need to be worried about.

I don't know the dimensions of Os. I think he probably got taller as he got older. But he had a very good Test series. I watched the three Tests back to back recently, during the first Covid lockdown, and he had a very, very strong Test series. That collision was probably at the halfway point of the three games, but it was definitely a watershed moment. When I knocked him over and spun out and offloaded to Jeremy Davidson, it really kept us in the game and kept pressure on them because it resulted in Jenks kicking a penalty.

Everyone in their team looked to Gary Teichmann for inspiration and once his head dropped, I could see everybody else's head drop. The moment their body language changed, I started to get super excited. I was constantly taunting Gary Teichmann and the back rowers – 'Run at me, you dickhead!' – and Jerry would gently pull on my jersey and go, 'Shut the fuck up, will you. You're winding them up.' And I'd say, 'Exactly!'

**Jeremy Guscott:** The fuckers would then run at me.

**Alan Tait:** That's the league mentality. When I first went to league, I couldn't believe the banter and the verbals they used to give each other. 'Run at me!' they'd be shouting at each other. 'Run at me! I'm going to knock your fucking head off, run at me!' And it would have an impact on you. I used to shake my head, going, 'These boys are nuts, like,' but it was all part of that sort of psychology of 'I'm on top, you can't hurt me.' It was something I learned, too. I remember taking a few big tackles on the tour – there was one against Western Province when I got properly buried – and the key was to get up and just say, 'Aye, good shot, pal,' because that upset them more than throwing a punch. If you can just get up and say, 'Yeah, good shot, but I'm not bothered,' that used to wind them up more than anything.

**Neil Jenkins:** I've known Gibbsy all my life. We're the same age. Played together, played against each other. He's a horrific man to tackle, I'm telling you straight. He's so quick, so strong, so agile. You try and brace yourself for him – if he comes straight at you and you're half-cocked, you're in a ton of shit. I'm not lying, a *ton* of shit. But then he can also sidestep you as well. He'll be going full tilt and then decide, 'I'm not going to go through you, I'm just going to sidestep you this time.' He was exceptional and he was always like that from a young age. The size of him, you know – his legs, his physicality. He was a fantastic player, Gibbsy, one of the best I ever played with.

The Lions were one point behind, the man from Pontypridd keeping them in the game with his unerring boot, but there was a response coming. Having already fluffed his lines under the bomb that had led to Montgomery's try, Jenkins was found wanting again less than a minute after the restart. Honiball launched a huge up-and-under into the Lions' twenty-two and as it came back down from outer space Jenkins didn't lay a glove on it. It bounced in no-man's land and the Boks were quickest to react, regaining possession through the chasing Honiball. It was only when André Venter flew off his feet at a ruck five phases later, with the line just metres away, that the Lions got a reprieve, but Jenkins' vulnerability under the high ball was fast becoming a concern.

The Lions escaped, but not for long. With fifty-five minutes on the clock, Honiball floated a wide pass to Joubert that caught Bentley flat-footed. The Springbok swatted Bentley aside and accelerated away from Jenkins to score in the corner – a third try for the Boks.

**Pieter Rossouw:** Juba bumped off Bentley and went through. I was running on his shoulder, looking for the pass, but he went and scored. It was fitting that he scored – in Durban, in front of his home crowd. He was an unbelievable player.

**Jim Telfer:** Bentley's error was unforgivable – he went far too high. And a faster full back would have caught Joubert.

**Ian McGeechan:** But that's the trade-off we made for

manufacturing Jenks into a full back. He was weak under the high ball and he was slow for a fifteen, but he brought us benefits that other full backs couldn't.

Kings Park was rocking again. Joubert had played below his best in the series, but he had just produced a piece of pure class when it mattered most. He sucked on a water bottle as he walked back, the ball in the crook of his arm. The kicking duties had now been passed to him. He set it down just inside the touchline, a horribly difficult angle. He tried to keep it low and scud it through the posts, but it was a poor effort. They'd now had six pots at goal and six misses.

**Gary Teichmann:** We were all over the place with our kicking, for which I have to take part of the blame. We started off with Lem [Honiball] as the kicker, then Percy and then, by the end of the game, André. Maybe if I'd asked André to kick at the beginning, it could have turned out differently. I don't blame him for that conversion, that angle is as hard as it gets for a kicker.

**Percy Montgomery:** I wasn't the first-choice kicker and didn't think I would be kicking – that makes a difference to any player's approach during the week. Henry started the game as the goal kicker and after he missed twice, Gary handed me the ball and told me to give it my best. On the day, my best wasn't good enough and when we scored our third try to take the lead, André was given the responsibility and I was only too pleased.

You look back now and you have a different perspective on things, but even then it was a bit strange that there was no real emphasis on the goal kicking going into the Test. Henry and André were the recognised kickers and I'd kicked for Western Province in the pre-season tour to Argentina, in the Nite Series final against Boland and against the Lions, but that was the total of my kicking in 1997 and I never thought I'd be taking the kicks in my Test debut. There was not much intensity about how I practised my goal kicking that week. I'd have a few kicks with Henry and André after training and that was it.

**Jeremy Guscott:** Montgomery had just come on the scene, and he wasn't the kicker then that he was to become later on. Honiball was a bit hit and miss. I don't really know what Joubert was like at kicking, but he wasn't good that day either. You have days like that, don't you? Some days, even Jonny Wilkinson missed, even Neil Jenkins missed. You have off days and thankfully they were all having an off day.

**Percy Montgomery:** A lot of people have never forgiven me for those misses and don't seem to remember I wasn't the only one who missed that day.

**Gary Teichmann:** I have regrets, of course I do. I could have done things differently. Percy was new to international rugby and playing centre. Because of the guy Percy is, and the perception that was created, the public didn't like him, and his selection wasn't popular. So he must have felt massive pressure in what was his first series for the Springboks. I could have taken the pressure off him and given the goal kicking duties to André earlier, who didn't feel pressure the same way other players did.

And then I could perhaps have communicated better with the coaches and explained what they were doing wrong; I could have suggested different approaches and modes of behaviour. But I suppose if you look at the three of us – Carel, Gert and me – none of us are very communicative or forceful people. We were strong in our own ways, but not in the way that Nick Mallett was, for example. What I should have done is gone to Carel and

Gert and said, 'Look, we need a definite game plan here and we need to know who the kicker is and stick with him.'

**Os du Randt:** I don't think any of us were really that worried about the kicking at that stage. We were starting to play well and were getting into a good rhythm. We were breaking the Lions down and I felt like we were getting on top of them. With twenty-five minutes remaining we were leading 15–9 and everybody expected the Lions to get a hiding.

**Jeremy Guscott:** You thought, 'When are these guys going to stop coming?' They were just relentless and it was all defence on our side.

The Lions changed tack slightly and began to ping the ball to the corners, trying to gain some territory. Townsend's kicking came to the fore here and he used a variety of deft chips and booming punts to pin the Boks back in their half. As one of these bounced into touch on the South African ten-metre line, the electric sideline boards went up to signal a change in the Lions' back-row. Neil Back was coming on for the exhausted Richard Hill. Immediately, Back slotted into the role of Canute trying to hold back the sea.

**Joost van der Westhuizen:** We were all over them. I can't remember any Test where one side enjoyed so much ground advantage over the other.

Sixty-five minutes had passed when Townsend sent a low torpedo kick from just inside his own half down past the Springbok ten-metre line. Snyman ducked to gather it on the run, but Didier Mené deemed that he had knocked on in the process – and the green and gold sections of the Kings Park crowd loudly voiced their disagreement. At the subsequent scrum, Venter broke his bind early – a misdemeanour he had already been penalised for twice during the game – and Johnson pointed at the posts.

**Gary Teichmann:** André was getting so frustrated. He'd been penalised for the same thing a few minutes earlier, when we were on attack, and neither infringement had had any material effect on the play. I remember him throwing his hands up in the air at the ref and saying, 'I just don't understand this.' It felt like we were being whistled out of the game.

**Martin Johnson:** Didier Mené was a lovely guy, a little Frenchman with little round spectacles on, who looked like a maths teacher from your local secondary school. But I think the big South Africans, in the heat of the Test match, didn't want to listen to him. And obviously he's French-speaking and they're Afrikaans-speaking mainly, so English is a second language for both of them, and they're trying to communicate and it wasn't really working that well. André Venter and Ruben Kruger were starting to annoy Mené. He was trying to tell them things and they wouldn't listen or they didn't understand or whatever and I thought, 'We'll get penalties here.' And we did.

**Neil Jenkins:** When I was taking kicks, my thoughts always drifted to where I'm from in Church Village, my pitch in Cae Fardre. I practised there all my life, and that was always the best place for me to be. Wherever I've played – Cardiff Arms Park, Twickenham, Paris, Newlands or anywhere in Australia or New Zealand, I've never ever imagined I was actually there. That's how I made things easy for myself. If I actually thought and understood what I was *actually* doing, I probably would have crumbled and had a shocker. If you want to be a good goal kicker, you have to have the best temperament. If you haven't got the temperament, you ain't gonna be a goal kicker. It's plain and simple. I was always very good at transporting myself back to where I practised. I was never at any of the big stadiums; I was just a kid again practising back at Cae Fardre. You know, you kick your goals for fun. That's what it comes down to. Technically, you'll work hard and get yourself right and comfortable, but your temperament is by far the most important thing. If you can combine technical excellence with the right temperament, chances are you'll become a world-class goal kicker. Like my dad and I have always said, 'Pressure is for other people'. Any opportunity for you to step up and win the game, that's what you practise all week for, and that's where the fun comes. If you've grown up thinking about doing that, I guess it becomes second nature.

Amid a clamour of whistles and boos, Jenkins sent the ball through the posts yet again; 15–12, the Lions were inching back into the game again.

There were just eight minutes left when the Lions decided to throw caution to the wind and began to redeploy their offloading game. Tim Rodber carried to the Springboks' ten-metre line and slipped it to Lawrence Dallaglio, who charged into space. Gregor Townsend and Paul Wallace came into the attack, the prop accelerating onto the ball and rampaging up to the twenty-two. A few moments later, Mené did Teichmann for hands in the ruck. Jenkins made it 15–15.

**Gary Teichmann:** Throughout that game, it felt like we couldn't do anything right in the ref's eyes.

**Neil Jenkins:** The pressure mounted with each kick, but every time I just took myself away to Cae Fardre. Same routine and, thankfully, same result. People always ask about pressure kicks, but that is what goal kickers live for. You don't hope the chance never comes, you pray it does. The fifth and final penalty was probably the most important of my career, but I approached it as any other and managed to keep the pressure at bay. I nailed it.

**Tim Stimpson:** Neil Jenkins is arguably the most mentally tough goal kicker there has ever been. He played so many games with so little ability. I'm joking, obviously – I love the guy. But he didn't have power, he didn't have pace. He had an ability to go to the line and pass the ball and he did his basics really well, but he didn't offer a threat on his own apart from being mentally hard as nails when it came to goal kicking and that proved absolutely critical. If Henry Honiball had been Neil Jenkins, we'd be talking about a three-nil whitewash for the Springboks, wouldn't we? Tough Test matches don't come down to twenty points, it's always one or two points.

**Jeremy Guscott:** Jenks in that series, he was better than Jonny Wilkinson at his peak. It was just metronomic to watch. Boom, boom, boom: between the posts, between the posts, between the posts. He was a fucking machine.

**Keith Wood:** This is a good story that no one knows. I tore my ankle ligaments in the first match and we strapped it. I kept strapping it for training and it was sore but it was manageable. I went over it a couple of times in the second Test. With maybe fifteen or twenty minutes to go I went down, I was shattered. That's not a place you ever want to be. Scott Gibbs caught my eye and I was convinced that he thought I was giving up. And he shouted at me, 'Woody, get back up on the line and make the next fucking tackle.' And I jumped up and I got back into the line and I don't know if I made the next tackle or not but I was there for it. I said this to him about ten years ago and he said, 'I'm glad you picked that up. I knew you were fucking chickening out.' And I said, 'I thought I was gone, I thought I was empty, I thought I had nothing left to give,' and I didn't have anything left to give, but out of embarrassment, I got up.

**Gregor Townsend:** I played pretty controlled rugby throughout the game, but I did do one thing and Jim's reaction was captured on the video: 'No, no, Gregor you're wrong, you're wrong, man!' Stuart Hogg always likes to say that to me. I ran and got turned over. I could probably hear Telfer, even though he was up in the stand. 'No! Kick the ball to touch!'

Joost van der Westhuizen dinked a chip over the top of the ruck, but Bentley was onto it. Against all perceived logic for the position he found himself in, he began to run across field, weaving his way past defenders. He was closed down by Teichmann and threw a loose pass to Tait that bobbled across the ground. Tait gathered it and then tried to toe-poke it down the line. The ball was leapt on by Honiball and Guscott leapt on him. Four Springbok forwards converged on the ruck. On the other side, Back burrowed his way in behind Guscott, barely visible amid the mass of huge green shirts. Somehow he emerged with the ball and laid it back on the Lions' side.

**Martin Johnson:** I'd given the ball up for dead. I didn't go into the ruck. You know, no point committing, it's gone. So Neil's in the ruck by himself with about five Springboks and he steals the ball.

**Lawrence Dallaglio:** I don't think any other player in the world could have pinched it. He was always exceptional at the breakdown. Good running lines got him there quickly and because he's small it was hard for referees to know whether he was on his feet or not. He was very canny and didn't attract the referee's attention the way a bigger man would, yet he was virtually impossible to knock off the ball. Total class.

Dawson was screaming at the touch judge to signal that his side had won the ball and that play should be allowed to continue. When he turned back to pick up the ball he saw that it was gone. Keith Wood had picked it up and, in the blink of an eye, box kicked it downfield.

**Fran Cotton:** We turned them over at a ruck, Woody kicked through and chased incredibly well, forcing Percy Montgomery to hack the ball out, giving us the throw inside their twenty-two. That was a game-changing moment.

**Jim Telfer:** It was all Neil Back's doing. Richard Hill had gone off and Neil came on and won the turnover on halfway. I'm not normally a fan of hookers kicking, but Keith Wood put in a pearler that got us down into their twenty-two.

**Keith Wood:** The ball popped out and I just kicked it. And then I went, 'Jesus, I have to run after it now.' I ran up and Montgomery ran it into touch. He probably didn't realise it was me and how fucked I was. If he had, he could have sidestepped me no bother, but he gathered the ball and ran into touch and I just fell over. Absolutely shattered. It's actually so embarrassing for me to look back on that clip because I'm so fucked. My ankle is absolutely screaming, my lungs are on fire, I have nothing left. But now I have to try and gather myself to throw in at the lineout. Jesus, you talk about pressurised moments . . .

**Jeremy Davidson:** Johnno called the throw to me. We had to win it. How long was left? Four and a half minutes? All-square.

This could be our last chance down here. Fair dos to Johnno for being objective and being able to call the right options for the team. He had confidence in me, which was huge because I was only twenty-three. Up I went and won it cleanly. Step one, done.

**Gregor Townsend:** We mauled it from the lineout and made it about six or seven metres from the line. I remember seeing Tim Rodber holding in Van Heerden at the side of the maul and creating a space. There was a gap between the first defender and maul that hadn't been closed, so I went really flat and Daws passed me the ball and I got half through.

**Keith Wood:** Rodber gets hit with a swinging punch from Van Heerden that splits him over the eye, a big cut. And Rodber stops, cocks his fist and then goes and cleans out the ruck. He never hit him. And that, for me, that discipline at that moment in time is extraordinary. You're talking five minutes to go in a Test match, you're talking guys that are running on fumes, so tired, very few subs used in those days, absolutely wrecked, and you get hit, and you could almost see the gears cranking to the decision: 'No, clear the ruck.'

**Gregor Townsend:** It was one of those moments where you're kind of spinning and pumping the legs and I wondered about whether to try and lunge for the line. In a previous season for a different team I might have tried to lunge and hope my strength could get me over. But in a situation like that, you don't go for the risky play; you can't have the Test series decided on a selfish act like that, so I set up the ball.

**Ian McGeechan:** Gregor took a brilliant line back at them which is why he wasn't there when the ball came out, but what he'd done was put them on the back foot.

**Gregor Townsend:** As soon as Jenks saw me go he drifted in straight behind the ruck, into the pocket for the drop goal, and Guscott came into first receiver just to the right as another option. Daws gets the ball and you can see on the video that he looks at both of them as he comes up with the ball. He shapes to give it to Jenks and then changes his mind and passes it out to Jerry.

**Fran Cotton:** When Jerry got the ball I remember thinking, 'Well, there's no way Jerry Guscott is going to miss this.'

In the maelstrom, Guscott didn't just retreat into a pocket when taking Matt Dawson's pass, he entered his own little world where doubt played no part, where only certainty existed. He didn't notice the Springboks charging at him in a mad frenzy, he didn't notice the crowd, he just struck a ball high and true like he was doing it on a training night at the Rec. No sweat, no panic. He did what he was born to do. The Lions led 18–15.

**Gregor Townsend:** Drop goals are a lot to do with confidence. If you think about it too much or worry about a guy charging you down, you're not going to follow through. But with Jerry it was just, 'Give it to me, I'll whack it over.' He had the most confidence of anyone in that group. The right player at the right time.

**Jeremy Guscott:** Austin Healey was outside me and he always maintains that he would have been in for a try if I'd passed it.

**Austin Healey:** I reckon I would have had pretty much a clear run to the posts if he'd passed it.

**Jeremy Guscott:** Thank fuck that didn't happen. Can you imagine if Aus had been the one that won the series?

**Austin Healey:** The one thing he would have been able to hear was me shouting: 'You greedy bastard!'

**Jeremy Guscott:** Some people say 'it had to be you' and it's like '*fuck*, it had to be you' or '*why* did it have to be you?' because their perception would be 'we're not going to hear the last of it'. The reality is, 'thank fuck it was you, because who else could have dropped it over. Thanks for doing it.' There are any number of thoughts in that way, but all I am is someone who did it. There's no more or less. It's a nice bit in a fantastic story, but it's a grain of a much bigger story. The story is the Lions. It's part of Lions history, but everyone on that tour will be part of it. My bit – that drop goal – will be underlined a little bit more than anything else.

**Gary Teichmann:** That drop goal is one of those rugby moments that's going to be etched on my memory forever. I can remember every moment of the build-up. The kick downfield from Keith Wood, the lineout, the carry from Townsend. I remember shouting that we had to watch Neil Jenkins going for the drop goal because he'd dropped deep into the pocket, but the ball went to Guscott instead. I can still remember reaching out to try and charge him down.

**Jeremy Davidson:** I've got a picture of the drop goal and you can just see one of my feet sticking up out of the ruck before it. I've watched it on video so many times since and it still gives me shivers down the spine.

**Jeremy Guscott:** If you'd seen me spraying drop-kicks all over the pitch in training during the previous week – off the outside of my foot, off the inside of my foot, off the end of my toes – you would have bet as much money on me putting it over as you would on a one-legged man in a backside-kicking competition. But I'd played fly-half from the ages of seven to nineteen, and the natural decision was made when Matt Dawson passed me the ball. I saw it unfolding and made the decision without anyone saying anything to me.

That drop goal – I've seen it so I know what happened, but I couldn't talk you through what was going through my head. I was just part of a team and I ended up being where I was. I don't remember consciously thinking, 'I must get into the first receiver position', I just did it. I don't want to make a song and dance about it. If someone had jumped in there before me, who I felt was capable of catching the ball, I'd have just moved out. But if someone like Paul Wallace got in front of me, I'd have told him to fuck off because there's no way he'd have caught the ball.

It went end over end, it went through the middle, it was going up as it went through the posts. It was more like a punch golf swing. I punched it. It wasn't like a big follow-through of a kick. There wasn't any follow-through. It was more of a shunt. I didn't feel like I had a lot of time. I knew what I was going to do. It came out, and *boom*, I just knocked it through. It's a moment in time. I like the feeling it gives me when thinking about what happened.

**Keith Wood:** Guscott is magic and he's cool as a breeze, but he's shy and the cool as a breeze thing is maybe his safety blanket. He's a great guy, like a really great guy, and I may have seen more of Guscott than I have of any of the other guys who I played in the Lions with, working with him on the BBC for years and a few other different things that we do together: I see a lot of him. He played really well in the midweek matches because we were playing with space and, I mean, he was the most beautiful runner, he just had this gliding run. I mean, Jesus. But in the Tests, he didn't get a chance to shine. He didn't get a huge amount to do. He had a quiet series.

This is totally random, but maybe it fits. I watched Newcastle play once and Alan Shearer was up front. He was offside eight times. Miles off. Didn't make a huge effort to get onside either. I was thinking, 'Jesus, that guy is so lazy, he doesn't give a shit.' It's 0–0 late in the game and then, *bang!* Goal for Shearer. They win 1–0. He had one chance. That was Jerry in the Test series. One chance. *Bang!* We're not playing a game that suits him at all. And he's not getting the run of the game. Nothing's coming his way, but he manages to keep his concentration when a game has been almost the anti-Jerry Guscott game and he's still present in the moment when he needs to be. That's world class. He was an assassin.

And then I tore my groin with about two or three minutes to go – and that's a bad injury. I tried to go off and they wouldn't let me go off, so I scrummaged a couple of scrums with a torn groin. You ask about tiredness. When Jenkins kicked it into the stand on full-time there's pictures of people running and jumping all over the place, but there's very few of me. I had nothing left. I was in agony. I was glad it was over. I was glad we'd won, but it was the most tired I ever felt in my life. There was nothing left in the tank.

**Ian McGeechan:** Of all my rugby moments, the sound of that final whistle in Durban in 1997 was probably the sweetest, perhaps even shading the Scotland Grand Slam in 1990.

**Gary Teichmann:** I felt instantly drained. It was so hard to accept that we'd lost a match that we'd completely dominated.

**Os du Randt:** At full time? Devastated.

**Keith Wood:** Did I understand how devastating it was for the Springboks? I didn't care. I didn't. I couldn't even appreciate my own excitement. All I wanted to do was go in and sit down. The day after, I put a disc out in my back bending down to pick up my shoes.

**Ian McGeechan:** When we were dissecting the game afterwards we had to admit that we hadn't played at all well, we'd not set up our own game and, on occasion, we'd been bullied. But we'd stayed the course and won the series in the face of a relentless South African onslaught.

**Gary Teichmann:** We dominated long periods of the game and scored three tries to nil. Each player hit his personal targets. Yeah, we missed a few try-scoring chances and we could have been more physical at the beginning, but no one let us down on the day. It was also the most disappointing day of my entire rugby career. Even now I find it hard to understand how we lost. We deserved to win by twenty points. I'm not exaggerating. Forget about the goal kicking. We were the better team in every phase of the game.

**Neil Jenkins:** I felt for South Africa's kickers because it's probably the loneliest role in rugby. You're out there, in front of 50,000 people, knowing you could make a complete fool of yourself and cost your side the match. But it's only rarely that I felt the pressure to succeed. I liked to pick out a spot in the stand directly behind the middle of the posts and aim for it. Then it was just me, the ball and the posts.

**Os du Randt:** They had so little possession compared to us, yet they'd won by three points. It felt like we'd lost the Test rather than them winning it. But when you look at the passion they had on the field and then you saw all the footage from behind the scenes afterwards, in the end their desire to win was simply greater than ours. That's why they could defend for longer periods than we could. They worked hard for each other; their scrum was solid; their basics were solid – and their confidence grew from that.

**Gary Teichmann:** You look back and think that if we'd landed just two of those six kicks, we'd have won. People said afterwards that we shouldn't have gone into a Test without a top goal kicker, but all three players were recognised goal kickers and, either before or after, each of them won Test matches with his boot. We won the 2007 World Cup because of Percy's kicking. We just had terrible luck that all three of them had an off-day, but that's what happens when you're struggling for confidence.

**Keith Wood:** The thing that still frightens me is that we could and should have lost all of them. South Africa is just so difficult. As forwards, we played really, really well early on in the tour, we played with great ambition and when we got to the Tests it became a more straitened version of that. There was interplay and there was different things, but it wasn't as joyful as the play that we had had in the earlier matches. But that, in many respects, is the difference between a Test and a tour match. The pressure that you have in the Test is magnified by a number.

**Jeremy Guscott:** Geech has a phrase – 'Test match animals' – it means having the ability to turn in your best performances at the highest level, keeping a cool head while playing at your highest intensity and making the right decisions under pressure nine times out of ten. I think that the whole of the '97 squad had that about them. You had some of the hardest men ever to play for the Lions – Johnno, Gibbsy, Dallaglio, Hill, Rodber, Davidson, Wallace, Smith, Wood – and some real skill out wide. But the real key was that we played for each other – we went to war for each other and we formed a bond that will never be broken. It's amazing what can happen in the space of a few weeks.

**Tom Smith:** The whole night was nice, a really special memory. Everyone together. It was the old days, no iPhones, no cameras, no Facebook, just mixing with the supporters and enjoying ourselves.

**Jeremy Guscott:** Some people remember the night out better than me. I think I was sharing with Jenks. He'd remember more than me. The series was done so there was a bit of mayhem. The England players all had mobile phones back then and we had free calls, so you'd lend your phone out to people so they could call their families back home.

Most of us got back at varying times the next day, early morning, and gravitated towards the team room, picked up some beers and went down to the beach in Durban where we were staying. We chatted and drank and generally had a good time. Geech said, 'Don't think about the third Test, just enjoy this. Have a blow-out. Don't think about tomorrow – just enjoy this moment with each other right now.'

And that's exactly what we did. We went over all that had happened, talked about what a brilliant tour it had been and we didn't even think about the third Test, we just really enjoyed that moment together. It was cool. Really cool.

# CHAPTER TWENTY

# COME ON JIM, WE'RE LEAVING

'LIONS BREAK BOK HEARTS' read the headline in London's *Sunday Times*. 'Acclaim the most astounding defensive performance, the most remarkable courage in adversity, in rugby history,' wrote Stephen Jones in the article that followed. 'Acclaim the counter-attacks of the last ten minutes when the siege was raised and, with a short, stabbing, yet soaring drop-goal by Jeremy Guscott, the Lions took the lead. Acclaim the 1997 British Lions, victors in the Test series in the home of the world champions. Now we have seen it all. The lot.'

'Lions in the land of legends' boomed the headline in *The Independent*. 'The Lions rewrote history in staggering fashion in Durban yesterday and not just rugby history either. Quite how anyone could simultaneously defend Rorke's Drift and the Alamo will forever remain a mystery but Martin Johnson's band of bravehearts managed to perform the feat under more pressure than they could ever have imagined possible.'

'The dreams, aspirations and commitment to a cause that came from the heart have been realised,' wrote Edmund van Esbeck in

*The Irish Times.* 'First nurtured almost two months ago, when the 1997 Lions assembled in a London suburb to prepare for the tour to South Africa, those dreams came to glorious fruition on a foreign ground, appropriately named Kings Park, in Durban on Saturday . . . The Lions of 1997 had given us something which we can in the days and the years ahead tell stories of and glory in at having been present on a humid and historic day on a stretch of turf that lies adjacent to the Indian Ocean. What the Lions have achieved will reverberate across the seas.'

For the victorious Lions there wasn't a lot of time to bask in the glory of their achievement. Not a lot of time either to recover from their sore heads after an all-nighter on the gargle. On the Sunday afternoon they took a flight north to the small industrial Transvaal city of Vereeniging, remembered as the place where the second Boer War ended in 1902 and where François Pienaar was born in 1967. For the most part its place in history is recorded for the nearby town of Sharpeville, scene of the horrific Sharpeville Massacre, the 1960 police attack that killed sixty-nine anti-apartheid protestors and injured 180 others. The penultimate game of the trip would be against Northern Free State.

**Keith Wood:** Vereeniging? Jesus. It was grim.

**Rob Wainwright:** Fucking horrible place.

**John Bentley:** They deliberately wanted to go somewhere far away from Joburg to get us away from the supporters so that we could focus on the third Test. They were probably expecting us to be one-all in the series with all to play for and didn't want any distractions, but we'd already gone and bloody won it. Ideally we should have been in Sun City for a big last week.

In a players' meeting on the Monday, Johnno cut a relaxed figure. 'Personally, I don't think we need to get heavy this week,' he said. 'We can relax and enjoy it, but I'd like to go out on Saturday and play some rugby – play the sort of rugby we've played in the non-Test matches. If we can beat them 3–0, it will be brilliant. If they beat us on Saturday it will be: "I told you so," and all that shite coming out of them and they'll still think they're the top side. If we can beat them 3–0, it's never been done.'

It was a point re-emphasised by Geech. 'Nobody has ever whitewashed the Springboks. Nobody.' But in order to achieve that goal, they needed the midweek team to put in one final performance before the third Test.

**Allan Bateman:** It was absolutely freezing cold, you couldn't do anything, it was miles away from anywhere and they took us there for a week. That was the only thing on that tour that was possibly not the right thing to do. People started to get bored, and instead of focusing our minds it caused us to lose our concentration. Instead of looking forward to the game, we were stuck up there in the middle of nowhere.

**Scott Gibbs:** It was at altitude and the weather was awful and nearly half of the squad went down with flu-like symptoms all week. Admittedly, we all partied and celebrated after the second Test on the Saturday, and some on the Sunday, and Wally maybe on the Monday, but we went from Durban up to the veldt, into a smaller lodge type hotel which wasn't luxurious and at least a dozen started to have flu and got worse as the week went on, so the playing pool shrunk considerably.

**Tom Smith:** I understand it was the same hotel that the All Blacks stayed in before the World Cup final, a place called Vanderbijlpark. It was the equivalent of the outback in Australia, a place to gather ourselves before what everyone thought might be a decisive third Test. There was a lot of illness. Training was cancelled or a lot of people missed it. I guess at the end of a long tour, an emotional come-down and a very big Saturday night in Durban, everything sort of collided.

**Ian McGeechan:** Fran had picked it. He'd come out with a fella from the Lions in the previous October, which was during the summer, and this place was by a river and there were boats on it and all sorts of things going on, but he'd forgotten that we would be there in the middle of winter and absolutely nothing he had seen would be there.

**Neil Jenkins:** You've done what you've come to do, but we did want to win that third Test as well. There'd been a few issues in the week, we had another midweek game against the Purple People Eaters, as they were known.

**Allan Bateman:** Their supporters – you'd walk down the street throughout the tour and they'd be saying, 'We're going to have you.' And even when we'd won the first two Tests, it was like, 'We'll still get you the next time.' They were in denial all the way through because they couldn't believe we were beating them. They were pretty vitriolic, some of the supporters. I'm not sure they really meant it, but it's just their demeanour. They're naturally very confident.

**Jim Telfer:** The big focus for us that week was not to lose focus, if you know what I mean. It was important that the midweek team didn't just chuck it in or think we didn't care about them now that the series was won. And we didn't want them getting fixated on it being the last time they might play on tour or the last time they might wear a Lions jersey. So the mantra we kept repeating was: *This is not your last game as a Lion. It's your next game as a Lion.*

The game was at Welkom, a mining town two and a half hours south-west of Johannesburg. The North West Stadium was on the outskirts, its playing surface hard and scattered with yellowing grass. Tony Underwood scored a first half hat-trick and Neil Back was absolutely everywhere, linking play, making tackles and stealing ball on the ground as he had done so crucially in the second Test. As positive as they were in attack, however, the Lions' defence was the worst it had been all tour. They scored ten tries but conceded five in a madcap 67–39 win. It was the highest number of points the Lions had ever conceded in a single game, not that anybody was all that bothered at that point.

**Martin Johnson:** You just can't replicate the edge that would have been there if the series was on the line. You can't.

**Rob Wainwright:** The tour was won and then there was a real off-tour feel to that week, and I don't think we were hugely helpful to the Test team. The forwards weren't doing their job quite the way Jim wanted and I remember him losing his temper with us a wee bit when we were having wine with dinner or something. In that final midweek game, the edge wasn't there in defence but the backs were just playing champagne rugby and we scored some sensational tries.

I think one of the overriding lessons of a Lions tour, particularly in those days when we were playing a lot more games, is that everyone in the squad has got a pretty high probability of playing a Test. A number of guys who had played in the first two Tests were in pieces. If you're still able to take the field by the third Test, there's a very good chance you're going to be selected, because the injury rate is so high and the intensity of the rugby is so high, so there was still a lot to play for in that final game.

As the Lions searched for the motivation to go back to the well one more time on the Saturday, the Boks were in an advanced state of self-analysis and self-torment. 'If we'd kicked just fifty per cent of our achievable penalties, we would have won comfortably,' lamented Du Plessis. He was drawn and pale and seemed to have aged visibly over the course of the series. 'The forwards gave everything, the backline struggled again but there was very little wrong with our overall performance. Future Springbok teams will play much worse and finish on the winning side. I know that.'

**Joost van der Westhuizen:** Carel came in for a lot of criticisms for not picking a dedicated kicker. I always felt that was unfair. He was coming from an amateur background and expected that the guys who were supposed to be able to kick, like Henry and Juba and Percy, would be able to kick.

**Percy Montgomery:** Carel was dejected and so was Gary, but both of them were dignified in the changing room afterwards. Neither blamed anyone for the defeat and both gave me the reassurance that I'd done well, even if the conversation was limited to a few words.

There was also no blame among the other players. There were long periods of silence and reflection. We all knew the media were going to be harsh and Carel seemed to be preparing for the worst. I felt sorry for him and I felt I'd let him down because if just two of our six kicks had gone over, we'd have won, but none of them had and we'd lost. If you asked me before the game if I thought it was possible that between Henry, André and myself, we would miss six out of six, I would have said never, but it happened.

**Carel du Plessis:** I gave Gary Teichmann the green light to use Honiball at first, if he was feeling confident. If Honiball struggled, then Teichmann was to bring in Montgomery. In the week before the Test, both Montgomery and Honiball were successful with seventy per cent of their kicks in training. Honiball was used initially because he'd kicked for South Africa before and was playing on his home ground.

**André Venter:** You look back now and . . . do you know, at no point during that second Test did I think we were going to lose. I still don't understand it.

**Gary Teichmann:** I agree one hundred per cent. We were so dominant. And I kept thinking, 'Sooner or later we're going to get one of these kicks over.' And if we had, this whole story might have been completely different.

**Joost van der Westhuizen:** Above all, the players felt sorry for Carel. He'd worked very hard and he'd shown himself to be a decent person. He'd only been in charge for three games but already the knives were coming out.

**James Dalton:** I'm sorry to say this, but I have to tell the truth – we lost that series to the Lions for one reason and one reason only, and that is because Carel du Plessis just wasn't a coach. He is a lovely man, but he just didn't have what it takes to coach an international sport.

We would sit in team meetings and listen to him lecture and we would all be looking at each other: 'What is this guy talking about? Is this rugby he's talking about, or some other sport, because we don't recognise it.'

We were so confused. We wasted far too much time on theory, and it was tiring and literally put some of the players to sleep.

Make no mistake, Carel is a very clever man, but he didn't know how to put his ideas across. It is very important that the coach keeps you engaged. There has to be a sense of respect, which is different from fear. As long as a coach has those elements, he will get the team to perform for him.

That's where many coaches lose the plot, which, unfortunately, has happened a lot at Springbok level. I believe it has cost our country a lot of Test matches. The coaches rule by fear, and it becomes more pronounced as more pressure comes to bear on them, or they just lose your attention with bad game plans, a lack of insight into the game, and poor or biased team selections. I experienced that as often at Springbok level as I did at provincial or schoolboy level.

**Carel du Plessis:** I've been told my message wasn't getting through to the players, but I don't see it like that. The results were the problem, not the game we were playing. If you are not successful, you cannot initiate anything new, as losing undermines confidence. If you are winning, then people don't question your playing style and you can get on with it. But we lost the second Test when we really shouldn't have. We played a lot better than in Cape Town and were just let down by terrible kicking and by some 50/50 calls that went against us.

**Mark Andrews:** How could you appoint a coach with no coaching experience to an international team? Yes, maybe Carel shouldn't have taken the job, but it's hard to turn a job like that down when it's offered to you.

I don't think Carel was a good coach and I don't think that at that stage of his career Gert was either, but they both worked incredibly hard and no one could fault their commitment. They used to slip a synopsis on the performance of each player under our doors at night. That took a lot of time and they always seemed to be working. But in the end, they just weren't ready for the job. It wasn't Carel's fault; he should never have been appointed as coach. He had no experience. It was a waste for us to lose an iconic series that we should have won, given the relative strengths of the two teams. The Lions side that beat us was very average.

**Russell Bennett:** We should have beaten them 3–0 in the series, there's no question about it.

**Mark Andrews:** I missed the third Test through concussion, and for the first time in my career, I was actually grateful that I wasn't going to be playing. Carel never liked me, but that wasn't the problem I had with him. He just wasn't a coach and didn't appear to value the Springbok ethos or anything related to it. He was no motivator and had no clear plan. He was just wishy-washy. And from what I recall, we had no defence under his coaching. Not that I recall a lot from that period. I think I've blocked out most of the time I spent with him. People who survive wars actually block parts of it from their memory. I think I did the same with Carel du Plessis.

**Gary Teichmann:** The mood in the camp started to deteriorate badly. Players retreated to old provincial groups, blaming other teammates for the series defeat. It had become a disaster for South African rugby. People can look back and blame me for the Lions defeat if they want. As captain, I accept responsibility, but, in all sincerity, I can't look back and say I could have done this or I could have done that and we would have won. I tried everything I knew and gave everything I could.

**Os du Randt:** The guys were hurting so badly. But we came together and said, 'Let's salvage something from this series.' All we had to play for was our pride – but that was still a powerful motivator.

**Pieter Rossouw:** It was maybe different for the Lions, but for us we had to win that game. It was no dead rubber. We had to restore some pride. We were disappointed to lose the series but there was no way we could lose 3–0. Absolutely no way.

Although some changes were forced upon him by injury, Carel du Plessis still took an axe to his team, making six changes to the side that lost in Durban. The front-row, which had been expected to destroy the Lions almost single-handedly, was broken up. Os du Randt held on to his shirt, but out went hooker Naka Drotske and tight head prop Adrian Garvey to be replaced by James Dalton and Dawie Theron. Injuries to Mark Andrews and Ruben Kruger saw promotions for Krynauw Otto in the second-row and a debut cap was handed to Rassie Erasmus at blindside. In the backline, Henry Honiball was ousted for another debutant, Jannie de Beer, at fly-half and then, late in the week, André Joubert went down in training with a groin injury and had to be replaced by Russell Bennett, the man who scored the try that never was at Newlands.

**André Snyman:** There was this cartoon in the newspapers of Carel playing darts and on the bullseye of the board was Percy Montgomery's name. And the bullseye was the size of the dartboard and the rest of the team were these tiny little names around the edge of the bullseye. The point being that Carel would pick Percy first and then pick the rest of the team. So that's what the media thought of the whole selection process – they thought it was a joke. 'He doesn't know who to select, he just throws a dart at a board and whoever's name he hits, that person is in the team.'

**Percy Montgomery:** Carel seemed happy with the way Danie and I had gone against the Lions and told us to ignore what was being written and said in the media. He said we had to work hard on minimising defensive errors and never stop believing in ourselves when we got the ball. Before every Test, he told me to back my pace and to attack my opposite number on his outside shoulder because none of those guys would be adequately prepared for my pace.

**Rassie Erasmus:** If you get to play against the Lions, as a Springbok in a Test series, or as a provincial player, it's a lifetime highlight. I was incredibly fortunate to get to do both – first for Orange Free State and then to make my Test debut against them at Ellis Park.

**Gary Teichmann:** Rassie Erasmus was a player ahead of his time. He spent hours each day in the video room analysing the opposition. He was calm on and off the field, probably because he had done his homework and had left nothing to chance. He had a very good feel for the game and usually popped up in the right place at the right time. He'd played fly-half when he was at school in Port Elizabeth before moving to the flank, which meant that he could read the game incredibly well and he had great skills – handling, kicking, the whole lot. When he came into camp you saw immediately how good he was going to be.

The Springboks had won more possession and enjoyed a greater territorial advantage in both Tests, not that it mattered a damn. On both occasions the Lions had come from behind in the final ten minutes to win. Doing so had been a testimony to their spirit and never-say-die attitude – and was equally damning of the Springboks' inability to kill off opponents they had dominated for the majority of both matches.

**Jim Telfer:** The South Africans were very predictable. Ian had worked out that Carel du Plessis was very inexperienced and his way of playing was completely frustrated by our defence. Because he hadn't coached them before, he didn't know how to adjust the game plan to change what they were doing. There wasn't a plan B. Honiball wasn't a kicker and it was in the third Test that they finally changed it and went with a kicker. But they were found out tactically. Ian's idea of the way to beat them was the right one. And they couldn't respond – I don't think du Plessis was confident enough in changing them.

The Lions had also made some significant changes of their own. Out with injury were Keith Wood, Alan Tait and Gregor Townsend. They were replaced by Mark Regan at hooker, Tony Underwood on the wing and Mike Catt at fly-half. The only tactical change was to hand Neil Back the starting jersey at openside in place of Richard Hill.

**Martin Johnson:** What impressed me a great amount as a young captain was that the coaches didn't just go, 'Oh, well, brilliant lads, you won the series, everyone plays again next week.' It was, 'No, where do we get better? We need to improve our attacking, we need more of a cutting edge, what can we do?' Do we pick Neil to steal those balls for us out wide and put them under pressure? Do we give Jenks a run at ten? He'd played so well there when he had a chance. Or do you go with Catty at ten? So for every guy that played, there was another guy who could have played who would have done a job. They might have done it slightly differently, but they would have done a job. That was another aspect that made that tour so special.

**Scott Gibbs:** The message was to go for the jugular, but we were struggling towards the end for fit bodies. Thank God we had secured the series by then because you could never have predicted that a little virus could have come into the camp and decimated the squad. Obviously, it's a much poorer excuse to say that we were depleted by numbers because guys fell ill, but genuinely when we arrived that week – I think a lot of the guys were really tired. It's not that we didn't prepare well. We prepared. We were sharp and we were ready for the third Test, but some of the bodies were sore.

**Gregor Townsend:** I think there were four or five of us down injured – would we have stitched ourselves together for one more game if the series had been on the line? Your body would probably have found a way. I was gutted I didn't play in the third Test because it was more like the build-up games, it was really open and I would have loved to have played in it. But our bodies were battered and other guys were fit and it was the right call to go with them.

**Barry Williams:** The last week was different. The series was won. Once you've won something, when it comes to those really tight games, their hunger might have been a bit more than ours. We did have a good week, like. You want it, right, but is your mind as hungry as it was on day one of the tour? You know you're going to be home in a week's time after eight weeks on tour. You'll give it your all, whatever, but you don't know, do you, because your mind does start to wander.

**Alan Tait:** Fran and a few of the lads tried to maintain that there was still a lot to play for in the third Test, but I think they knew in their hearts it was kidology. It was different perhaps in 1974, when the Lions kept the momentum going to maintain an unbeaten tour record by drawing the final Test. By the time the series was won many of us were hanging together with bits of tape.

**Barry Williams:** You look back on that rivalry Ronnie and I had and I suppose he had the last laugh really because I was on the bench for the first two Test matches. Keith Wood got injured and was struggling for the third Test. And I was told, 'We're not playing you on the Wednesday because you've got a good chance of playing on the Saturday in the third Test.' Ronnie had a very good game on the Wednesday before the Test match and he got the nod. To be honest, you get highs and lows when touring . . . I've got to admit, when I found out he was in and I wasn't, it was bittersweet. They spoke to me, said he'd had a good game on the Wednesday and said, 'We've gone for him instead of you.' It's just one of those things, you know what I mean? They didn't have to win the last Test, they didn't have to play entertaining rugby, so I was still on the bench. I was on the bench for three games and never went on.

He had a cracking Wednesday game. I take my hat off to him, he had a very good game. It's just one of those things. You're bigger than that, you've just got to dust yourself down and get on with it. It felt like my world had fallen apart on the Thursday morning, but by Friday you'd have to pull yourself together.

**Rob Wainwright:** In my case, it was slightly different because Tim Rodber came down with a stomach bug and I got called up to the third Test about four hours before kick-off because Tim's stomach hadn't settled down.

**Scott Gibbs:** The pre-match rallying cry from the coaches before the second Test was: 'We can go out and finish it off right here.' With the third Test, the focus was on being a little bit more expressive because the South African press were obviously keen to say that we shouldn't have won the first Test and, had they had a kicker, we shouldn't have won the second Test. So the third Test was always about proving the squad's calibre as a football-playing team. And we did play a lot of football in that third Test; but we were looser as a squad because the combinations hadn't played with each other for the last couple of weeks.

**Martin Johnson:** I was warming up for the third Test at Ellis Park and I was thinking, 'The nerves and the tension and the anxiety and all those things from the previous two weeks aren't there.' I just thought, 'You feel flat. You feel flat here.' It was such a bizarre feeling because the adrenaline and nerves and everything should just be crackling through your body. We didn't really play like that, you know?

Roared on by 61,000 fanatical supporters, the Springboks enjoyed another barnstorming start. They landed two penalty goals within ten minutes to immediately justify the selection of Jannie de Beer after the kicking calamity of Kings Park. Then, after sixteen minutes, Percy Montgomery scorched in for a try. The Boks were thirteen points clear. Enter Neil Jenkins and his magic boot. By half-time, the deficit had been reduced to just four points.

**Allan Bateman:** At half-time, everybody was fine, and ready to go back out when Geech said to me, 'Get changed.' I said, 'What's up?' He said, 'Jerry's broken his arm.' And I thought, 'Oh, there's a bit of luck.' It was just like 'get on the field'. It's a great stadium. A very high, steep stadium. There was a sea of red there.

Robbed of Tony Underwood after thirty-one minutes and Jeremy Guscott at the interval, the depleted Lions struggled. Eight minutes into the new half, the Springboks got their second try when Van der Westhuizen darted from the base of a ruck and split the Lions' defence, beating four defenders on his way to scoring. Out on the far right-hand touchline, Jannie de Beer kicked a pinpoint conversion to extend his side's lead to 20–9. Where were you in Durban, Jannie? The fly-half landed another penalty a few minutes later; 23–9 to the Springboks.

There was one last surge from the Lions when Matt Dawson scored but the day belonged to the driven hosts, the men who needed this victory like they needed their next breath. André Snyman and Pieter Rossouw both scored late on as the Lions flagged. Mentally, they were already on their way home, their work done, their achievement written in history. It ended 35–16.

**Ian McGeechan:** Myself and Jim were put in among the South African supporters. That's when Jim got into the argument with the Springbok fans. He was calling them Nazi bastards. I had to get him out. 'Come on Jim, we're leaving. Now.'

**Rob Wainwright:** The team had slightly lost its mojo. You know, there was a lot of talk about, 'Let's whitewash them,' but it just never really felt like that in the third Test. It was a mammoth physical battle again, but ultimately not everyone was firing on all cylinders.

**Martin Johnson:** I think we'd squeezed everything possible out of ourselves by then – and they were desperate not to be whitewashed. And they wouldn't have deserved to have been whitewashed. Don't get me wrong, I'd have taken it – but I think it played out as it should have. And we had nothing left to give at that stage. To bring out emotional performance after emotional performance after emotional performance, we did it and we got there and we won the series, *just*, but then to do it again, when we knew we'd already won it, you just can't. I couldn't do it. I just couldn't emotionally get to the same place.

**James Dalton:** With the series lost I finally got my chance to play in the third Test and it reminded me of the final Test during the previous year's series against the All Blacks. The atmosphere was similar, the opposition seemed to have one foot on the plane home and we were psyched. Ellis Park, as a venue, inspires the Boks as much as it intimidates the opposition. We smashed them.

**Pieter Rossouw:** There maybe wasn't the same focus from the Lions, having won the series, but we really played well. I was man of the match in that game, which was a nice accolade to receive, but the thing I was most pleased about was that I played well and hoped that it would be enough to keep me in the Springbok set-up.

**Jeremy Davidson:** Yeah, they were very good, but we were battered and bruised and there was that raging illness that came through the troops in the build-up. I think the tour had just taken its toll.

**Neil Jenkins:** It would have been nice to have won the series 3–0, but if you'd said before we went that we were going to be 2–0 up going into the third everyone would have ripped your arm off. They'd have gone, 'Thank you very much. We'll take that, no problem.'

As the Lions basked in the delirium of their travelling fans, Joost van der Westhuizen was summoned to the sideline for an interview that was broadcast over the stadium's public address system. The scrum-half had captained the Boks for the last seven minutes of the match after Gary Teichmann was taken off injured. Asked to pay tribute to the tourists who had defied all expectation by claiming the series win, Van der Westhuizen was emotionless. 'Ja, well,' he said, 'we wanted to give them a *klap* [a slap], and I'm pleased we did that today.'

The Lions fans booed, but it was a typically honest – albeit truculent – answer. The Springboks felt that they were the better team. With the series so closely contested, it was a fair enough appraisal – either side could have emerged victorious.

**Os du Randt:** How do I reflect on the series? The '97 Lions were a side who made the most of the talent at their disposal. Their coaching staff and management were outstanding and the team spirit was exceptional, but many of us still wonder today how a team who scored nine tries to three could lose a series.

I don't think we underestimated them; I just think, tactically, we played wrong. The coaches decided to play with a more attacking fly-half in Henry Honiball when we should maybe have stuck with our physical strengths and picked a strong kicker – if you look at all the opportunities we missed in front of goal, we should probably have won the series 3–0. Or at least 2–1.

But that's in the past, we can't change that. Playing against the Lions was really an honour, you know. To be lucky enough to fall into that twelve-year window, it was very special. I look back on my career and I won the Tri Nations, the World Cup in '95 and '07, I won the Currie Cup. That's almost all the cups that you want. But the one elusive thing, the one I missed out on was a series win against the Lions. So it hurts. I was fortunate to have other things to soften that disappointment, but only a tiny bit.

# CHAPTER TWENTY-ONE

# TRAGEDY OF THE FALLEN BOKS

IN THE WAKE of the series defeat it was only a matter of time before Carel du Plessis was removed from his position. 'It was the coaching staff who took most of the blame and the criticism for us losing that series to the Lions,' said André Snyman. 'You know, South African supporters are very hard, they always want to win and if you lose they're quick to pull the trigger and tell you how bad you are. And then the next week you play better and that same person will tell you how great you are. It's just the way it is. But the knives were soon out for Carel.'

The news broke on Saturday 6 September. Carel du Plessis, the Springbok star once christened the Prince of Wings by an adoring Cape Town fanbase, had been sacked from his role as South African coach barely halfway through his twelve-month contract. Following the Test series defeat to the Lions, the Springboks suffered a poor Tri Nations campaign. Although they picked up a thumping 61–22 victory over Australia in Pretoria, on Du Plessis' watch, the Boks lost five out of eight games – an unacceptable return in the Republic. He was replaced by Nick

Mallett, the former Oxford University number eight who played alongside Du Plessis for Western Province. Mallett's appointment felt to many like the righting of a wrong from when he had been overlooked in favour of Du Plessis following the ignominious departure of André Markgraaff.

In November 2019 it was announced that Du Plessis had undergone brain surgery as he continued a battle against cancer. If he didn't always have the support of his players on the field in 1997 then the opposite was the case as he fought the biggest fight of his life. 'Patience and perseverance are tested on all fronts,' he said. 'I'm spiritually strong and fully trust in God and his word at this time.'

By the end of the series Gary Teichmann was thinking about retiring from international rugby and dedicating himself wholly to the Sharks. He'd been through so many coaches and had so much grief in such a short period of time that he felt like he'd reached the end of the road. He remained steadfast in his view that the Lions were not a great side and that the Springboks should have beaten them. That angst lived with him.

'As captain, I felt exposed by the lack of assistance and support from the team management. Carel and Gert were both quiet by nature, and our team manager, Arthob Petersen, was not the type of man to take hold of such a difficult situation. Sarfu officials were conspicuous by their absence. I'm not making excuses, and I'm not suggesting the problems were everyone else's fault but mine. But it's important to make clear that professional sports teams lean heavily on their management to create the right mood within the camp. The Springbok teams of 1996 and 1997 were not afforded these circumstances. Carel, Gert and I were all quiet, reserved guys and we didn't give the team the confidence that they needed to get the job done. We had the wrong mix. I look back on the series now and it's such a disappointment. A Lions tour is a once-in-a-lifetime experience and we blew it. It was a dreadful feeling. The lowest point of my career.'

He describes the whole scene around the Springboks in those years as a 'shambles'. But it changed when Nick Mallett took over. Teichmann stayed on as player and captain as the Springboks rampaged once again. He won a record-equalling seventeen Tests in a row including three victories against the Wallabies, two against the All Blacks, two against England and two on a tour to France. He was controversially left out of the South Africa World Cup squad of 1999, an omission that brought the curtain down on his Test career after forty-two caps, thirty-six of them as captain. He spent two years with Newport in Wales, a happy period that is remembered fondly by all those fans who were to witness his leadership and his class.


Joost van der Westhuizen became a Springbok immortal in the summer of 1995 when South Africa won the World Cup and nothing the Lions did two years later could take a shine off that extraordinary achievement. He played for his country for another six years, finishing in 2003 with eighty-nine caps and thirty-eight tries. He has gone down in history as one of the finest rugby players of all time.

Van der Westhuizen lived a controversial life, admitting to an extramarital affair and drug taking in his autobiography of 2009. There were sordid tales of sex tapes and strippers. SuperSport, the television channel that employed him as an analyst, promptly sacked him when the revelations were made public. He was a wondrous rugby player but was also capable of bad behaviour, particularly towards those closest to him. However, everything in his world started to change in May 2011 when he was diagnosed with motor neurone disease.

Remarkably, he said that MND changed him for the better. He set up the J9 Foundation to raise funds for research into what is an incurable condition. 'There is no time to worry about death,' he said. 'There is no time to stress about the petty things, like money. There is no time. I'm a better person now. People are surprised when I say that, but during my career I became an arrogant person and now I'm back to the reality of life and what is important.' In the first week of February 2017 Joost van der Westhuizen passed away. He was forty-five.

'I spent a lot of time with Joost before he died and he was the first to say, post his career, that he had regrets in the way that he handled himself whilst he was playing,' said Matt Dawson, his opposite number in 1997. 'But then, you know, can you create a player like Joost without having that ego, that character, that confidence? I don't think so. You can't. He was a sporting icon. He moved the dial in an era which changed the sport in the country and you're not going to do that by being a wilting lily. You've got to be a real strong, confident guy and sometimes it did verge on arrogance and he did get found out a couple of times, but I just think that added to the amazing character that he had.'

André Venter called the summer of 1997 'a disaster' for South African rugby, which was saying something because Venter was rarely the type to express emotion of that kind. His teammates didn't call him Ironman for nothing. 'Jeremy Guscott's drop goal broke our hearts,' he said. 'We were gutted to lose like that and more so because we knew we were the better team. That wasn't a great Lions team. We made up for it a bit by winning convincingly in Johannesburg in the last game of the series and in that match we showed just how much better than them we were, but it didn't change the end result.'

Venter went on to win sixty-six caps and was at the heart of the Nick Mallett revolution, playing in sixteen straight victories between August 1997 and November 1998. He was in the back row when South Africa won the Tri Nations championship in 1998 and when they finished third at the World Cup in 1999.

He is remembered as a Springbok great, a man who inspired awe for his athleticism and power, a player who had to be dragged off the training ground by his coaches. 'He's no oil painting, but look at him working the blindside like a pop-up toaster,' said Bill McLaren once.

His last cap came in 2001. In July 2006 he was diagnosed with a degenerative syndrome of the central nervous system, later revealed as transverse myelitis, a spinal condition that has led to paralysis. When Rassie Erasmus, his old teammate, took over as Springbok coach in 2018 one of the first things he did was to invite Venter to present the jerseys to the players ahead of their next Test. Venter may have lost the series against the Lions, but his legend is undimmed.


In a team with numerous enforcers, Mark Andrews was one of the principal hard men. 'I like to think I was a psycho on the field,' said the World Cup-winner. Plenty of his opponents would have stories to back up that view. Having made his debut in 1994 at the age of twenty-two, Andrews, like a few others, came to a crossroads after the Lions series in 1997. He believed that Carel du Plessis' brand of rugby was outdated and that time had passed him by,.

'At the end of Carel's stint, myself, Gary Teichmann, Henry Honiball and André Joubert had officially retired,' he recalled. 'We didn't want to play for South Africa again until there was a new coach so that we could do justice to the Bok jersey. When Nick Mallett took over he flew to Durban and met us at a beachfront hotel where he convinced us to play on. He told us the Boks needed us.'

Andrews played on for another four years, winning seventy-seven caps. At the time he was the most capped Springbok forward in history – and one of the most memorable.

The hardest thing for any sportsman is to give up the game. You not only lose the fame and the money that comes with it, you lose the chance to do something you do best of all. James Small had written his name into Springbok legend on the day he played so brilliantly when taming the great Jonah Lomu in the 1995 World Cup final. After rugby, Small worked in property and invested in businesses including e-sports, but life away from the game that had given him such purpose and structure was difficult. He had a high-profile, tempestuous on-off relationship with Christina Storm, a model he met on a photoshoot in 1997 and to whom he was twice engaged and with whom he had a daughter, Ruby. Shockingly, he admitted to occasions of domestic abuse but said in 2009 that he was a changed man, having been through therapy. Life continued to be a rollercoaster. There were suicide attempts and he was in part saved thanks to the intervention of Nelson Mandela, who phoned him after one suicide attempt to tell him that he had much to live for and was still a hero to millions. Small played forty-seven times for the Boks and scored twenty tries but still the demons haunted him. On 10 July 2019, while attending an 'upmarket gentlemen's club' in Johannesburg, Small suffered a massive heart attack and was rushed to the Life Bedford Gardens hospital where he died. He was fifty.

Os du Randt can lay claim to being the greatest loose head prop there's even been, despite losing to the Lions. Even in a country of huge men, Os was different. A monster scrummager but a ball-player, too. A phenomenal physical force but one who could carry. He could do the grunt but there was always way more to his game than attrition. His thoughts on 1997 are slightly different to other players'. He doesn't wish to lay all of the blame at Carel du Plessis' door. Far from it.

'I couldn't help feeling sorry for Carel. He's the perfect gentleman – quiet, honest, genuine and intelligent and we as players respected him for that. We also respected him for his knowledge and insight into the game. After the Loftus Test there was consensus that the players at last had caught onto Carel's vision on the field and thrashed the Wallabies in spectacular fashion during his last game in charge. Everything Carel had been trying to convey all came together on that day. In many ways it was a shame Carel wasn't allowed to carry on, but Nick Mallett built on these foundations and pushed us into a new level.'

After the 1999 World Cup – South Africa beat New Zealand to third place – Os endured one injury after another. He didn't play rugby for three years. The end looked nigh. It was Rassie Erasmus at the Cheetahs who persuaded him to go again for one last push – and this time it worked. Os got a break from his injury problems and started to look like his old self again. After going four and a half years without playing for the Boks he made his return in the summer of 2004. And he was immense.

Os became a key man in Jake White's Springboks and in 2007 South Africa played England in his second World Cup final. He was the last man standing from 1995 and here he was at the pinnacle of the sport a dozen years later. The Boks beat England to become champions once more. Os became the first Springbok to win two World Cups. He was thirty-five years old and it was to be the last of his eighty Tests. He bowed out on the greatest high imaginable.

Desperate tragedy has befallen some of the 1997 Springboks and Naka Drotske, a substitute in the 1995 World Cup final and hooker in the first two Tests against the Lions, came frighteningly close to being added to the sad stories when four armed assailants in balaclavas shot him twice while he was in his brother's house in Pretoria. It was December 2018 and whatever he achieved on the field in his six-year, twenty-six-cap career with the national team, Drotske excelled on an altogether more profound level when those intruders struck.

Drotske was sitting in his brother's back garden enjoying a braai with family. Os du Randt, his great Springbok mate and business partner in their sports supplement company, was also there. There were young children in the house and Drotske felt everybody's life was in danger when the madness began. He acted on instinct. 'I just decided to attack them,' he said. 'I targeted the middle man – the leader – and took the other two or three with me down the stairs and onto the lawn. I was wrestling on top of him when he shot me in the stomach, another guy shot me through the arm and a third attacker shot but missed. My adrenaline was pumping and we all rushed back into the house and locked it. That was when Os saw me and said, "I think you've been shot." I assessed the wound and told him to get me to a hospital quickly.'

He underwent operation after operation. 'The doctors said it was touch and go at one stage, which you only really hear afterwards. They even called the family together to maybe start preparing them, but with God's grace I got through it. This incident changed my life. When you are so close to death you do have a different perspective. It makes things like rugby results seem trivial.'

Drotske won his last cap in 1999. He was twenty-eight. Five years later he captained and won man of the match as his beloved Cheetahs beat defending champions the Blue Bulls to win their first Currie Cup in thirty years. That was arguably his greatest performance – until those masked gunmen burst into view with the sorely mistaken impression that nobody would be brave enough to stand up to them.

Adrian Garvey was the third member of the celebrated Springbok front row that was expected to obliterate Tom Smith, Keith Wood and Paul Wallace. Garvey was a turbo prop who'd won ten caps for his native Zimbabwe before winning another twenty-eight for South Africa. He was in the vanguard of Nick Mallett's team from 1997 to 1999 when he bowed out of the international arena and headed for a spell with Newport in Wales. In 2001, Garvey scored his team's only try in a Principality Cup victory over Neath at the Millennium Stadium. His captain, once again, was Gary Teichmann.

There's a simple story told about Ruben Kruger that encapsulates the straightforward passion he brought on to a rugby field. It dates back to some dog days for his Blue Bulls team when they couldn't buy a win and when confidence and motivation was beginning to become an issue. Kruger addressed his fellow players in the dressing room, his vice-captain Jacques Olivier by his side. 'Jacques and I will play our hearts out today,' he said. 'It's up to you to decide what you do.' Then he got up and walked out to play. His team followed him with a renewed focus. The Bulls were fine that day.

It was typical Kruger. No great oratory, no clever one-liners, no pomp, no circumstance, no bullshit. Kruger was an exceptional rugby player, a flanker of massive ferocity with an engine the size of a house. He won thirty-six caps between 1993 and 1999. In 2000, while playing for his club at Loftus

Versfeld, he blacked out. 'I tackled the guy and couldn't remember anything else,' he said at the time. 'It was a hard knock, not a big one, but the lights went out and I thought that was strange because they'd gone out in the previous match. I'd had big knocks before without the lights going out. They took me for a scan and found a second-grade tumour in my head. I knew it was all over. You play one day, then the next day you're finished. I'd been playing since I was six years old and I didn't understand Saturdays without rugby. It's a great game but it's not so nice that I want to spend the rest of my life in a wheelchair. Giving up is a small price to pay. I've had a nice innings but I was in a state of shock for four or five days. Some people phoned me up and they seemed to think I was already dead! I said: "No, it's not going to kill me. I'm still alive, still kicking."'

In early 2009, the cancer returned. Kruger fell ill on a family holiday resulting in a five-hour operation in which surgeons removed a tumour the size of a man's fist. In June, it resurfaced. On 27 January 2010, Ruben Kruger died. He was thirty-nine.

Henry Honiball was thirty-one when the Lions clinched the series and had just about had enough of life with the Springboks. He was one of the group of players that Nick Mallett went to see in Durban when word reached him that they were about to retire. Mallett got another two years out of Honiball and they were two of his best years. In the run of seventeen straight victories from 1997, the fly-half played in fourteen of them. In the autumn of '97, the Boks beat France 52–10 at the Parc des Princes, Honiball scoring a try, kicking one penalty and seven conversions. Unlike in the summer, he could hardly miss that day.

He played his last Test in the third/fourth place play-off at the World Cup in 1999 before heading to Bristol the following season. Saying that his body was talking to him and telling him that it was time to stop, he retired from the game in July 2000.


André Joubert, the Rolls-Royce of full backs, only won thirty-four caps but it should have been more. He made his Springbok debut against a World XV in the days of isolation. Carel du Plessis and Gert Smal were teammates. That was in 1989 and he was twenty-five years old. Because of isolation, he had to wait another four years for a second cap.

Juba was class personified, the finest full back in world rugby at one time. He had an effortless calm about him, was a rock at the back and had a graceful and lethal presence in attack. He didn't run, he glided. In full flow, he had a mesmeric quality. His place in Springbok folklore was secured even before winning the World Cup. In the quarter-final against Samoa he was hit late in the tackle when setting up a try for Chester Williams and broke his hand. He underwent surgery that night, spent time in a decompression chamber and was fit for the semi-final against France a week later. He wore a personalised hand brace. Nothing was going to stop him.

He only played one more game for the Springboks after defeat to the Lions. He left the stage in August 1997 after a 61–22 pummelling of the Wallabies. As exits go, it wasn't the worst.


Percy Montgomery made his Springbok debut in the second Test in Durban and scored a try, not that it did any good. All those missed kicks cost his country dear. 'I had felt lonely when I walked into a Bok change room, but the feeling of being in a losing Bok change room is far worse than loneliness,' he said. 'I looked at these icons around me and wondered if I would get to know the feeling of victory in a Springbok jersey. We'd lost the

Test and the series and not only had Jeremy Guscott finished us off with a drop goal, he'd also humiliated me by refusing to swap jerseys after the Test. I was stunned when he said no as I'd assumed it was the done thing. I thought he was a prick for saying no.'

Montgomery needn't have worried about experiencing the sensation of victory. He would experience it often over the next eleven years. He played 102 times for South Africa, scored twenty-five tries, broke the national points record and won the World Cup in 2007 and yet that covers just a part of his Springbok story.

Over the years Montgomery was a regular target of venom among sections of the South African rugby public who saw him as spoilt and privileged, an unfair depiction but one he had to endure. 'I've never gotten the resentment they feel towards me,' he said. His father, Percy Snr, went further. 'You know how many times I have gone to the pub to watch the Springboks and I have to hear the shit they talk about him. There have been times when I have come close to klapping [hitting] an oke because of the kak they talk about him.'

In 2003, while playing for Newport against Swansea in a sojourn in Wales, Montgomery lost the plot and pushed an official to the ground. The ban he received meant that he missed the World Cup. Four years later, he kicked twelve of South Africa's fifteen points in the final against England and, regardless of whether some sections of the support liked him or not, he joined the pantheon of Springbok greats.

Almost twenty-five years on, André Snyman reflects on his old teammates. 'We've lost a few players in the years since that Lions tour,' he says, softly. 'Ruben Kruger, Joost van der Westhuizen and James Small . . .' Though he never played in the Test series in

1997, Chester Williams has also gone, the wing and only black player in the World Cup-winning team of 1995 suffering a fatal heart attack in late 2019.

'It's scary. It's scary to lose these players. Joost was an absolutely fabulous player, he was my roommate for seven years and it was so sad to lose him as a friend. To see him die from motor neurone disease, to see him wither away like that. It was awful. Although the circumstances were different, I was just as sad when James Small died because he was also a close friend.

'It's sad when you sit here and you reflect in one moment about how many of my old teammates have died and how many have been sick – André Venter's in a wheelchair because of a flu virus that attacked his spine. Jesus, Naka Drotske got shot. He's alive, but the impact of that incident has been huge. Poor Carel du Plessis got a brain tumour. It's terrible. It just shows you how precious your life is.

'Sometimes when you're a professional rugby player, the whole culture of being a rugby player can consume you and you forget about the people that matter around you. You realise very quickly when that is taken away that the people around you were there to support you without you knowing it. With Joost, for example, I think that when he got sick he realised that when you took away the fame and everything else, what was left over were the people that cared for him – his friends and his family. And that humbled him and it made him a better person in his final years. It was a terrible disease that took him, but I think he found peace and happiness in his final years that he had never had before. I suppose there's a powerful lesson there for the rest of us.

'You look back and you realise how lucky we were; lucky to enjoy all those incredible moments under the lights, playing international rugby in front of tens of thousands of screaming fans and millions of people watching on TV – but they're not the moments that really count. It's the people around you that matter most. Your family and friends and those men who you went out to play with who become your brothers for the rest of your life.'

Speaking to the South African writer, Donald McRae, in 2017, Nick Mallett reflected on what had happened in his country since François Pienaar and Nelson Mandela shared a stage in a moment of unimaginable beauty and glory and hope. 'The World Cup united the nation and there were remarkable scenes of black taxi drivers dancing with white supporters,' he said. 'But I remember thinking: "This is not the reality of South Africa." The next day the privileged and wealthy went back to the suburbs and the poor and the unemployed returned to their areas. So it masked the problems we faced later.'

As much as people wanted to believe it, it was not the game that changed a nation. Pienaar's team had one black player, Chester Williams, and the process of transformation – finding others to follow in Williams' stead – was a painful one. When Mallett took over from Carel du Plessis he didn't need to be prompted by government to commit to change – but government prompted him anyway – and so for the 1998 Springbok tour to the UK and Ireland, Mallett selected Owen Nkumane in his squad. His selection had been greeted with derision by white South Africans. 'I was surprised to be picked, but a group of us had played for SA Under-20s,' he said. 'We were just on tour for experience but it was still a proud moment. I remember walking along a London street and a South African stopped me and said: "You're doing this for all of us." That hit home.'

That pressure must have been tough to bear. Nkumane played some midweek games on that trip but wasn't deemed good enough to be tried in any of the Tests against Wales,

Scotland, Ireland and England. Nkumane's time at the top came and went in the manner of a light switch being flicked, from on to off.

The colour game became excruciating and divisive, but it was a journey the nation had to go on. Every year brought examples of why South Africa needed to root out the cancer of racism.

**March 1998:** Former president Nelson Mandela and then sports minister, Steve Tshwete, accuse Sarfu of racism, nepotism and financial mismanagement and launch a commission of inquiry. Mandela gives evidence for five hours. As a consequence of the investigation, race quotas are introduced at all levels of South African rugby. By law, each team has to field a certain number of black players.

**April 1999:** Springbok prop Toks van der Linde is sent home from a trip to New Zealand after calling a black woman a 'kaffir'.

**April 2000:** Sarfu's black president, Silas Nkanunu, claims racism is behind an alleged plot to oust him. The Lions and the Bulls are fined are for breaching quota regulations. It emerged that they had asked their black players to feign injury early in matches so they could be replaced by whites.

**March 2001:** Nine members of the Noordelikes Rugby Club are implicated in the murder of a black man they found poaching on their land. Two of the nine are found guilty.

**October 2002:** Chester Williams, the one black player in the 1995 World Cup team, writes a book in which he says his career was dogged by racism and that he had been regularly abused by teammates and opponents. He said that James Small, from the World Cup-winning team, once rounded on him during a game at Twickenham. Small was alleged to have said: 'You fucking kaffir, why do you want to play our game? You know you can't play it.' Williams said that the whole Rainbow Nation image was a sham and that white South Africans in positions of power at the governing body only tolerated black players because it made it look like they had embraced change. 'Much of it was born of the belief that being white in South Africa somehow made you superior to anyone born black.'

Progress came slowly. Four years after the great day with Pienaar and Mandela, the 1999 World Cup squad had four black players. Four out of a squad of thirty was just a tiny baby step forward. Four years after, at the 2003 tournament in Australia, the number remained at four. In eight years, the advancement was snail-pace slow and the tension around transformation was viciously high.

Jake White's World Cup-winning Boks had six black players in the squad – an improvement, but only two of them played in that 2007 final against England. When White left the job, he was replaced by Peter de Villiers, the first ever non-white to become Springbok coach. De Villiers was given to outrageous and inappropriate comments and rarely impressed in the role. One of the exceptions was when the Lions returned to South Africa in 2009.

Geech was back in the chair as coach by this time and, against De Villiers' team, the outcome went in reverse. The Boks won the first two Tests and the Lions won the third. At the 2011 and the 2015 World Cups there were six and seven black players respectively. Allister Coetzee, the second black coach of the Boks, took over for two ill-fated years until, mid-crisis, Rassie Erasmus was sent for.

Erasmus had made his Springbok debut in the third Test against the 1997 Lions and had gone on to be an illustrious flanker and coach. He was in charge of Munster when his homeland called and in 2019, in Japan, he led the Boks to their third World Cup victory. A hugely clever man, Erasmus had twelve black players in his squad with six of them starting in the final. The group was captained by the brilliant Siya Kolisi, the first black man to hold the position. Kolisi became a symbol of what was possible in a new South Africa. Pienaar's triumph in 1995 has been immortalised by Hollywood, but it really wasn't until twenty-four years later that the nation got a champion team that reflected the country in all its bewildering wonder.

# CHAPTER TWENTY-TWO

# WONDERWALL

THE LIVES OF the 1997 Lions changed forever that summer. Their exploits on the pitch endeared them to rugby fans all over Britain and Ireland but when *Living with Lions* was released the love people had for the tour reached another level. Its footage was so intimate that viewers almost felt part of the trip themselves, even if they'd never set foot outside of the four nations.

**Martin Johnson:** People look back and say, 'Oh, you were a great captain in '97,' but I wasn't a great captain in '97. We had a really good bunch of players, a good bunch of senior players, we had a great management – and we wanted to win.

**Lawrence Dallaglio:** The bottom line is that Martin Johnson was a world-class second row forward. People often ask what made him such a good captain and I'd say: 'Strip away the captaincy and see what you've got.' That's the starting point of his captaincy, his excellence as a player. Everything was built on that. And all the time, he developed as a captain. In the early days, he disliked the trappings, the media responsibilities and other formalities. I understood his reservations. When you're captain, you're always centre stage, being asked irritatingly obvious questions or questions thrown at you to get a negative response. That used to get to him, and he would retreat behind those eyebrows.

It used to affect his demeanour, and there were times when you thought, 'He doesn't smile very much.' But it suited him to be like that; the more people saw him as forbidding, the less they pestered him. Over time he grew into the public role. I guess it comes with growing up as an individual, becoming more rounded, as we all do. At the World Cup in Australia in 2003 he was at the peak of his powers, comfortable with his responsibilities – the best rugby captain England have ever had. He even enjoyed it and allowed people to see that he is an intelligent, funny guy. What I will remember is the warrior, the guy who, more than anything, wanted to win. I liked his style, too, totally unfussy and very tough. He didn't just turn up, he came to play. Uruguay or the All Blacks, it didn't matter to him. He wanted to be on that field for every minute of every game.'

**Gregor Townsend:** The more I look back on that tour the more it grows in my mind as the most special thing to have happened in my rugby career. I assumed there would be more of this to come, but I didn't make the 2001 tour and if you look at the next three tours, they had nothing like the success of that 1997 trip – so I was incredibly lucky to be a part of it.

**Alan Tait:** I had played a lot of big games – especially in rugby league, which is really hard-nosed about going out there and doing a job – so I think that helped me take it all in my stride. But now I look back at it I can see that I didn't appreciate at the time just how special that experience was. Now, when I see the Lions go off every four years to try and achieve what we managed to achieve and just about always coming up short, it really hits home how much it means to a lot of people. It was just another day at the office, but I should have been looking at it as a massive, massive achievement. And every four years the size of that achievement gets bigger and bigger.

**Ian McGeechan:** There's no doubt that the 1997 Lions tour is my favourite experience as a coach. To win in South Africa is always such a colossal achievement. Don't forget that in more than a century of trying, on tours that were long and regular, the All Blacks had won just one Test series in South Africa. It was in 1997 that we got closest to the style of rugby that I have always wanted a team to play. We probably reached the highest level of all my Lions tours that year. The key was that we surprised them with the style and quality of the rugby we played in the provincial games and the knock-on effect was that we took that attitude and confidence engendered into the Test matches. In fact, I think we surpassed South African rugby in every way.

**Matt Dawson:** That tour changed my life, but I think it was significant to *everybody* who went on it. It didn't matter whether you were the kit man or you were Jerry Guscott kicking the winning drop goal, it had a significant impact on all our lives. And it was significant for the Lions too, because before the tour it was being touted as the last Lions tour ever. We had so much backing from all the fans that followed us and I remember speaking to mates when I was in the changing room after the Tests and they were telling me that everyone watching in the pubs and rugby clubs all around the country back home were going completely bonkers. Ever since then the mania around a Lions tour has been incredible.

**Keith Wood:** I know now that when I meet a Lion from my tours – or any of the other tours – you've shared something. Something that's very special.

**Tim Stimpson:** It's England, Ireland, Scotland and Wales against the world champions in their back yard. Playing for a group of guys that took nothing for granted and put everything on the line for me and for the shirt. By far and away it's the highlight of my sporting career, and I'll always be grateful for being given the chance.

**Scott Quinnell:** My memories of that tour are fantastic despite the injury. It was incredible to be around those guys. That's what gave me the confidence to go and play in the three Tests in 2001 – the fact I'd been on one tour and found out what it's all about.

**Barry Williams:** It was nearly twenty-five years ago, but as soon as 'Wonderwall' comes on, it all floods back. Not so much the playing of the games, but the memories of the tour – hanging out, going to restaurants, just being with one another. You're like brothers and you never forget that. I was so fortunate to be a part of that. It's probably the same as going to university in that years later you've still got a bond with some of those people because you went through different times, special times. From day one to the end, there were a lot of great memories.

How many people can say that they had their stag party with the Lions? I had my stag with the *'97 Lions*, right? We'd just won the Test series. Can anyone say that? It's unique. That day, they stripped me off to my pants, taped me to a lamppost. They let me back in after a couple of hours. Everyone was laughing. Great memories, I've got to admit. Fair dos, they put some tape down my pants to make me look very well endowed. You've got to give it to the boys.

**Ieuan Evans:** My first tour was in 1989 and I loved every minute of it. Scoring the winning try in the Test series – it's hard to beat that. And 1993 was probably when I played my best rugby. They all have elements. My frustration in '97 was that I didn't play in the second Test but do you look back with fondness? Yeah, bucketsful. I talk about positive scar tissues. You look back and think, 'Special times, special people, special occasions.'

**Dai Young:** Once you've been on a tour like that, there's always a relationship with the guys you went with. You play against guys that you don't like on occasion, from Ireland or Scotland, or England, and it's quite ironic that you go on a Lions tour and end up spending most of your time with the guys you thought you didn't like. There's always something there when you've been on a Lions tour. I've been on three and there's never been a single guy I haven't got on with. It's a fantastic concept and long may it continue.

**Allan Bateman:** That tour is a memory that will never escape you. You knew everybody on tour, you were there for eight weeks in amongst all the same people, and I go to internationals now, go to functions up in London or wherever, and it's not far off what Geech said, you know – you'll catch an eye, and exchange a smile, and you might catch up and have a couple of words but you don't need to. You respect everyone who went on that trip and you never forget it. It's the best of the best in the UK and Ireland, so it's obviously got that prestige. To be selected for the Lions, and being amongst players of that calibre, that was a real highlight.

**Lawrence Dallaglio:** If you ask any player, he will tell you that being picked for the Lions is the pinnacle. Playing for the Lions changes you as a player and as a person.

**Jeremy Guscott:** No rugby is ever the same once you've been on a Lions tour. Nothing in rugby can compete with it. The atmosphere is different and it's always really hard to adjust down a gear after the Lions.

**John Bentley:** If I'm honest I found rugby life difficult after the Lions, it was such a career high. I wasn't comfortable with the high profile and limelight, and got into a contractual dispute with Rob Andrew, which I now regret and which ended my career at Newcastle before its time. We all learn some hard lessons as we grow up.

I went on the tour determined to be remembered on the field rather than off it for once. I'm a bit of a clown and bit of a joker and I have got to be honest – when I first got back, I got thrust onto a pedestal that I wasn't accustomed to sitting on.

Suddenly I was famous for a short period of time and I found that hard to cope with. You've been in a bubble on tour in South Africa; we didn't realise how big it was back home. I wasn't used to that level of attention. I was uncomfortable with it and for a short period of time I lost sight of what I actually was; I was just a rugby player, I wasn't some movie star. It was hard but I've always had a good family to keep it real. But I'm glad I experienced it because it made me a better person.

I joined Rotherham and later enjoyed some happy playing days back at Cleckheaton down in the lower leagues, but to the world at large my rugby career seemed to end after South Africa. Not a bad place to end, mind.

**Barry Williams:** I lost my way after that Lions tour. At twenty-three I should have kicked on for another one, but instead I had a three- or four-year block in which nothing happened. I had things too quick, too soon, mainly because the game had just gone pro and some clubs were doing stupid stuff. When we got back from South Africa, Richmond paid a record £130,000 transfer fee to get me from Neath. Richmond was great, and I'd never turn the clock back, but for a couple of years I went right off the boil. When Richmond went under in 1999, I went to Bristol and after that back to Neath, which eventually became the Ospreys.

I won twenty-four caps for Wales before retiring from Test rugby in 2002. I was only thirty, but I'd given Wales almost ten years, and only two nights a week at home during the Six Nations wasn't enough with a young family. I also wanted to prolong my career. If I'd carried on with Wales I don't think I'd have played for the Ospreys for as long as I did. I managed to play on until 2008, became the first player to play over 100 games for the region and won the Celtic League. But the question is, if I hadn't quit playing for Wales, would I have won fifty caps? I don't really know.

I'm not in touch with many of the boys anymore. When rugby's over, it's over. I've drawn a line under it. I've got my cap in a box. The only thing I've got on display is a crystal rugby ball on a marble stand. It says 'Lions tour 1997' and it's the only thing I've got up. I've got a Lions shirt, a Welsh shirt and a Baa-baas shirt in a different room but apart from that, all I've got are the memories in my mind, and no one can take them away from me. In 2019, we had our caps sent to us and that brought great memories flooding back.

Looking back, the '97 Lions tour was the highlight of my career. It was a fantastic experience. An honour. Jesus, what a time.

**Tim Rodber:** At the beginning and middle of my career, I thought I was invincible. That's the arrogance of youth, right? We go out, we play a game of rugby, we have a good game, we come off and we go, 'I'll do that again.' Actually, it's bloody hard to back up top level performances one after the other. I remember Jack Rowell pinning me to the wall at Marlow Rugby Club in

1994 – this was back when Twickenham was being redeveloped and we were training at Marlow – and he took me out of the changing room, pushed me against the wall and he said, 'Every time you play well, England win. And every time you play badly, we lose. But you're being a prick. You're arrogant,' and so on and so on, and he dressed me down. At the time I didn't really sit and digest it, but now I look back at it and think, 'Wow, he was in his fifties, he was chief executive running Golden Wonder, he was running Bath who were the best side in the country, he was managing England and he really knew what he was talking about – and he could probably see my potential, but I wasn't living up to it.'

I was lucky enough to play in teams that were good – England in the early 90s were pretty much unbeatable. And I'm not trying to be flippant about it because I worked my arse off, I loved it, and I don't reflect on it often enough, but if I'm honest, when I think 'good', I think Johnno, I think Lawrence, I think Sean Fitzpatrick and Richie McCaw. I achieved a lot, but I don't count myself as 'good' because I wasn't in that bracket.

When I think about the highs and lows of my career, the Lions was incredible, but it had an impact on me. I was the midweek captain, we won all of our games and I expected to be in the twenty-one for the first Test and then I opened my letter and I wasn't in. Eric then got ill and I got in the starting team. History will say: I played in that first Test and I had a really good game and we won; we won the second Test and I played well again – but I was starting to realise, 'You're not as good as you think you are, mate.'

I stopped playing when I was thirty-one; I could have carried on, I was pretty fit, but I didn't want to stay in rugby because I realised that I wasn't good enough. When I first stopped, it took me about two years before I didn't feel guilty on a Friday night about what I ate and drank . . . I met my wife and she helped me realise that you don't need to feel guilty about having a glass of wine or missing a training session – but it can take a while to break that complete obsession. Over the years you dilute, dilute, dilute. You still have in your DNA 'I'm going to be successful, I'm going to fight my corner, drive performance in myself, drive performance in my people at work, my team,' and you've got to then dilute that down into day-to-day life.

I've kind of walked away from rugby, really, which is a shame. You start to get philosophical the older you get, but you sometimes need help to do that – not only from family but sometimes professional help. You can get dark moments when you wish for something you don't have anymore. For me, the fact that I wasn't always in the England team, the fact that I wasn't a regular with the Lions, the fact that I got dropped – these are the things that I remember and it's what drives me on, it's what drives me to want to be successful. It's all shaped me for who I have become.

**Eric Miller:** I was only on the pitch for a few minutes at the end of the second Test but I took a big bang because the next day I woke up and had some pain in my thigh. By the Wednesday I was ruled out of the third Test. I was so naive at the time. I looked at it with a long-term view, thinking I'd have a couple more Lions tours ahead of me. As a twenty-one-year-old I thought I'd come again, but it didn't happen that way.

A lot of very good things happened to me early in my career and I then struggled to cope with having experienced such highs. I probably took a bit of a lax attitude as we had won the series and missing that third game wasn't a huge deal at the time. I wasn't as disappointed as I should have been.

I'd have hoped to go in 2001 and 2005 but it didn't flow like that. Every four years I go through a period of mourning. The senses are heightened when the Lions are playing and you want to jump back on the pitch and do it all again. When you retire you still have an emotional attachment to the game and it's hard to watch as you feel you're missing out, but I'm at a stage in my life where I can appreciate it all and watch on. I'll never forget that tour because not only was it the Lions but as players we were allowed to go out and play with freedom and express ourselves. You only realise how huge it was as the years pass.

**Lawrence Dallaglio:** Everything about a Lions tour is set up to fail. You come together, you get a week to prepare and then you fly off and you play one of the best sides in the world in their back yard. So the odds are fairly stacked up against you. It's the greatest honour you can receive in rugby. But it's a challenge collectively and individually because every single player who is picked for a Lions tour is used to being the number one player for their international side, more or less, and you go on tour and you think that's what you're going to be as a Lion. And you go through this sort of eight/nine-week period and you have to fight it out.

**Martin Johnson:** That's all part of the magic of it.

**Neil Jenkins:** When you see some of the boys now, it's like you've only just played the game. You can catch up with them and pick up from where you left off in '97. It's an incredible feeling. No matter where you are, you always say hello and shake hands. I saw Will Greenwood just before the England game in 2020 and Will's no different. I always remember Geech saying that – there might not be any words spoken. It might just be a nod and a wave, and you'll know. And he was right. It's an incredible feeling.

**Tom Smith:** Geech was spot on. You bump into people over the years and there is always that kind of connection, that you did something special, were part of something special, something important.

**Jeremy Davidson:** The squad just bonded together so well, and what Geech said was so, so true; you know, some special moments are easy to make: special moments with your family, but special moments with a rugby team in South Africa, beating the world champions, there's not many people who can look back on those memories.

**Rob Wainwright:** The bonds are extraordinary. Those players are friends for life; you are bound by a special moment in time and I suppose the sadness is that a lot of these bonds we're dealing with at the moment are to do with sad news, and Tom and Doddie having their battles. But wherever we are, we're still bound together by our involvement in an incredible theatre which remains frozen in time – which is an amazing thing to be involved in.

**Neil Jenkins:** It's scary to think it's more than twenty years ago. I don't think anything will come close to that trip again. The amount of games, the fact the series was won, the quality of the players, the characters, the fact it was part-professional, part-amateur. Now it's just totally professional. Nobody knows anything about amateurism anymore. I played half my career as an amateur. It'll never be like that ever again. That series was a complete one-off. If you're ever fortunate enough to win a series as a Lion, you'll cherish it for the rest of your life.

**Jim Telfer:** The last time I saw Geech was in Glasgow at a big function where he was being inducted into the Scottish Sports Hall of Fame and I did the bit to introduce him. I hadn't seen him in a while but it was as if we'd never been apart. We had a lot of shared history in 1990 and again in 1997. Those weeks in South Africa were among the most special of my life. My history of being on Lions tour three times and failing three times and then finally succeeding, those were happy moments with tremendous players and tremendous men.

**Scott Gibbs:** It's the embodiment of the responsibility that you have for the badge and all the guys that have come before you, and all the guys that come after you. That's what I love about the Lions. We're always going to follow the future Lions of the game, but those future Lions are created by those guys of the past, aren't they?

**Doddie Weir:** It's difficult to find the words for what rugby has done for myself and my family since I was diagnosed with motor neurone disease. It's allowed us to raise £5 million in under two years. And the awareness of the disease is growing in a big way. You get a lot of people talking about MND now, which is great news for other people suffering with it. It's all very sad that there still isn't a drug on the market that can help; but saying that, the journey that we've been on has been amazing.

I saw Tom Smith at the Hong Kong Sevens a few months before he was diagnosed with cancer and he looked so fit and so well and all of a sudden you hear this terrible news about his illness. But he's an amazing guy. His resilience to try and get better, rumour had it he wanted to get chemo at twice the power you normally get it. He just said, 'I can do it. For my kids and my family, I can take it.' But the doctor said, 'No, sorry Mr Smith, you're not allowed.' But that just shows you the will that boy's got. That's what rugby does to you – especially at that level.

I remember when Geech said that 'thirty years' time' thing and thinking, 'What are you on about, Geech?' But it's very true. You might not see each other for years, but when you do you pick up as if it were yesterday. And not just the Lions – it's true of every rugby team. I had a fundraising event in Battersea in 2018 and it was great to see everyone again – and we did it again for Tom in 2020. I keep saying we should have these reunions more often – but happy reunions would be good.

**Scott Gibbs:** During the first coronavirus lockdown, Sky re-ran all the Lions Tests. My friend invited me over and we ended up watching all three from 1997. It's the first time I've ever watched them, and it's funny – how you think the game unfolded in your mind bears no resemblance to what actually happened. Two different games. It threw me. I was on the edge of my seat because it was a gripping Test series whatever way you look at it. From going ahead, going behind, going ahead again, and all that. It was sad as well, because we've lost Ruben Kruger and James Small and Joost van der Westhuizen since then.

**Doddie Weir:** It was tear-jerking to see Joost in his final months. A boy who used to run around being the best rugby player on the planet. That's the humbling part of it. That's my prognosis down the line and that's the bit where we've got to try to make a difference. The rugby world has been overwhelmingly supportive.

I'm still here. If I go back over my life, I've had one of the best ones. No regrets. I was in a national team as a teenager, travelled the world for fourteen years, met a lot of lovely people in the amateur days, which were totally different to the professional game, which I also enjoyed. And all at someone else's expense, which is always good. Not being able to look too far ahead now – that's the sad part, but I wake up in the morning and think, right, let's get on. I'm lucky. I'm still here. I'm still going.

# THE '97 LIONS WILL BE REMEMBERED FOREVER

**Johnny Sexton (Lion #791, toured 2013 and 2017):** I'd have been twelve years old at the time and it was the first Lions tour that I really remember. I watched some of the games with my dad in Kiely's in Donnybrook and Keith Wood was our big hero. We had Paul Wallace, Jeremy Davidson and Eric Miller as well, but Woody was the Irish superstar. Himself and Scott Gibbs were my favourites. I loved watching Scott Gibbs. I'd been to some Ireland games by then but this felt way bigger, even though we were only watching it on telly. It's one of my favourite childhood rugby memories. Then, the *Living with Lions* video came out and as a young kid I can safely say I watched it hundreds of times.

**Sam Warburton (Lion #800, toured 2013 and 2017):** My first Lions memory is from 2001, watching Jason Robinson bursting down the touchline to score in the first Test. That set my world alight. To play for the Lions became my ultimate ambition. I then wanted to find out all I could about the previous tours and it was then that I watched *Living with Lions*. Oh my God,

I must have watched it 1,000 times. It sounds pretty awful to say this, but I remember my dad coming home from work one day with a questionnaire that the son of one of his colleagues needed filled out for a homework project. He handed it to me and my brother to fill out and I can remember exactly what I wrote. Name: *Sam Warburton*. Age: *Fourteen*. Hobbies: *Football and rugby*. Ambition: *To become a Lions legend*. I cringe telling you that, but it's all I wanted to be. I wanted to win a Test series for the Lions and play an important part in doing that. I wanted to be Martin Johnson and Lawrence Dallaglio and Keith Wood and Jerry Guscott and Neil Jenkins all rolled into one. That's the impact that tour had. They were heroes; they set the bar that all the rest of us wanted to reach.

**Paul O'Connell (Lion #738, toured 2005, 2009 and 2013):**
Never mind wanting to be a Lion myself, the 1997 Lions played a massive part in my desire to be a rugby player full stop. I must have watched *Living with Lions* a hundred times. Two hundred. I was obsessed. I watched it before I went training, I watched it before I played games.

I grew up wanting to play for Munster and wanting to play for Ireland, but before 1997, I didn't really have much of a handle on what the Lions were. We didn't have many players featuring in the two previous tours and I wasn't getting up in the middle of the night to watch the games in 1993. And I didn't see any of the games live in 1997 because we didn't have Sky. But then when the documentary came out, it was just this amazing, brand new thing that I didn't know was important – and it suddenly became incredibly important. One of the reasons was that Woody was in the video; he played for Garryowen, a club that my club hated, but he was from my town and it was amazing to see him play such a big role in that team. And there was Wally and Eric Miller and Jeremy Davidson, who was the best forward on the tour, and it just fed that connection. Then there were all these guys you barely knew but they were suddenly just as important to you as the guys you grew up watching. There's now this thing called the Lions in your conscious mind and its massive and special and magic. That video had a huge impact on me and it made me fall in love with the game because I wasn't too bothered about rugby until I was sixteen/seventeen/eighteen years old. But then that video came out and it genuinely made me fall in love with rugby.

**Mike Phillips (Lion #762, toured 2009 and 2013):** I grew up watching the '97 Lions. It was awesome, wasn't it? I used to end up watching *Living with Lions* every other day. It was something you always wanted to do and achieve and emulate. 'This is your fucking Everest, boys.' It still gets me. Four countries coming together, the best of the best players. It's epic, really. And to then go to South Africa and be a Lion myself twelve years later and play the world champions, just like they did, was amazing. I was proud of the way I performed but we just missed out on winning the series, which was bitterly disappointing. And it still hurts. Even after winning a series in 2013, you wanted to be remembered like those '97 guys in South Africa. There's something different about them.

**Tommy Bowe (Lion #752, toured 2009 and 2013):** The '97 Lions is probably my earliest rugby memory. Watching that tour was when I really fell in love with the sport. I sit here now and I think back to my younger self watching that tour, watching *Living with Lions* over and over again, and I can barely believe that I went on to follow in their footsteps. It's an incredible thing. It still makes me want to pinch myself.

**Kyle Sinckler (Lion #814, toured 2017):** 'This is your Everest!' I think I've watched that speech alone a hundred times. At least.

I watched it as a kid all the time, Telfer sitting down talking to Martin Johnson, Lawrence Dallaglio, Tom Smith, Paul Wallace. On the 2017 Lions tour the other players all asked me to do renditions of that speech. I'm a Lions superfan because of that tour. It was a massive thing for me to put on that same jersey.

**Brian O'Driscoll (Lion #697, toured 2001, 2005, 2009 and 2013):** I watched the 1997 Lions series on television while finishing my final-year exams at school in Dublin. If someone had told me then that I'd be involved in the next one, I'd have laughed at them. I felt a world away from the standard of the top players, but it just goes to show how quickly things can happen when you're young. Within two years I was playing for Ireland and in another two I was a Lion. Unbelievable. There's a magic about a Lions series that puts it above all other competitions in rugby. And for me it started with '97.

I was fortunate enough to go on four Lions tours. As a concept, it shouldn't come off: sworn enemies from four nations come together for seven weeks to become the best of teammates and take on one of the southern hemisphere giants. Somehow, though, it really does work, and the weight of that tradition makes it completely unique. But you've got to win a series to be properly remembered. Until you win a series it's difficult to place yourself in that elite group of great Lions players. It's not enough to produce one-off performances or be nearly-men. When you become a Lion, you want to be like the '97 Lions. I've talked to Matt Dawson about that dummy over-the-head pass that secured the first Test win – what an iconic moment. How many times have people spoken to Scott Gibbs about his big hit on Os du Randt? These moments are timeless – but they're only timeless because of the victory that followed. To be considered a great and a custodian of Lions rugby you have to achieve that success – and the '97 Lions will be remembered forever.

**Jamie Carragher (Liverpool and England footballer):** Someone got me the DVD of '97 and, listen, I must have watched that five or six times already. It's brilliant. Probably the best documentary I've seen on a sports team. I was involved with a behind-the-scenes thing with Liverpool that was embarrassing in comparison – it was cheesy and American and nothing on the level of the Lions' one. And the one person who stood out for me was Jim Telfer, listening to the way he spoke to players. There's something about the Lions that grips me. When the Lions play I always watch and I want to go on a Lions tour.

**Duncan Humphreys:** I think the film helped create the kind of myth of the Lions for the professional era, and so consequently, it had its role to play, not in saving the Lions, but it certainly popularised the Lions in a way that I don't think they expected. It showed what being a sportsman was like; you go into battle, and all the little bits of Paul Wallace retching, all of those things, and Jenks being sick before the matches, it had a realism that struck a chord with a generation, and it stayed with them.

**Tendai Mtawarira (117 Springbok caps, 2008-19):** I was the right age when the 1997 tour happened, I was a kid and just watched the whole thing. It was *the* rugby tour and it inspired me. I was still in Zimbabwe and running around as a school kid but it left its mark on me, that's for sure. To be a part of a Lions series twelve years later was surreal. I was a youngster in 2009 and just starting off my international career, so to be selected to face the Lions was an honour. I remember running out and seeing this sea of red in the stands. Kings Park was packed and the noise was incredible. It was like a different world and it was quite overwhelming – it wasn't easy to take everything in. To win that series was incredible. The only thing that's probably better than that moment was winning the World Cup.

**Schalk Burger (86 Springbok caps, 2003-15):** We all remembered watching 1997. All of us remembered Gibbs bouncing Os du Randt. The Boks losing. It scarred us. So to get the opportunity twelve years later to play the Lions was incredible. What an experience. It's so special.

**Bryan Habana (124 Springbok caps, 2004-16):** I was fourteen in 1997 and only just got into rugby at that stage, so I was only just starting to recognise certain players and understand the game. But it was exciting to see the world champs come up against this massive thing called the British and Irish Lions. I wasn't too sure about the history and tradition, but I remember watching Percy Montgomery get his first cap and I remember Martin Johnson and the emotion he brought to the series.

I played a school match in Johannesburg in the morning and was home in time for kick-off, watching it on my bed. Looking back at those memories, it really was an unforgettable experience. Seeing Guscott drop that goal in that second Test, I was as gutted as anyone. We as South Africans were really let down by what happened in 1997. The focus for us in 2009 was to right the wrongs of 1997.

**John Smit (111 Springbok caps, 2000-11):** It was more than that – it was an obsession. We'd been waiting twelve years to have another crack at them. That series in 2009 was the most pressurised situation I had in my career because of how much it meant to South Africa to make amends for '97.

**Rory Best (Lion #793, toured 2013 and 2017):** The drama of that 1997 series was incredible. It was one of the most loved tours of all time because of what they did against this incredible force that was the Springboks but also because we saw their personalities on the DVD later on. It was probably the first time that people got an insight into what it was like on tour.

You'll never get another rugby film like it. Nowadays if that happened you'd get players behaving differently in front of the camera. They'd either be guarded in what they do because of what social media would do to them, it's a minefield, or you'd have people playing up to the camera. It wouldn't be natural, whereas in 1997 it was almost innocent. We're used to cameras being everywhere now but those guys weren't. That tour was a major influence on a lot of international players that came after. Everybody's watched that film.

**Peter O'Mahony (Lion #832, toured 2017):** I watched the '97 tour DVD to death when I was a young fella. Seeing the craic, it was the change-over period from amateur to professional, I loved it. You couldn't be filming that sort of stuff anymore – the nights out and that kind of thing. Not for any particular reason, just that it couldn't be done now. It's a snapshot of amateur rugby coupled with some of the greatest players to have played the game at that time.

**Keith Wood:** Johnno mentioned this to me a while ago. He said that when he went in to have a look at *Living with Lions* while they were still editing it he saw the scene where I was cursing non-stop in the dressing room. He told the boys that they'd have to edit out some of my curses. They said they already had. This was the finished version. Apparently I said 'fuck' thirty times in thirty-four seconds and they cut it back to fifteen or sixteen. I love that.

**Martin Johnson:** In the original, he was like, 'For fucking fuck sake, what the fuck are we doing, fuck!' My brother used to do him, my brother used to do impersonations of Woody saying fuck. Brilliant. Absolutely brilliant.

# ACKNOWLEDGEMENTS

During lockdown, the weeks and months tended to blend into one another, but at some stage during this disorientating life we picked up the phone to Martin Johnson and started talking about the Lions tour of 1997. Three hours later we were still talking. Johnno was, of course, a colossal player and captain and his memory for the detail, the colour and the vibe of that summer was exceptional. And not just that summer. His understanding of the history of the Lions runs deep. He quoted extracts from books written about tours going back to the 1950s. The chances are that had we quizzed him on the goings-on when the Lions – then a British team – first went to South Africa in 1891 he'd have told us that they sailed on the *Dunnottar Castle* and that they brought with them a trophy gifted to the most impressive team they faced on tour, a trophy that is now known as the famous Currie Cup.

He calls himself a 'bit of a rugby nerd'. And he says it with pride. The day after we talked to Johnno, we spent an afternoon talking with Keith Wood, one of Johnno's key lieutenants. Woody laughed when the rugby nerd line was repeated to him. 'You see, there's a superfluous word in there,' he said. 'Johnno isn't a rugby nerd. He's just a nerd.' The warmth between them is as strong now as it was back in 1997 when they were younger men up against the odds. 'Johnno's just magnificent,' said the hooker of the lock. 'I love him to bits.'

That warmth was evident everywhere we turned. The Lions won an unforgettable series that summer and in doing so a bond was created for life. It's as Ian McGeechan said in one of the most storied pre-match speeches of them all – time will pass, no words will be exchanged but when these men see each other again they'll be immediately transported back to South Africa 1997 and the memory of what happened there will bring them close again.

The cast of characters was incredible and we managed to speak to the vast majority of the Lions and a good number of the Springboks. The book-writing game can be a tough gig but spending time talking rugby with Geech, Jim Telfer and dozens of others was no chore. Alas, lockdown meant that all of our interviews had to be done over the phone or on Skype, or Zoom or Google Meets or Microsoft Teams – the smorgasbord of platforms that is now part of our daily lives. The generosity of all of these players and coaches and other key people in the story was much appreciated. It was a privilege to spend time with them and we wish them well, particularly those who are currently fighting profound battles in their own lives. Our thoughts are with Doddie Weir and Tom Smith.

As well as doing our own interviews, we had help from Gavin Rich, Ross Harries and Brendan Nel for others. We drew on myriad sources – books, magazines and the writings of our friends and colleagues in newspapers in the UK, Ireland and South Africa. Thanks to all of them.

**Tom English:** My greatest love and thanks go to my late mother, Anne – the most fantastic and unforgettable woman. Mam passed away at home in Limerick in March 2021 with her three children by her side. I'll feel her loss forever, but I'm so glad that I had her for so long and I'm so grateful for everything she did for me. Dad will be watching out up there. That celestial poker game just got very interesting. There's a new player at the table now – and she's probably holding a kicker.

To my brother, Alan, and my sister, Sinead, and their families – you're amazing. Hilt HQ is a home from home now. We'll see you back there soon. A heartfelt thanks also to my wider family of Franklins,

Englishes and Beveridges, to my friends in Ireland and Scotland and to all the terrific folk at BBC Scotland.

I couldn't do what I do if it wasn't for the love and support of Lynn, Eilidh and Tom. Enormous thanks for everything. We'll be back in Yaliskari the minute the coast clears. Promise.

**Peter Burns:** To Julie, Isla and Hector, thank you so much for putting up with the thousands of books, magazines, newspapers and match programmes that littered our house for so many months while Tom and I wrote this book. Thanks also for rolling your eyes only occasionally when *Living with Lions* was once again being played on the TV (although I'm afraid it will continue to be watched on a regular basis until the day I die) and for putting up with me roaring with laughter or just generally making a racket while on a Zoom call to yet another of my rugby heroes.

Thanks also to my dad, Richard, for his excellent proofreading skills. Dad, it felt fitting that you got to read an early draft of this book as it was you who introduced me to the '97 Lions – we were on a trip to London in May 1997 and we sat in a hotel bar to watch the Lions take on Eastern Province in Port Elizabeth. I can still remember you shrieking in delight when Jerry Guscott drifted onto Gregor Townsend's pass to score. A golden memory of a golden summer and the starting point for my deep love of the Lions.

# BIBLIOGRAPHY

*BBC Sport*, '"Pretty Boy" Johnson and his All Blacks double-life' by Tom Fordyce, 7 October 2011

*British Lions Tour: The Official Magazine,* May 1997

*Bullet Proof: The James Dalton Story* by Mark Keohane

*Cape Argus,* 'Beauty in hands of master tactician' by Andrew Longmore. 29 January 2000

*Chronicle Live,* 'Face to Face: Mark Andrews' by John Gibson. 28 February 2013

*ESPN,* 'The try that changed my life: John Bentley's solo effort in South Africa' by Euan Reedy. 11 June 2017

*For the Record* by Gary Teichmann

*Joost: For Love and Money* by Edward Griffiths

*Joost: The Man in the Mirror* by David Gemmell

*Landing on My Feet* by Mike Catt

*Le Mond,* 'The Francois Pienaar affair betrays the unease of South African rugby' by Frederic Chambon. 29 October 1996

*Lionsrugby.com,* 'Tendai Mtawarira: "It was a tough road to face the Lions."' by Charlie Bennett, 3 May 2020

*Mail & Guardian,* 'Rugby exposes SA's resistance to transformation', 1 June 2018

*Monty* by Mark Keohane

*Os: The Autobiography,* by Os Du Randt

*Planet Rugby,* 'Life after Rugby: John Bentley', 7 September 2017

*Rugby Vavel,* 'John Bentley: The pride and pitfalls of being a British and Irish Lion' by Danial Kennedy, 5 July 2017

*Rugby World,* August 1997

*The Cape Times,* 'Du Randt the ox who anchored Boks to 1995 glory' by Mike Greenaway, 14 June 2020

*The Cape Times,* 'Rassie is the renaissance man for the Springboks' by Mike Greenaway, 17 August 2019

*The Chosen: The 50 Greatest Springboks of All Time* by Andy Colquhoun and Paul Dobson

*The Greatest Game with Jamie Carragher podcast:* Episode 11, Martin Johnson, 16 January 2020

*The Guardian,* 'McGeechan braces himself for the toughest ever Lions tour' by Donald McRae. 19 May 2009

*The Guardian,* 'Mike Phillips rewinds to dreams of childhood for Lions inspiration' by Owen Gibson, 25 May 2013

*The Hard Yards: My Story* by Simon Shaw

*The Herald,* 'Karate kick puts Weir's career on the line'. 6 June 1997

*The Independent,* 'A Crying Shame for Howley' by Chris Hewett. 15 June 1997

*The Independent,* 'Court backs Mandela inquiry' by Kieran Daley, 11 September 1999

*The Independent,* 'Du Randt' by Chris Hewett, 20 June 1997

*The Independent,* 'History casts a long shadow' by Chris Hewett. 17 May 1997

*The Independent,* 'Lions made in the McGeechan mould' by Chris Hewett, 16 June 1997

*The Independent,* 'McGeechan's creed: team and sympathy' by Chris Hewett, 25 May 1997

*The Independent,* 'Rugby boss forces Mandela into court' by Mary Braid, 20 March 1998

*The Independent,* 'SA rugby coach quits over racist outburst' by Mary Braid, 19 February 1997

*The Independent,* 'Tom Smith: "I played right after one seizure – not a good idea"' by Chris Hewett, 25 April 2009

*The Irish Independent,* 'The life and times of Francois Pienaar' by Vincent Hogan, 20 November 2000

*The Irish Times,* 'Keeping it in the family', 4 April 1998

*The Irish Times,* 'Lions fashion heroic victory', 23 June 1997

*The Irish Times,* 'Racism still deeply rooted in SARFU' by Patrick Laurence, 21 February 1997

*The Irish Times,* 'Selectors picked the right men' by Edmund van Esbeck. 8 July 1997

*The Irish Times,* 'Sluggish Lions fail to recover from poor start' by Edmund van Esbeck, 9 June 1997

*The Irish Times,* 'The thin red line refuses to capitulate' by Edmund van Esbeck, 30 June 1997

*The Mail & Guardian,* 'South Africa, Coach makes the mother of all mistakes' by staff writer. 18 October 1996

*The Mirror,* 'Bok sending off will haunt me for rest of my life', by Colin Price. 19 June 1997

*The New York Times,* 'Something Amiss with Springboks' by Ian Thomsen, 15 October 1996

*The Observer,* 'Guscott shines bright' by Mick Cleary, 25 May 1997

*The Observer,* 'Johnson on Johnson' by Bill Burrows. 5 October 2003

*The Observer,* 'No hiding place as Stoker Jim hots up the furnace in session from hell' by Mick Cleary, 8 June 1997

*The Rugby Paper,* 'My Life in Rugby: Nigel Redman' by Nick Verdier. 6 December 2012

*The Sunday Times,* 'A new lease of life' by Nick Cain, 14 January 2007

*The Sunday Times,* 'The big interview: Martin Johnson' by Paul Kimmage, 20 April 2003

*The Sunday Times,* 'What Johnno did next' by Stephen Jones, Sunday 10 October 2004

*The Telegraph,* 'Former Lions coach Andy Keast giving something back to South Africa' by Brendan Gallagher, 25 June 2009

*The Telegraph,* 'John Bentley relives golden moment of 1997 South Africa tour' by Brendan Gallagher, 3 June 2009

*The Telegraph,* 'The day when rugby nearly cost Will Greenwood his life' by Will Greenwood. 5 June 2009

*The Times,* 'And the van played on' by Mark Souster. 7 November 2003

*The Times,* 'Bryan Habana hoping for shot at revenge' by Owen Slot, 27 June 2009

*The Times,* 'How Bentley's magic changed game in 1997' by Owen Slot, 3 June 2009

*The Times,* 'Mad, bad and dangerous to know' by Lawrence Dallaglio. 12 October 2003

'After the Whistle' podcast with Lewis Moody and Leon Lloyd: *Tim Rodber*

*Winter Colours* by Donald McRae

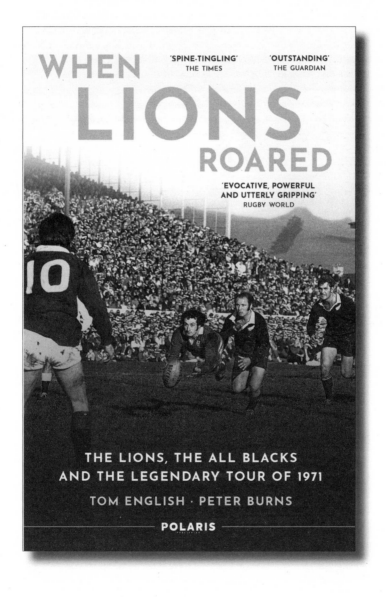